Digital Libraries and Information Access

Research Perspectives

Digital Libraries and Information Access

Research Perspectives

G. G. CHOWDHURY
and SCHUBERT FOO, Editors

An imprint of the American Library Association

Chicago 2012

First published in the United Kingdom by Facet Publishing, 2012. This simultaneous
U.S. Edition published by Neal-Schuman, an imprint of the American Library
Association, 2012.

16 15 14 13   5 4 3 2 1

ISBN: 978-1-55570-914-3 (paper)

Contents

Foreword

Christine L. Borgman

This collection of chapters on digital libraries complements other important new books in the Facet Publishing series on digital libraries, information access and data services. Digital libraries have matured over the 15+ years since the term was coined, yet the term 'digital libraries' has never come into general use outside a select group of conferences and journals. The research area is expanding, but not always under this term. Some digital libraries research has been subsumed under the rubric of cyberinfrastructure and e-research, other parts under webscience, and yet others under social informatics.

The chapters presented here return to the debate I stoked about the difference between the (digital) library of the future and the future of (digital) libraries (Borgman, 1999). It is indeed time to ask whether a focus on technology has obscured the larger questions of social practice that surround digital libraries, or whether digital library research is at an inflection point, in a pivotal position to respond to the next wave of challenges for an information society.

Chowdhury and Foo return to these early definitions and debates in their opening chapter, providing the necessary historical context to understand current issues. While framed as a book on digital libraries research, chapters range in style from the analytical to the tutorial. Some describe individual research projects and case studies; others synthesize the literature in specific areas. Collectively, the chapters span the scope of current research themes: user interfaces, architecture, equity, technology, organization, curation and social policy.

An edited book on research issues has to balance currency and comprehensiveness, which the editors have done well. Most of the chapters are devoted to foundational matters such as technology and usability, avoiding coverage of breaking topics that may be outdated by the time the volume is in print. That said, they have introduced current issues such as crowdsourced data analytics, open access, intellectual property and scientific data policy. The latter is the focus of my own research, and even here they have framed the emerging concerns of data policy and practice (Borgman, 2012, forthcoming). The book closes with a projection of research trends in digital libraries.

Two other strengths of this book are notable: first is the international body of authors represented. Digital libraries research, while international in scope, is all too often parochial. These authors span Europe, Asia, Australia and North America. They are well known within their respective regions, but often not elsewhere. Bringing them together in one volume introduces a rich array of perspectives. Second, a consequence of the first, is the extensive bibliography on digital libraries research. The authors cite work from their own regions and well beyond.

Professors Chowdhury and Foo are to be commended on assembling this thoughtful body of work on digital libraries from around the world. The volume is a valuable addition to library collections, digital and otherwise.

Christine L. Borgman
Professor and Presidential Chair in Information Studies
University of California, Los Angeles

References

Borgman, C. L. (1999) What are Digital Libraries? Competing visions. *Information Processing & Management*, **35** (3), 227–43.

Borgman, C. L. (2012, forthcoming) The Conundrum of Sharing Research Data, *Journal of the American Society for Information Science and Technology*.

Editors and contributors

Editors

Gobinda Chowdhury

Gobinda Chowdhury is Professor of Information and Knowledge Management and Director of the Centre for Information and Knowledge Management at the University of Technology, Sydney (UTS). After acquiring an honours, a postgraduate and two PhD degrees he worked as an academic and a researcher in different parts of the world for over two decades. Before joining UTS in 2008 he was a Senior Lecturer at the University of Strathclyde in Glasgow, UK, and prior to that an Associate Professor at Nanyang Technological University, Singapore. He has written several books and journal/conference papers in his research areas on information retrieval and digital libraries and has served as an editorial board member of the *Journal of Documentation, Library Review, Journal of Information Science, World Digital Libraries: an International Journal* and *Online Information Review*. He has chaired international conferences and has also acted as an international programme committee member at various international conferences, including the Joint Conference of Digital Libraries, International Conference on Asian Digital Libraries, International Conference on Digital Libraries, International Society for Knowledge Organization and ACM SIGIR.

> **URL:** http://datasearch2.uts.edu.au/fass/academic/group/journalism/details.
> cfm?StaffId=7488

Schubert Foo

Schubert Foo is Professor and Associate Dean (Graduate Studies), College of Humanities, Arts and Social Sciences, Nanyang Technological University, Singapore. He received his BSc (Hons), MBA and PhD degrees from the University of Strathclyde, UK. He is a Chartered Engineer, Chartered IT Professional, Fellow of the Institution of Mechanical Engineers and Fellow of the British Computer Society. He has served as a Board Member of the National Library Board, and the National Archives of Singapore Board. He has also served on the Editorial Advisory Board of the *Journal of Information Science, Journal of Information and Knowledge Management* and *International Yearbook of Library and Information Management,* among others. He has published more than 200 international conference and journal papers, book chapters and books in his areas of research in internet and multimedia technology, multilingual information retrieval, digital libraries and knowledge management.

URL: www.ntu.edu.sg/home/sfoo

Contributors

Gobinda Chowdhury

See p. ix.

Sudatta Chowdhury

Sudatta Chowdhury is currently a researcher at the University of Strathclyde. Previously she was a lecturer at the University of Technology, Sydney (UTS). She gained her MPhil degree from the University of Sheffield, UK, and her PhD degree from the University of Strathclyde, UK. She has been involved in teaching and research for more than a decade and has worked in different parts of the world, including Africa, Australia, Singapore and the UK. She has been involved in a number of research projects on digital libraries, including two UK Higher Education Academy projects and two European projects. Her research interests include digital libraries, information seeking and retrieval, and knowledge organization. She has a good publication track record that includes several papers in peer-reviewed journals and international conferences, and five books.

URL: www.strath.ac.uk/cis/research/currentstudents/sudattachowdhury/

Milena Dobreva

Milena Dobreva is a Senior Lecturer in Library, Information and Archive Studies at the University of Malta. She was the principal investigator of European Commission (EC), JISC and UNESCO-funded projects in the areas of user experiences, digitization and digital preservation and is a regular project evaluator for the EC. From 1990 to 2007 she worked at the Bulgarian Academy of Sciences, where she earned her PhD degree in Informatics and served as the founding head of the first digitization centre in Bulgaria. She was also a chair of the Bulgarian national committee of UNESCO's Memory of the World programme. In 2007–11 she worked for the University of Glasgow and the University of Strathclyde. She was awarded an honorary medal for her contribution to the development of the relationship between Bulgaria and UNESCO (2006) and an Academic Award for young researchers (Bulgarian Academy of Sciences, 1998).

URL: www.linkedin.com/pub/milena-dobreva/7/752/767

Angel Durr

Angel Durr is a Library and Information Sciences (LIS) Masters student at the University of North Texas (UNT) and Research Assistant to the department. On completing her degree in spring 2012, she will be a PhD student in the UNT Interdisciplinary LIS Program. Her interests include knowledge management, minority relations, and the politics of information.

> **URL:** http://angelkdurr.pbworks.com/w/page/36944960/
> AngelKDurrFrontPage

Schubert Foo

See pp. ix–x.

Michael Fraser

Michael Fraser, AM, is Professor of Law and Director of the Communications Law Centre, University of Technology, Sydney (UTS). He obtained his BA (Hons) degree from Sydney University and his LLB (Hons) from UTS. He was a founder and CEO of Copyright Agency Limited (CAL) for 21 years and a founding director of national and international copyright management companies and NGOs. He is Chairman of the Australian Communications Consumer Action Network (ACCAN), President of the Australian Copyright Council, President of International PEN – Sydney Centre, Chairman of the Stolen Generations Testimonies Foundation, Member of the Telephone Information Services Standards Council and Member of the Steering Committee for the Review of the Telecommunications Consumer Protections (TCP) Code. His research interests include responsible freedom of expression, copyright, access to content and digital rights management, libraries and knowledge management, access to indigenous cultural productions, privacy, cybercrime and media, the internet, telecommunications and broadcast regulation.

> **URL:** http://datasearch2.uts.edu.au/fass/staff/listing/details.cfm?StaffId=7482

Dion Hoe-Lian Goh

Dion Hoe-Lian Goh is currently Associate Chair (Graduate Studies), Wee Kim Wee School of Communication and Information, Nanyang Technological University, Singapore. He has a PhD in Computer Science from Texas A&M University, USA. He has extensive experience in the areas of collaborative information access in web and mobile environments, information retrieval and mining, evaluation of information systems and services, and serious games. His work has been widely published in international journals and conference proceedings in these areas. He has been involved in several funded projects in varying capacities as principal investigator, co-investigator and collaborator.

Examples of his funded projects include the use of games for motivating mobile content sharing, collaborative querying for web and mobile environments, e-community building tools for portals, usability techniques, geospatial digital libraries and web-based information extraction.

> **URL:** http://research.ntu.edu.sg/expertise/academicprofile/pages/
> StaffProfile.aspx?ST_EMAILID=ASHLGOH

Suliman Hawamdeh

Suliman Hawamdeh is a Professor and Department Chair in the College of Information, University of North Texas (UNT). Prior to joining UNT in August 2010 he taught and co-ordinated the Master of Science in Knowledge Management in the School of Library and Information Studies at the University of Oklahoma. He also founded and directed the first Master of Science in Knowledge Management in Asia in the College of Communication and Information at Nanyang Technological University, Singapore. He was the Managing Director of ITC Information Technology Consultant. He has authored and edited several books on knowledge management including *Information and Knowledge Society*, published by McGraw Hill, and *Knowledge Management: cultivating the knowledge professionals*, published by Chandos Publishing. He is the editor of a book series on innovation and knowledge management published by World Scientific. He is also the founder and editor-in-chief of the *Journal of Information & Knowledge Management*.

> **URL:** www.hawamdeh.net/profile.htm

Jeonghyun Kim

Jeonghyun Kim has been Assistant Professor at the Department of Library and Information Sciences, University of North Texas, since 2010. She obtained her PhD from Rutgers University in 2006, and MA and BA degrees in 1998 and 1996 respectively, from Ewha Womans University, Korea. Her research areas are human information behaviour, human–computer interaction, digital libraries and museums, and emerging technology in education.

> **URL:** https://faculty.unt.edu/editprofile.php?pid=2846&onlyview=1

Chern Li Liew

Chern Li Liew is currently Senior Lecturer with School of Information Management, Victoria University of Wellington. She obtained her PhD from Nanyang Technological University, and her MSc and BA (Hons) degrees from Loughborough University and the University of Brighton respectively.

She conducts research in a number of areas with an evident interrelationship. Her research interests are motivated by a desire to understand and enhance user–information interaction in digital information services, particularly those concerning digital cultural heritage. Informing and supporting this research interest is an ongoing, coherent research programme that focuses on information interaction and information use, adding value to digital content, context-sensitive information seeking and knowledge discovery. A related interest is social informatics theory and applications, particularly those related to the dynamics of socio-cultural contexts. She is a member of the editorial advisory boards of the *International Journal of Digital Library Systems* and *Online Information Review*. Liew is a member of the Executive Committee of the Consortium of iSchools Asia Pacific.

    URL: www.victoria.ac.nz/sim/staff/chernli-liew.aspx

Elena Macevičiūtė

Elena Macevičiūtė is a Professor at the Swedish School of Library and Information Science (SSLIS), Gothenburg University/Borås University College, as well as a Professor at Vilnius University in Lithuania. She obtained a PhD from Moscow University of Culture and Arts in 1990, and was habilitated at Vilnius University in 2005. She worked at Vilnius University from 1977, teaching and doing research in a range of topics in information and communication science, as well as leading international projects, which she also did at the University of Borås from 2000. Her primary research interests are in digital library management, organizational information practices and digital preservation. She supervises the Master's programme in Digital Libraries and Information Services at the SSLIS and takes part in a number of research projects related to management of digital services, digital preservation (SHAMAN 2008-2011), and information behaviour in organizations. Eight doctoral students have successfully defended their PhD dissertations under her supervision. She is also a regional and review editor for the international electronic journal *Information Research*, and a supervisor for a number of doctoral students in both Sweden and Lithuania.

    URL: www.hb.se/wps/portal/research/researchers/elena-maceviciute

Natalie Pang

Natalie Pang is an Assistant Professor with the Division of Information Studies, Wee Kim Wee School of Communication and Information at Nanyang Technological University, Singapore. She obtained her PhD in Information Management in 2009 from Monash University, where her research was also awarded the Vice Chancellor's Commendation for doctoral thesis excellence and the Faculty of IT doctoral medal. Her research interests are: heritage informatics, collective action and new media, the digital public sphere and knowledge commons, and user processing of information problems. She has worked on research projects in Singapore, Malaysia, Australia, China and Italy and has served as a Research Associate of Museum Victoria (History and Technology) and the Victorian Association of Tertiary Libraries, and as Research Fellow of the Centre for Community Networking and Research (CCNR), Monash University.

She teaches courses in social informatics, advanced qualitative methods, organizational records management and information behaviour.

URL: www.nataliepang.com

Jung-ran Park

Jung-ran Park is currently an Associate Professor at the College of Information Science and Technology at Drexel University, USA. Her research areas are computer-mediated communication/online discourse and knowledge organization and representation; she has published widely in these areas. As the principal investigator, she has been engaged in research projects funded from the Institute of Museum and Library Services. These projects centre on modelling interpersonal discourse for digital information service and metadata quality evaluation for digital repositories. She is currently editor-in-chief of the *Journal of Library Metadata*, which is published by Taylor & Francis Group.

URL: www.cis.drexel.edu/faculty/jpark/index.html

Dinesh Rathi

Dinesh Rathi is Assistant Professor at the School of Library and Information Studies, University of Alberta, Edmonton, Canada. He has a PhD in Library and Information Science, and an MS in Finance from the University of Illinois at Urbana-Champaign, Champaign, IL, USA. Before joining the PhD programme, he did a Post Graduate Diploma in Business Administration (PGDBA) from Narsee Monjee Institute of Management Studies, Mumbai, India, and received a Bachelor of Engineering (BE) degree in Mechanical Engineering from Karnataka Regional Engineering College, India (now known as National Institute of Technology Karnataka). His research interests are in the area of knowledge management, social media, digital libraries, human–computer interaction, text mining, e-marketing, e-mail-based customer support and helpdesk systems.

URL: www.drathi.com/

Raivo Ruusalepp

Raivo Ruusalepp is a lecturer at the Institute for Information Studies at Tallinn University and has been a digital preservation consultant with the Estonian Business Archives for ten years. His consultancy projects cover both electronic records management and digital archives. He has been part of several digital preservation research projects on the EU level (DigitalPreservationEurope, Protage), with the Digital Curation Centre and JISC in the UK and with national archives in the Nordic countries. He was co-author of two digital preservation assessment tools – DRAMBORA and DAF – and his current research interests lie in the area of applying risk management methods in digital preservation.

URL: https://www.etis.ee/portaal/isikuCV.aspx?TextBoxName=raivo+ruusalepp&PersonVID=57046

Ali Shiri

Ali Shiri is currently an Associate Professor in the School of Library and Information Studies, University of Alberta. He obtained his PhD in Information Science from University of Strathclyde, UK, in 2004. His professional memberships include the Canadian Association for Information Science and the American Society for Information Science and Technology (ASIS&T). He has served as a programme committee member for the Joint Conference on Digital Libraries in 2011 and 2012. He is the digital library section editor for the *Journal of Digital Information*. His research interests centre on users and their interaction with information retrieval systems, digital library user interfaces and new information organization environments such as digital libraries, subject gateways and portals. He has taught courses in the areas of digital libraries and knowledge organization.

URL: www.ualberta.ca/~ashiri/

Hussein Suleman

Hussein Suleman is an Associate Professor in Computer Science at the University of Cape Town, where he directs the research of the Digital Libraries Laboratory. He completed his undergraduate degrees and MSc at the then University of Durban-Westville and finished a PhD at Virginia Tech in the USA in 2002, in the area of component-based digital libraries. He actively advocates for open access in South Africa and works closely with the Networked Digital Library of Theses and Dissertations (NDLTD), which promotes/supports the adoption of electronic theses and dissertations and digital libraries generally worldwide. Hussein's main research interests are in digital libraries, information retrieval, internet technology and high-performance computing.

URL: www.husseinsspace.com/

T. D. Wilson

T. D. Wilson is Professor Emeritus, University of Sheffield, UK. He holds visiting appointments at Leeds University Business School, the University of Borås and the Faculty of Engineering in the University of Porto. He received honorary doctorates from Gothenburg University in 2005 and from the University of Murcia, Spain, in 2010. He was the founder and first editor of the *International Journal of Information Management* and is founder, editor and publisher of *Information Research*, an online journal for information science. He is best known for his research and writing on human information behaviour and is one of the most-cited authors in the field. In 2000 he was the recipient of the ASIS&T SIG USE award for 'outstanding contributions to information behavior' and in 2008 was designated 'Bobcat of the year' for 'outstanding contributions in promoting European library and information science' by EUCLID, the European Association for Library and Information Education and Research.

URL: http://informationr.net/tdw/

Christopher C. Yang

Christopher C. Yang is an Associate Professor in the College of Information Science and Technology at Drexel University, USA. His recent research interests include health informatics, security informatics, social media analytics, web search and mining, knowledge management and digital libraries. He has chaired at many international conferences, such as ACM SIGHIT International Health Informatics Symposium, IEEE International Conference on Intelligence and Security Informatics, ACM Conference on Information and Knowledge Management, and International Conference on Electronic Commerce, and is the founding co-chair of the International Conference on Asia-Pacific Digital Libraries. He is also frequently serving as an invited panellist in National Science Foundation and other government agencies' review panels. He has published over 200 referred journal and conference papers in *Journal of the American Society for Information Science and Technology*, *IEEE Transactions on Systems, Man, and Cybernetics*, *ACM Transactions on Intelligent Systems and Technology*, *IEEE Computer*, *IEEE Intelligent Systems*, *Information Processing and Management*, and more.

URL: www.ischool.drexel.edu/faculty/cyang/

CHAPTER 1

Digital libraries and information access: introduction

Gobinda Chowdhury and Schubert Foo

Introduction

Systematic research and development activities in digital libraries began just over 20 years ago, and during this short period of time the field of digital libraries has progressed significantly. Over the past two decades a large number of digital libraries have appeared in different countries that cover different subjects, and disciplines from health to science, engineering to arts and culture, and others. Likewise, digital libraries have been designed, developed and used by a wide range of user communities that include school children, academics, scholars, scientists and the general public. Different types of content have been created and stored in these digital library repositories, ranging from basic digital objects like photographs, music and film to more research-oriented scholarly, scientific and research data.

Alongside this, a significant amount of resources and efforts have been invested in research into digital libraries that have given rise to over 8000 journal and conference papers and a large number of books, theses, research reports and other kinds of scholarly publications. Experts from a number of disciplines, like library and information science, computer science, engineering, psychology, business management, law, economics and others, have joined hands to address and resolve a variety of research issues and challenges associated with digital libraries.

The field of digital libraries has evolved significantly over the past two decades, both in terms of the nature and characteristics of research and in terms of the objectives and functionalities of digital libraries. While the first phase of digital library research in the early 1990s put the focus on building technologies for management of large volumes of digital information for remote access, this focus subsequently shifted to users, usability and impact studies, open access and so on. Subsequently, with the rapid progress in web and social networking technologies, the focus of digital library research has been extended to new and upcoming challenges such as semantic access, social information retrieval and social network analysis (see for details, Theng et al., 2009; Borgman, 2007; Goh and Foo, 2007). Furthermore, digital library research that once focused primarily on content – books, journals, music, video etc. – is now being extended to managing research data as well as research output, i.e. scholarly publications, in order to take a holistic view of research and scholarly activities and to develop information management systems that support all such activities (Borgman, 2011).

What is a digital library?

The term 'digital library' has been defined differently within the research communities, and over the years its definition has changed, reflecting the shifting focus of digital library research. Several researchers have discussed and analysed different definitions of digital libraries (see, for example, Arms, 2001; Borgman, 1999, 2000; Chowdhury and Chowdhury, 1999, 2003; Lesk, 2005). An earlier definition that came out of a workshop in 1994 (Gladney et al., 1994) considers a digital library as:

> an assemblage of digital computing, storage, and communications machinery together with the content and software needed to reproduce, emulate, and extend the services provided by conventional libraries based on paper and other material means of collecting, cataloguing, finding, and disseminating information.

It is clear from this definition that earlier digital libraries aimed to emulate conventional analogue libraries. This is more obvious from the second part of the definition, which emphasizes that:

> A full service digital library must accomplish all essential services of traditional libraries and also exploit the well-known advantages of digital storage, searching, and communication.
>
> (Gladney et al., 1994)

Of course there are other definitions that point out other functions of a digital library; for example, the following one provided by the Digital Library Federation emphasizes the service as well as preservation activities:

> Digital libraries are organizations that provide the resources, including the specialized staff, to select, structure, offer intellectual access to, interpret, distribute, preserve the integrity of, and ensure the persistence over time of collections of digital works so that they are readily and economically available for use by a defined community or set of communities.
>
> (Digital Library Federation, 2004)

These early definitions emphasize that a digital library:

- is an organization, rather than a service
- provides access to digital works rather than information and data

- promises to provide future access, i.e. it has the responsibility of preservation and
- should provide access to digital works easily and economically.

However, the perception and connotation of a digital library have changed with the progress of research in digital libraries and, consequently, the emphasis has shifted from managing documents to managing information and data. The complexity of the notion of a digital library grew as more and more researchers joined the field from different disciplines. According to the digital library manifesto produced by the DELOS network of excellence (Candela et al., 2007):

> Digital Libraries represent the meeting point of many disciplines and fields, including data management, information retrieval, library sciences, document management, information systems, the web, image processing, artificial intelligence, human–computer interaction, and digital curation.

The DELOS digital library manifesto (Candela et al., 2007) defines a digital library as a combination of:

1   An organization: A possibly virtual organization that comprehensively collects, manages, and preserves for the long term rich digital content, and offers to its user communities specialized functionality of that content, of measurable quality and according to codified policies;
2   A system: A software system that is based on a defined (possibly distributed) architecture and provides all functionality required by a particular Digital Library. Users interact with a Digital Library through the corresponding Digital Library System; and
3   A Digital Library Management System: A generic software system that provides the appropriate software infrastructure both (i) to produce and administer a Digital Library System incorporating the suite of functionality considered foundational for Digital Libraries and (ii) to integrate additional software offering more refined, specialized, or advanced functionality.

Furthermore, the DELOS manifesto points out that,

> For every Digital Library [DL], there is a unique Digital Library System [DLS] in operation (possibly consisting of many interconnected smaller Digital Library Systems), whereas all Digital Library Systems are based on a handful of Digital Library Management Systems. For instance, through DILIGENT it is possible to build and run a number of DLSs, each realising a DL serving a target community.
>
> (Candela et al., 2007)

The above definition indicates that a digital library uses a variety of software, networking technologies and standards to facilitate access to digital content and data to a designated user community. However, a digital library is much more than an online search and retrieval system comprised of hardware, software, standards and networking technologies. Lagoze et al. (2005) comment that while search and access are its basic functions, a digital library 'facilitates the creation of collaborative and contextual knowledge environments'. The same notion of the digital library as a place for activities and collaboration has been put forward by other researchers as well. For example, Pomerantz and Marchionini (2007) argue that libraries have always been places that are dependent on the functionality, community and personal experiences of users, and digital libraries support new kinds of functionality for much broader communities and thus bring emerging senses of place.

Research in digital libraries

Many researchers have reviewed research and development in digital libraries and identified major areas of research interests and trends. In the first comprehensive review of digital library research during the first ten years (1989–99), Chowdhury and Chowdhury (1999) grouped digital library research papers into the following areas: collection development; development methodology and design issues; user interfaces; information organization: classification and indexing; resource discovery: metadata; access and file management; user studies; information retrieval; legal issues; social issues; evaluation of digital information; evaluation of digital libraries; standards; preservation; and management. They commented that while certain areas such as metadata, indexing and information retrieval, were well researched during the first decade, certain other areas, such as social issues of digital libraries, and the evaluation and impact of digital libraries were not studied widely. In a more recent study, Liew (2009) analysed research papers published during the decade 1997–2007 that focused primarily on social, cultural, legal, ethical, organizational and use dimensions of digital library research. She observed that while there is a significant body of research in the use and usability of digital libraries, as well as on the organizational, economic and legal issues, there is a lack of research on the ethical, social and cultural aspects of digital libraries.

It should be noted that while the first decade of digital libraries focused more on the organization and retrieval aspects, research in the second decade moved on to user and usability issues and the corresponding organization, economic and legal issues. However, until a few years ago, the social and cultural issues were not studied extensively. Of late there is an increasing amount of interest in the social and cultural aspects of digital libraries, as can be gleaned from the themes of the major digital library conferences; for example, cultural heritage is the main theme of two major international conferences on digital libraries to be held in 2012, viz. TPDL (Theory and Practice in Digital Libraries, formerly ECDL, European Digital Library Conference) and ICADL (International Conference on Asia Pacific Digital Libraries).

In another piece of research, focusing primarily on curriculum development for digital library education, Fox and his collaborators at Virginia Tech University in the USA have developed the 5S model of digital libraries, where each of the five 'S' stands for (Pomerantz et al., 2006):

- **S**treams that describe all types of content – text, image, audio, video – and communication channels
- **S**tructures that describe various schemes of organization of information such as catalogue codes, metadata schema, taxonomy, etc.
- **S**paces that describe tools and techniques used in indexing, browsing, searching and interfaces
- **S**cenarios specified as system states, and events including machine processes, and
- **S**ocieties that include human users, system managers and machines.

The digital library curriculum based on the 5S model proposes 18 modules that cover different aspects of digital libraries, ranging from digitization and digital objects to metadata, thesaurus and ontology, architecture, searching and information seeking, filtering, summarization, visualization, archiving and preservation, intellectual property, etc. More recently Chowdhury and Son have attempted to create a knowledge map of digital library concepts, which contains 21 main topics and 1015 subtopics (for details, see Nguyen and Chowdhury, 2011).

Information access in digital libraries

Many large digital libraries exist today and the volume of their content and their growth rate are quite amazing. For example, the European Library (2011) provides access to 200 million records held in Europe's national libraries; the Europeana (2011) digital library, established in 2008, now has a collection of about 20 million digital objects; Trove (2011), a digital library service of the National Library of Australia, has over 250 million records; and so on.

Digital libraries are created to facilitate access to digital information by local or remote users. To be more precise, a digital library is created for a designated local or remote user community so that users can easily search, retrieve and use digital information that is relevant to their specific information needs. Thus information search and access is at the heart of digital library research and development activities. However, the concept of a designated user community is also very important here. All the activities related to the search, retrieval and use of information in a digital library should be designed to meet the information tasks and needs of a designated user community. Thus, information access has a broader scope than information retrieval. Agosti (2008, 2) comments:

> The approach to the modeling of the information retrieval process has dramatically changed over the years, mostly in a positive and evolutionary way, with the final aim of

passing from an information retrieval approach towards an information access one where the real user is the focus of interest.

Thus, we may say that information access is the *raison d'être* of any digital library, and as an area of study it includes all the typical information retrieval processes and activities, ranging from content and data selection, and processing and indexing by a digital library, to search and retrieval, and use of information and data by a designated community of users in order to meet their information requirements. This books aims to cover research and development in different areas related to information access in digital libraries.

About this book

As discussed so far in this chapter, the field of digital libraries continues to be a very important area of research and development. The pervasive nature of the internet, the multi-disciplinary nature of digital libraries, and the myriad of information available through different forms of devices and channels provide a rich avenue for further studies, learning, innovation, research and development (R&D) and use. Research challenges and issues continue to evolve as researchers and developers are expected to meet the increasing demands of users, and therefore need to develop more user-friendly interfaces, intelligent search and retrieval capabilities, well endowed metadata description and content organization in scalable system architectures. The number of digital libraries around the world, and the amount of money invested in digital libraries R&D, have continued to grow over the past two decades. The field of research attracts a large and diverse audience and many new books on the subject have appeared since the early 1990s. In addition, there are several academic conferences focusing on digital libraries – notably the three established annual conferences taking place in different parts of the world: the ACM/IEE Joint Conference on Digital Libraries (JCDL), TPDL (formerly ECDL) and Asia's ICADL.

Over the years several texts and references on different aspects of digital libraries have appeared, a number of which have been published by Facet Publishing. However, the emergence of new research findings and the future importance of digital libraries provide a constant scope for new books on the subject. Furthermore, given the diversity of the field and the extensiveness of research in it, it is not always easy to provide a comprehensive view of the entire spectrum of digital library research in one book. Consequently, many recent books on digital libraries focus on one or more specific aspects of digital libraries. In a similar vein, this book focuses on information access and interactions in digital libraries.

However, given the diversity of digital libraries and the extensiveness of research, it is not always easy to provide a comprehensive view of the entire field of information access in digital libraries by just one or two experts. Keeping this in view, and based on the editors' experience and an understanding of the level of research by various experts in relevant areas, an outline was prepared for this book that addressed the key areas of research in information access and interactions in digital libraries. A list of renowned experts in the field was then drawn from around the world to produce an up-to-date and authoritative resource on digital libraries that provides truly global coverage in terms of both content and expertise.

Altogether there are 15 chapters in this book. This chapter provides the background and an introduction to the book, beginning with an introduction to the concept of the digital library and then providing a brief overview of research in digital libraries, and finishing with a brief introduction to the content of the book.

Access to information depends quite significantly on the architecture of a digital library. In Chapter 2, Suleman discusses various issues related to the architecture of digital libraries. Core digital library design considerations are presented first, followed by a discussion of how these principles are used to build large digital libraries. The chapter then discusses how various digital libraries are interconnected into larger, networked digital library systems, exemplified by international projects such as the Networked Digital Library of Theses and Dissertations (NDLTD). Various challenges related to integration and scalability are then discussed. This is followed by a case study of an architecture designed specifically for digital libraries in developing countries that as yet do not have reliable and high penetration of internet access.

Metadata forms the foundation of a digital library in that it allows us to design a structure for better organization of and access to information. Metadata standards are created by expert communities of practice that specify the data elements and the corresponding features to be created in order to design a digital library database of one or more specific types of content and data. In Chapter 3, Shiri and Rathi discuss the importance of metadata, with special reference to user interface and interaction features of digital libraries. They review four digital libraries in order to discuss new developments in the use of metadata and to explore the emerging trends and new features and functionalities, such as social tags, recommendations, reviews and ratings in digital library user interfaces.

In Chapter 4, Chowdhury and Foo discuss various issues related to information access in digital libraries. Using examples from several large digital libraries, they discuss how access to information and its use depend on different factors such as the nature of the content and data, users, search interface features and the overall objectives and business of the digital library and the organization responsible for the digital library service concerned. The chapter also provides a brief review of literature and research projects in order to show the trends in R&D activities in relation to information access in digital libraries. Thus, this chapter provides the background for discussions of various issues related to information access that come later, in subsequent chapters of the book.

Recent developments in the web and social networking technologies have had significant implications for the access and use of digital libraries, especially in relation to collaborative search and retrieval. In Chapter 5, Goh discusses collaborative search and retrieval in digital libraries. Drawing on the relevant research in information seeking and retrieval, he argues that collaboration with other users has always remained a central feature of information seeking. He then discusses research on collaborative querying, collaborative filtering and collaborative tagging or social tagging, which facilitate access to digital information.

In Chapter 6, Pang discusses how the penetration of the internet and social media, accompanied by the adoption of computing devices by the masses, has led to an increase in the amount of information accumulating online. She examines how social media technologies have implications for information access in digital libraries and points out a number of further developments of digital libraries in the online world.

Access to digital libraries requires extensive use of information and communication technologies (ICTs). However, there are significant gaps in our society in terms of access to technologies, as well as in users' information and digital literacy skills. Thus, various social issues such as the digital divide, social inclusion, information literacy and web accessibility are associated with access to information in digital libraries. In Chapter 7, Liew discusses these issues in the context of access to and use of digital libraries. Focusing specifically on the issue of social inclusion, she argues that the mere digitization of cultural heritage of a community does not guarantee social inclusion. She explores and seeks some answers to two major questions: what are the current barriers to a socially inclusive use of digital libraries, and what initiatives towards overcoming exclusion can be incorporated and implemented in digital library projects?

A digital library is created for users. Sometimes these users are well defined and their needs are known, while in most other cases the target user communities of a digital library could be anyone anywhere, and consequently their information needs and information behaviour are not well defined. Coupled with this, the rapid changes in ICT, especially in the area of web, mobile and social media technologies, have continuously reshaped and redefined users' needs and their interaction behaviour with digital libraries. In Chapter 8, Wilson and Macevičiūtė provide an overview of the current trends in research on the interactions between users and digital libraries. More specifically, they discuss the main results of user research in digital libraries and explore the applicability of existing models of information behaviour to the digital library sphere.

Many new developments have taken place that have direct or indirect implications for digital information access and use. Alongside the institutional and commercial digital libraries and information services, many new players have appeared in the digital information field such as Google Books and Google Scholar and Microsoft Academic Search, which have brought many new opportunities and challenges for digital library designers as well as for users. However, one technology that has permeated almost every sphere of today's society is the mobile technology. In Chapter 9, Kim, Durr and Hawamdeh discuss mobile technology for providing digital information services in libraries.

Parallel to the developments in commercial digital libraries and information services, a number of open access digital libraries have appeared and a variety of open scholarship activities have taken place over the past few years that have significantly influenced the digital library landscape, from both research and user perspectives. In Chapter 10, Chowdhury and Foo discuss the issues of open access and institutional repositories in the context of open access digital libraries. They briefly introduce the concept of open archives initiative and institutional repositories and then discuss how open access initiatives, coupled with recent developments in cloud computing technologies and associated developments, can help us to build digital libraries that are free at the point of use, and thus facilitate better access to and wider dissemination of knowledge.

A challenge is often faced in integrating several subject open access repositories and collections, like the National STEM Digital Library (NSDL), arXiv, Engineering Pathway and Internet Public Library, so as to enable the building of larger, interconnected and distributed digital libraries. In Chapter 11, Yang and Park discuss ongoing research on integrating and expanding taxonomy and subject categories derived from multiple repositories in science, technology, engineering and mathematics. They discuss the challenges involved in determining the semantic relationships between subject categories from different repositories through several text classification models and developing operations and processes for integration based on the identified subject category relationships from different repositories.

Usability is an important measure of the success of a digital library. Usability and user-centred design issues, their importance and the associated challenges and research issues, with particular reference to information access and interactions in digital libraries, are discussed by Chowdhury in Chapter 12.

Digital libraries provide access to a variety of information and data, but while some digital libraries can be accessed for free, such as the National Science Digital Library (NSDL) and Europeana, others require registration and payment of fees, such as the ACM Digital Library. In this respect, intellectual property and copyright are very important issues related to the design and management of digital libraries. In Chapter 13, Fraser discusses the economic challenges facing library and information services, open access initiatives and the provision of current copyright laws with regard to information services. After addressing the current debates on the economic viability of digital information services and the inadequacies of current intellectual property laws, he proposes a new framework for a digital copyright registry and discusses its features.

As discussed earlier in this chapter, one of the objectives of digital libraries is to ensure future access to information and data. This calls for preservation of digital information and data. In Chapter 14, Dobreva and Ruusalepp discuss current research and development activities in digital preservation and point out that ensuring interoperability among various systems and services remains a major challenge for future access to digital information and data.

In the last chapter of the book, Chowdhury and Foo summarize and discuss the trends in research in digital libraries, with special reference to information access and interactions. The digital library as a field of study is significantly influenced not only by research and developments within the field, but also by a variety of other factors, including the developments and challenges associated with the web, social networking, green ICT and cloud computing technologies, and various other socio-economic and political challenges, including the digital divide and digital literacy. In Chapter 15 Chowdhury and Foo address some of these issues and discuss how they will influence access and interactions in digital libraries.

Summary

As discussed in this chapter, research and development activities in digital library work have progressed quite significantly over the past two decades, giving rise to numerous large and small digital libraries, over 8000 journal and conference papers, and several books covering different aspects of digital libraries. Nevertheless, given the fast progress of research in the field and rapid developments in digital library tools, technology and standards and others, the need for more authoritative books is now felt more than ever. However, given the depth and diversity of research in the field, it is becoming increasingly difficult for any one author or any one book to cover the whole spectrum of research and development in digital library work. This book specifically covers the important aspect of information access and interactions in digital libraries. Written by a team of digital library experts from around the world, it aims to be an authoritative source for students, practitioners, researchers and developers in the field of digital libraries. The book is particularly well suited as a text and reference book, owing to the carefully selected scope of its coverage and its balanced focus on what has been achieved and what we can expect in the future, together with its identification of future challenges and trends in information access and interaction.

References

Agosti, M. (2008) Information Access Using the Guide of User Requirements. In Agosti, M. (ed.), *Access through Search Engines and Digital Libraries*, Springer, 1–12.

Arms, W. (2001) *Digital Libraries*, MIT Press.

Borgman, C. L. (1999) What are Digital Libraries? Competing visions, *Information Processing and Management*, **35** (3), 227–43.

Borgman, C. L. (2000) *From Gutenberg to the Global Information Infrastructure: access to information in the networked world*, ACM Press.

Borgman, C. L. (2007) *Scholarship in the Digital Age: information, infrastructure, and the internet*, MIT Press.

Borgman, C. L. (2011) The Conundrum of Sharing Research Data, *Journal of the American Society for Information Science and Technology*, http://papers.ssrn.com/sol3/papers.cfm?abstract_id=1869155.

Candela, L., Castelli, D., Ioannidis, Y., Koutrika, G., Pagano, P., Ross, S., Schek, H., Schuldt, H. and Thanos, C. (2007) Setting the Foundations of Digital Libraries: the DELOS manifesto, *D-Lib Magazine*, **13** (3/4), www.dlib.org/dlib/march07/castelli/03castelli.html.

Chowdhury, G. G. and Chowdhury, S. (1999) Digital Library Research: major issues and trends, *Journal of Documentation*, **55** (4), 409–48.

Chowdhury, G. G. and Chowdhury, S. (2003) *Introduction to Digital Libraries*, Facet Publishing.

Digital Library Federation (2004) *A Working Definition of Digital Library* [1998], http://old.diglib.org/about/dldefinition.htm.

European Library, The (2011) http://search.theeuropeanlibrary.org/portal/en/index.html.

Europeana (2011) www.europeana.eu/portal/.

Gladney, H. H., Fox, E. A., Ahmed, Z., Asany, R., Belkin, N. J. and Zemankova, M. (1994) *Digital Library: gross structure and requirements: report from a March 1994 workshop*, www.csdl.tamu.edu/ DL94/paper/fox.html.

Goh, H. L. D. and Foo, S. (2007) *Social Information Retrieval Systems: emerging technologies and applications for searching the web effectively*, Information Science Reference, an imprint of IGI Global.

Lagoze, C., Krafft, D. B., Oayette, S. and Jesuroga, S. (2005) What is a Digital Library Anymore, Anyway? Beyond search and access in the NSDL, *D-Lib Magazine*, **11** (11), www.dlib.org/dlib/november05/lagoze/11lagoze.html.

Lesk, M. (2005) *Understanding Digital Libraries*, 2nd edn, Morgan Kaufman

Liew, C. L. (2009) Digital Library Research 1997–2007: organisational and people issues, *Journal of Documentation*, **65** (2), 245–66

Nguyen, H. S. and Chowdhury, G. (2011) Digital Library Research (1999–2010): a knowledge map of core topics and subtopics. In Xing, C., Crestani, F. and Rauber, A. (eds), *Digital Libraries: for cultural heritage, knowledge dissemination and future creation, 13th International Conference on Asia-Pacific Digital Libraries, ICADL2011, Beijing, October 24–27, 2011*, 367–71.

Pomerantz, J. and Marchionini, G. (2007) The Digital Library as Place, *Journal of Documentation*, **63** (4), 505–33.

Pomerantz, J., Wildemuth, B. M., Yang, S. and Fox, E. A. (2006) Curriculum Development for Digital Libraries, *Proceedings of the 6th ACM/IEEE-CS Joint Conference on Digital libraries, JCDL 2006, June 11–15, 2006, Chapel Hill, North Carolina*, 175–84.

Theng, Y. L., Foo, S., Goh, H. L. D. and Na, J. C. (2009) *Handbook of Research on Digital Libraries: design, development and impact*, IGI Global.

Trove (2011) *One Search: a wealth of information*, National Library of Australia, http://trove.nla.gov.au.

CHAPTER 2

The design and architecture of digital libraries

Hussein Suleman

Introduction
••••••••••••••••••••••••

Digital library systems (DLSs) are software systems that support the operation of a digital library. As software systems, they are designed primarily to meet the needs of the target community using current best practices in software design and architecture. Digital libraries, like other disciplines, assert a set of design constraints that then affect the architectural choices for these DLSs. Key constraints include: generality, usability by different communities, interoperability, extensibility, preservation and scalability. Individually, these constraints are not unique to DLSs, but together they provide a framework for the development of specific DL architectures.

The DELOS Digital Library Manifesto (Candela et al., 2007) defines three actors in the architectural space of a DLS. The DLS is the software system that manages data and provides services to users. The Digital Library focuses on the collection, users, processes and services, with a DLS as one of its operational systems. Finally, the digital library management system (DLMS) is responsible for the management of the DLS, for example instantiation of collections and services.

This chapter focuses on the DLS and, to a lesser degree, the DLMS. Core design considerations are first presented, followed by how these principles are realized in modern reusable and custom-built DLSs. The next section deals with how these individual systems are interconnected into larger, networked DLSs, exemplified by international projects such as the Networked Digital Library of Theses and Dissertations (NDLTD). Scalability – how to deal with increasing volumes of data and increasing numbers of service requests – is then discussed. Finally, the chapter ends with a review of research directions and a case study of an architecture designed for the developing world.

Core design considerations
•••••••••••••••••••••••••••••••••••••

Core components
Most DLSs contain three main components: a digital object store, a metadata store and a suite of services to manage and provide access to the other two components. These

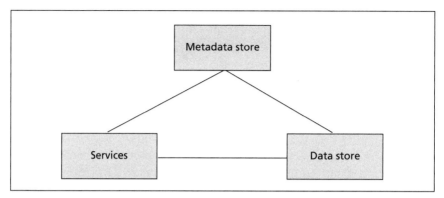

Figure 2.1 *Three main components of a DLS architecture*

are shown in Figure 2.1.

The data store and metadata store are typically implemented using a combination of file systems, databases, triple (data entities composed of subject–predicate–object) stores, etc. Services are provided by applications that execute both locally and via remote interfaces such as web-based interfaces. The exact mapping of services to applications varies across architectures. Typical services provided by a DLS include: search, browse, submit, annotate, manage, copy, authorize, import, export, link, filter and visualize (Gonçalves et al., 2004). Examples of different DLSs are presented in the following sections of this chapter.

Service Oriented Architecture

Service Oriented Architecture (SOA) is a popular paradigm in DLS architecture. Dienst (Lagoze and Davis, 1995) was one of the earliest examples of a designed distributed DLS with a strong emphasis on services and components. It was based on the Kahn/Wilensky Architecture (Kahn and Wilensky, 2006), which defined a set of simple primitives for abstract access to a DLS, and the Warwick Framework (Lagoze, 1996), which defined an abstract metadata container mechanism for genericity and multiplicity in metadata management. The influence of these frameworks has been carried forward into the Fedora repository toolkit (Payette and Lagoze, 1998). Fedora provides only a carefully managed repository with application program interfaces (APIs) and no user interfaces; the intention is that other systems will build on Fedora's strong foundation.

The emergence of the Open Archives Initiative Protocol for Metadata Harvesting (OAI-PMH) (Lagoze and Van de Sompel, 2001) (also discussed in Chapter 10 in the context of open access) led to more support for the idea of communicating components in a service-oriented architecture. Building on the success of OAI-PMH, the Open Digital Libraries (Suleman and Fox, 2001) and OpenDLib (Castelli and Pagano, 2002) projects attempted to define service interfaces for more than just harvesting.

As the number of components increased, management became crucial and two approaches were proposed. Diligent (Candela et al., 2006) extended OpenDLib to a grid environment in order to exploit the facilities provided by grid computing infrastructure. In contrast, Blox (Eyambe and Suleman, 2004) developed a minimal DLMS, based also on SOA.

These projects have illustrated the viability of components interconnected by means of well defined protocols as the core architecture of a DLS. Increasingly, this is becoming the norm in DLS architecture, as it is in many other domains. As examples, Greenstone 3 (Bainbridge et al., 2004) separates major components internally using SOA and the core of the Europeana system is based on externally accessible services (Concordia, Gradmann and Siebinga, 2009).

Digital library systems

Custom-built systems

Many early DLSs were designed to meet a specific goal and the software was considered to be specific to that goal. ArXiv.org, the first open access digital library (discussed in Chapter 10), is a central archive of preprints and postprints in the extended physics research community. The architecture of the system, the metadata and data it stores and the services it provides to its users are all driven completely by the needs of its user community only. The same holds for non-profit DLSs like the ACM Digital Library (www.acm.org/dl) and for-profit DLSs like SpringerLink. While all of these systems have been influenced by best practices in the architecture of DLSs, this is only noticeable in the external interfaces. For example, global identifier schemes for persistent linking are available in many such systems.

Institutional repository toolkits

The open access movement (discussed further in Chapter 10) has supported the design of reusable DLSs, as the use of a standard institutional repository tool is one part of an open access solution for an institution (Harnad et al., 2004). The most popular tools to serve as the support software for an institutional repository are currently EPrints (www.eprints.org) and DSpace (www.dspace.org). OpenDOAR (www.opendoar.org), a registry of open access repositories, lists 2160 repositories as of 12 December 2011. Of these repositories, 1739 each use one of 80 different named DLSs. Only EPrints and DSpace have more than 100 instances each. In fact, only 16 DLSs have more than 10 instances each, with a large majority of the DLSs having only a single instance. Thus, in practice, there are both large numbers of repositories with custom software solutions and large numbers of repositories using standard tools. Many of the systems in the former category were designed for specific projects and later generalized.

Both DSpace and EPrints, which together account for approximately half of the systems listed in OpenDoar, offer the following features:

- browse, search and submission services
- basic workflow management for submission, especially editing of metadata and accepting/rejecting submissions
- network-oriented installation (i.e., installation without a live network connection is not recommended)
- customizable web interfaces
- external import and export functions
- interoperability interfaces such as OAI-PMH (Lagoze and Van de Sompel, 2001) and SWORD (Allinson et al., 2010).

A major difference is that DSpace can only use qualified Dublin Core as its metadata format, while EPrints allows for the definition of arbitrary metadata formats.

Besides these systems, other repository toolkits have been developed with different design goals. Invenio (invenio-software.org), from CERN, provides a large suite of very flexible services but installation and configuration are not as simple as for DSpace or EPrints. Fedora (Payete and Lagoze, 1998), in contrast, provides users with a strong foundation repository but does not come bundled with any end-user interfaces or workflow management systems. Fez (fez.library.uq.edu.au) is an institutional repository tool built on top of Fedora, but its small user base means that installation and support are not on a par with DSpace or EPrints.

Commercial offerings attempt to deal with some of these problems, which appear to be largely about software configuration and management. Zentity[1] is a Microsoft toolkit that can be used to create a general-purpose repository with visualization as a core service. Hosted solutions are more popular: Digital Commons (digitalcommons.bepress.com), from BEPress, allows repository managers to completely avoid the problems of software systems by hosting their collections and services remotely and dealing only with the content-related aspects.

The remote hosting of collections occurs also in the open source community, where one institution may host the DLS of another that may not have the hardware or personnel to do so. This model is used in the South African National ETD Project (Webley, Chipeperekwa and Suleman, 2011), where smaller institutions have hosted collections at a central site.

Cultural heritage and educational resources

Systems for cultural heritage preservation use DLSs to preserve and provide access to digital representations of artefacts. These DLSs differ from the other repository toolkits because they offer specific preservation and discovery services for highly specialized collections of data.

The Bleek and Lloyd collection (Suleman, 2007) of Bushman stories was designed for distribution and access without a network and can be viewed from a DVD-ROM using a standard web browser. The Digital Assets Repository at Bibliotheca Alexandrina

(Mikhail, Adly and Nagi, 2011) was designed for large-scale storage of digital objects using a flexible, modular and scalable design. Besides such custom-built solutions, the Greenstone Digital Library (Witten, Bainbridge and Boddie, 2001) toolkit allows end-users to easily create their own indexed collections with search and browse functionality. The emphasis of Greenstone's design has been on universal applicability and minimal resource use.

Digital library systems have also been used for educational resources. The National STEM Digital Library (nsdl.org) is a large and interconnected system of repositories to gather and provide easy access to science, technology, engineering and mathematics resources for educators and learners. Unlike the previous systems, the architecture of NSDL is inherently distributed – the motivation for this and similar large-scale systems is presented in the next section.

Central vs distributed architectures
Motivation for distribution

A central DLS stores all its digital objects and metadata and provides services from a single hardware system in a single location. In contrast, a distributed DLS may store digital objects and/or metadata in multiple locations and/or may provide services from multiple locations. Popular DLS tools, such as DSpace and EPrints, create a central DLS but include services for interconnection into larger networked infrastructures.

Distributed DLSs are desirable for a number of reasons, including:

- central DLSs are resource-intensive, while in distributed DLSs the costs are shared among the distributed partners
- different collections of digital objects and metadata usually belong to different organizations and a distributed system maintains the links between organizations and their collections
- services may be provided by the most appropriate service providers, rather than by the data owners by default.

While distributed DLSs have clear benefits, end-users need cross-archive discovery and access services, as they cannot navigate the space of thousands of collections to find relevant resources. The simplest approach to provide such cross-archive services is a web search engine. Simply by virtue of having a visible online presence on the world wide web, a repository will be indexed by search engines that crawl the web regularly, e.g. Google and Bing. Provided that such search engines are able to distinguish high-quality digital resources from less useful websites, some useful services may be provided. Google Scholar and Microsoft Academic Search are examples of services based on crawled data. In both cases, the indices are of a relatively high quality, but neither uses the more complete metadata found in DLSs to provide higher-order services such as alerts or structured browsing, and neither can provide access to well defined subsets of digital objects, such as theses. Such higher-order and focused services are, arguably, best provided by direct interoperability among DLSs; most recently this has been accomplished through federation or harvesting.

Federation

Federation refers to services that access distributed sites on demand in order to satisfy a specific request. The most popular form of federation is federated search, where a query sent to a DLS is forwarded to one or more remote sites. The results from the remote sites may then be merged into a single result set using result fusion (Shokouhi, 2007). The set of remote sites to be queried also can be optimized by eliminating those sites that probably do not contain relevant results – a process known as source selection.

In practice, federated search requires that a DLS support a remote search protocol such as Z39.50 or the newer Search/Retrieval via URL (SRU) (www.loc.gov/standards/sru). SRU is a client-server protocol where the client sends URL-encoded query parameters to the server and receives an XML-encoded list of records as a result.

Early experiments with federated search were partially successful but the reliance of a DLS on multiple remote sites led to unreliable operation over time, with increasing unreliability with greater numbers of sites. This inability of federation to scale and remain stable over time led to harvesting as an alternative method of creating distributed DLSs (Suleman and Fox, 2003).

Harvesting and open archives

Harvesting is the periodic transfer of data from one machine to another. In the digital libraries community, the data being transferred usually takes the form of metadata that has been updated since the last harvest. Harvesting has been suggested as an alternative to federation because a DLS that collects all the metadata in one location does not need to contact each remote site on every query. The disadvantage is that all metadata has to be stored in one location – however the digital objects are usually not harvested, the central metadata store is easily replicated and metadata does not use much storage relative to the digital objects themselves.

The Open Archives Initiative (OAI) developed the Protocol for Metadata Harvesting (PMH) (Lagoze et al., 2002a) (also discussed in Chapter 10) as a mechanism for interconnecting distributed repositories using the harvesting approach. This is a client-server web-based protocol, where requests are URL-encoded and responses are contained in well defined XML documents. There are six possible requests in the OAI-PMH:

- **Identify** returns a description of the repository, including such information as the administrator's e-mail address, service end-point URL and name of repository.

- **ListMetadataFormats** returns a list of the metadata formats in which records may be disseminated.

- **ListSets** returns a list of subsets of the repository that may be harvested instead of the entire collection.

- **ListIdentifiers** returns a list of record headers, where each header contains the identifier of a record, its update date and the list of sets it belongs to.

- **GetRecord** returns a single complete metadata record for a specified identifier and metadata format, including header information and optional meta-metadata, such as provenance data.

- **ListRecords** is a combination of the ListIdentifiers and GetRecord requests, where the repository sends back a list of complete records instead of just their headers.

OAI-PMH relies on datestamps for incremental harvesting. A List-Identifiers or ListRecords request can specify a 'from' parameter that indicates the earliest datestamp of records to be returned. If all records are datestamped on accession or modification, a client can then harvest only the updated and new records on each subsequent harvest after the first. Since this is a stateless solution, multiple clients can harvest independently at different times. There is, however, one element of state in the protocol in the form of a resumption token. This is a special parameter that is returned in one of the 'List' responses to indicate that there is more data available and that the client should

Figure 2.2
Example of OAI-PMH request and response

send this token back to request the next instalment of data. This mechanism allows servers to send batches of records to clients without creating XML documents of an unmanageable size. Figure 2.2 illustrates a typical OAI request and response.

Examples of distributed architectures

National STEM Digital Library

The National Science Technology Engineering and Mathematics (STEM) Digital Library (NSDL; nsdl.org) is an American project to organize and provide access to teaching and learning resources in the STEM disciplines, spanning K-12 primary/secondary schools as well as university education. NSDL mostly stores metadata, but has also indexed full-text content where possible. The metadata used was either standard unqualified Dublin Core or an NSDL-specific variant (Lagoze et al., 2002b), so as to ensure that participation in NSDL had few barriers.

NSDL's technical architecture focuses on a central metadata repository that stores metadata from all its distributed partner repositories. The metadata in this repository is in turn shared with service providers, such as a local search service, via an OAI-PMH interface. Ingest into the repository takes place using one of three mechanisms: direct entry into the database; harvesting using OAI-PMH; or gathering from the web, a form of web-crawling. This 'spectrum of interoperability' was decided on so as to maximize participation – while harvesting was considered the normative interoperability mechanism, it was expected that harvesting is not as low a barrier to interoperability as is needed for repository sites with few human resources to set up and operate OAI-PMH interfaces. As of 2006, NSDL contained 1.2 million records and regularly harvested from 85 OAI-PMH servers (Lagoze et al., 2006).

Europeana

Europeana (www.europeana.eu) is a cultural heritage digital library project with an emphasis on gathering the heritage of different European communities into a single portal for easy navigation and discovery by end-users. As with other distributed digital libraries, the content is stored at the distributed partners but the metadata is shared with the central portal. This central portal stores metadata as a networked data system based on RDF (Resource Description Framework) so that the services can exploit the rich relationships among and within objects and collections (Doerr et al., 2010). Fundamentally, however, the data is either harvested using OAI-PMH or manually inserted into the central repository using a defined API (Concordia, Gradmann and Siebinga, 2009). In this way, the core data architecture differs from NSDL, but the core networked architecture is the same.

Networked Digital Library of Theses and Dissertations

The Networked Digital Library of Theses and Dissertations (NDLTD) operates a Union Catalog of metadata describing Electronic Theses and Dissertations (ETDs) from around the world (union.ndltd.org). Metadata is stored in a central metadata repository in either Dublin Core or ETD-MS formats (ETD-MS is a metadata format specific to ETDs). As in both NSDL and Europeana, metadata is harvested periodically from partner sites using the OAI-PMH. Sites may represent single institutions (e.g. Virginia Tech), consortia (e.g. OhioLink), country/regional projects (e.g. Australasian Digital Theses) or international collaborations (e.g. OCLC WorldCat). Given that these are overlapping organizations, the Union Catalog contains some repeated records so that de-duplication of these is an ongoing challenge. Services are provided at a higher level by independent service providers obtaining a stream of metadata from the Union

Catalog, again using the OAI-PMH. As of 2011, VTLS Inc. and Scirus provide discovery interfaces based on the metadata.

The NDLTD Union Catalog is strongly focused on a single type of resource but agnostic to the source of the metadata and the language and cultural differences in higher education systems around the world. Its architectural model is therefore a generic model for international focused DLSs. This is illustrated in Figure 2.3.

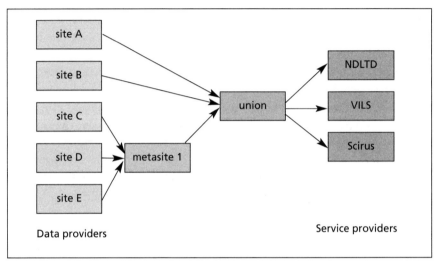

Figure 2.3 *NDLTD data and its service provider network*

Scalability

DLSs such as the ones presented in Figure 2.3 have to deal with three forms of scalability challenges:

- increasing numbers of service requests (or end-users)
- increasing amounts of data and metadata
- increasing numbers of repositories.

The first two forms of scalability have been explored recently, while the last is gradually emerging as more digital repository systems are created.

Compute clusters

Clusters of tightly integrated networked computers may be used for high-performance computing or high-throughput computing tasks, both of which are necessary as quantities of data and numbers of end-users increase. Suleman, Parker and Omar

(2008) performed experiments using a cluster of computers to provide typical DLS services and illustrated that it is indeed feasible to replicate services on multiple nodes in order to handle increases in the number of requests. Nakashole and Suleman (2009) showed that large quantities of data in a DLS can be indexed effectively in parallel using both fixed cluster nodes and dynamic grid-style nodes.

Cloud/utility computing

Utility computing allows for the creation of one or more virtual computers in a remote location, or the creation of arbitrarily large storage systems in remote locations. Any web-based DLS can exploit such services in its architecture to support scaling of services or data stores. Utility computing is either a pay-per-use service provided by commercial providers (e.g. Amazon) or a locally hosted service with the same interfaces but on a local computing cluster, referred to as a private cloud. The advantage of the former is that a popular service can quickly and relatively cheaply acquire large amounts of resources without having to deal with power and cooling concerns. Private clouds, in contrast, allow an organization to maintain full control of the hardware and data, where this is potentially an issue. In the DLS space, few projects have adopted utility computing as part of their architectures.

Volunteer thinking/crowdsourcing

Volunteer computing is a large-scale processing of data using the idle computational resources of volunteers. This has usually been applied to solve humanitarian, medical or scientific problems that require processing of large quantities of data. This approach has recently been generalized to volunteer thinking or crowdsourcing, where users are recruited to perform tasks that computers are not able to perform easily, such as image recognition. This has been applied in the context of digital libraries for the creation of high-quality metadata and transcription of handwritten text (Oomen and Arroyo, 2011). The advantage over automated techniques is that large numbers of volunteers can be recruited to deal with large quantities of data and repeated processing of the same data ensures high quality, in addition to high speed and low cost.

Scalable storage

Database scalability provides a trivial basis for scaling DLS storage where the metadata and/or data collections reside in databases. In addition, specific techniques may be employed to achieve scalability at higher levels. The Amazon Web Services (aws.amazon.com) utility computing infrastructure offers multiple services for data storage where the physical details are masked from the system. S3 is a service to store arbitrary amounts of data addressed with a logical identifier scheme. SimpleDB is a service to store indexed tuples and perform queries using a variant of SQL. Both services are provided as web-based APIs for easy integration into external systems or systems that run on the co-located virtual machine infrastructure (EC2). In the digital library community, DuraCloud uses multiple utility storage providers as a replication platform for preservation of digital objects as a commodity service.[2]

Instead of centralized storage, systems may opt to use multiple distributed storage systems to achieve scalability, flexibility and extensibility. This is the approach advocated by Storage Resource Broker (SRB) (Baru et al., 1998) and its successor, iRODS. Both mechanisms create abstractions of remote storage. Some repository toolkits, such as DSpace, support SRB/iRODS as an abstract storage layer.

SimplyCT
Motivation

SimplyCT is an alternative architecture for DLSs with a specific emphasis on low-resource environments, such as institutions in developing countries. Low-resource environments are environments where there are few staff; the staff are not highly skilled in DLSs; there are few servers and other computers available; the computers are not high end and are shared among multiple applications; and either there is no network available or the network is slow and unreliable. Taking all of these conditions into account, simplyCT has been proposed as an architectural framework that is potentially more relevant for developing countries.

The basic idea behind simplyCT is to encourage simplicity in all elements of the architecture. This strategy is borne out by the long-term success of Project Gutenberg, which has a stated preference for simple text in order to guarantee preservation of the data. The initial experiences of NSDL, where OAI-PMH turned out to be too complex, also support the notion that complex DLSs are not likely to be effective without large injections of resources (Lagoze et al., 2006).

SimplyCT is currently a proposal that is being evaluated experimentally and by direct application in production systems such as the Bleek and Lloyd Collection of Bushman stories and drawings.[3]

Design principles

SimplyCT is based on a set of design principles derived from the experiences of past DLSs. These principles are as follows:

- Minimalism. Only provide the bare minimum amount of infrastructure, as additional complexity increases development, extensibility and maintenance costs. This principle argues against highly layered and abstract architectures.
- Do not impose on users. Users may already use the data in particular formats and with specific structures and identifiers. The DLS should mould itself around the data rather than force users to changes structures, formats and identifiers. This

principle argues against enforced global identifiers.

- No API. Components should not need to use an API when basic file access is sufficient. This principle argues against web services for everything.
- Web or no web. DLSs should not require the use of a web interface where users may want to access data by other means. This principle argues against unnecessary layers for users to access data.
- Preservation by copying. It should be possible to preserve the data and services simply by copying a directory, as this form of data protection is widely understood and can be implemented using a wide range of technological solutions. This principle argues against the use of unnecessary databases.
- Any metadata, objects, services. There should be no constraints on what metadata formats are allowed, what digital objects are allowed or what services are possible. This principle argues against unnecessary restrictions on formats.
- Everything is repeatable. Even basic services should be repeatable, so that, for example, different search services can be provided over core metadata and annotations. This principle argues against fixed services.
- Superimposed information. Metadata should be stored as granular objects with additional layers of meaning specified as superimposed peer sub-collections. This principle argues against complex objects that conflate descriptive metadata with categorical metadata.

Structure

Figure 2.4 illustrates the file structure of a simplyCT archive. In this structure, 'archive' contains the digital objects and metadata files corresponding to each digital object; the metadata files have the same names as the digital objects but are suffixed with '.metadata'; 'index' contains indices for any services that require these, such as search; 'service' contains the code and/or configuration data for each instance of each service; 'static' contains any static files that are part of the user interfaces, like the home page of the collection.

Toolsets

Some tools have been constructed to manipulate and access data based on the simplyCT framework. The CALJAX project (Suleman et al., 2010) produced a web-based collection manager and AJAX-based search and browse tools for a simplyCT-structured collection. The access services were based on AJAX so that the collection could be copied to a CD/DVD-ROM without any loss in

```
/archive
    file1.jpg
    file1.jpg.metadata
    file2.jpg
    file2.jpg.metadata
/index
    search.1/ ...
/service
    onlinesearch.1/ ...
    offlinesearch.1/ ...
/static
    file1.html
```

Figure 2.4
Example of a simplyCT file layout

functionality even though there is no longer a web server intermediary.

The Bonolo project[4] produced web-based tools for both management and discovery of simplyCT collections. The two tools were developed to be independent, so that the management module could be used to maintain the collection while CALJAX's services are used for access. Further tools are under development.

Research challenges and trends in DLS architecture

Architecture of DLSs, especially of the large distributed DLSs, has evolved over time, and consequently several new technologies and standards, such as the OAI-PMH, have been developed in order to facilitate easy and seamless access to digital information that is distributed across several partner sites. However, several problems still remain unresolved. These are some current research challenges:

- Large data curation refers to the ingestion, management, querying and dissemination of large datasets. As datasets become very large, the standard algorithms for handling data change and new algorithms are actively being sought.
- Metadata and system interoperability is still difficult, at best. Experience with OAI-PMH has shown that, while it works in some communities, it is not a good general solution. Newer standards like OAI-ORE are significantly more complex than is probably necessary.
- Packaging of DLSs is often a source of frustration because dependencies and configurations are handled as out-of-band activities. Instead, modern packaging systems like FreeBSD ports and Ubuntu packages can provide system-wide management across all software systems. Integrating DLSs tools into operating systems can result in more widespread use and adoption.
- Cloud services are increasing in popularity. New services can provide annotation and linking capabilities and these should be provided in DLSs. In addition, there is a need for more evidence that cloud services are a good design decision.
- Any distributed or large DLS needs to monitor its metadata for duplicates and quality issues. Services to make such assessments are gradually being improved, but de-duplicating is still considered to be a difficult problem.

Summary

In summary, the architecture of a modern DLS is based on a metadata store, data store and service suite. The service suite typically follows a service-oriented architecture, which has been experimentally validated in various systems. Distributed DLSs are common, and interoperability is a key consideration for any system. Most systems are therefore not run in isolation but as one part of a larger networked information system, where scalability adds a new dimension to the architecture. Standards such as OAI-

PMH are crucial in enabling this interoperability for such systems.

However, even OAI-PMH has been demonstrated as too complex for some applications. In addressing this, simplyCT has been presented as an alternative architecture for DLSs, based on a set of principles and minimal services. It is hypothesized that an architecture conforming to these principles will stand the test of time and has greater universal applicability than existing designs for DLSs. This shows much promise in early experiments but is yet to be proved by ongoing research!

Notes

1   http://research.microsoft.com/en-us/projects/zentity.

2   http://www.duraspace.org/duracloud.php.

3   http://lloydbleekcollection.cs.uct.ac.za.

4   http://shenzi.cs.uct.ac.za/~honsproj/cgi-bin/view/2011/hammar_robinson.zip/ Website/.

References

Allinson, J., Carr, L., Downing, J., Flanders, D. F., Francois, S., Jones, R., Lewis, S., Morrey, M., Robson, G. and Taylor, N. (2010) *SWORD AtomPub Profile version 1.3: Simple Webservice Offering Repository Deposit*, www.swordapp.org/docs/sword-profile-1.3.html.

Bainbridge, D., Don, K. J., Buchanan, G., Witten, I. H., Jones, S., Jones, M. and Barr, M. I. (2004) Dynamic Digital Library Construction and Configuration. In Heery, R. and Lyon, L. (eds), *Research and Advanced Technology for Digital Libraries: ECDL 2004*, Springer, LNCS 3232, doi:10.1007/978-3-540-30230-8_1.

Baru, C., Moore, R., Rajasekar, A. and Wan, M. (1998) The SDSC Storage Resource Broker. In *Proceedings of the 1998 Conference of the Centre for Advanced Studies on Collaborative Research*, ACM Press.

Candela, L., Castelli, D., Pagano, P. and Simi, M. (2006) OpenDLibG: extending OpenDLib by exploiting a gLite Grid Infrastructure. In Gonzalo, J., Thanos, C., Verdejo, M. F. and Carrasco, R. C. (eds), *Research and Advanced Technology for Digital Libraries: ECDL 2006*, Springer, LNCS 4172, doi:10.1007/11863878_1.

Candela, L., Castelli, D., Ioannidis, Y., Koutrika, G., Pagano, P., Ross, S., Schek, H.-J. and Schuldt, H. (2007) *The Digital Library Manifesto*, DELOS, January, www.delos.info/index.php?option=com_content&task=view&id=345.

Castelli, D. and Pagano, P. (2002) OpenDLib: A Digital Library Service System. In Agosti, M. and Thanos, C. (eds), *Research and Advanced Technology for Digital Libraries*, Springer, LNCS 2458, doi:10.1007/3-540-45747-X_22.

Concordia, C., Gradmann, S. and Siebinga, S. (2009) Not (just) a Repository, nor (just) a Digital Library, nor (just) a Portal: a portrait of Europeana as an API. In *Proceedings of World Library and Information Congress: 75th IFLA General Conference and Council*, IFLA, 23–27 August, Milan, Italy, www.ifla.org/files/hq/papers/ifla75/193-concordia-en.pdf.

Doerr, M., Gradmann, S., Hennicke, S., Isaac, A., Meghini, C. and Van de Sompel, H. (2010) The Europeana Data Model (EDM). In *Proceedings of World Library and Information Congress: 76th IFLA General Conference and Council, IFLA, 10–15 August, Gothenburg, Sweden,* www.ifla.org/files/hq/papers/ifla76/149-doerr-en.pdf.

Eyambe, L. and Suleman, H. (2004) A Digital Library Component Assembly Environment. In Marsden, G., Kotzé, P. and Adesina-Ojo, A. (eds), *Proceedings of SAICSIT 2004, 4–6 October, Stellenbosch,* ACM Press, 15–22.

Gonçalves, M. A., Fox, E. A., Watson, L. T. and Kipp, N. A. (2004) Streams, Structures, Spaces, Scenarios, Societies (5s): a formal model for digital libraries, *ACM Transactions on Information Systems,* **22** (2), doi:10.1145/984321.984325.

Harnad, S., Brody, T., Vallières, F., Carr, L., Hitchcock, S., Gingras, Y., Oppenheim, C., Stamerjohans, H. and Hilf, E. R. (2004) The Access/Impact Problem and the Green and Gold Roads to Open Access, *Serial Review,* Elsevier, **30** (4), 310–14, doi:10.1016/j.serrev.2004.09.013.

Kahn, R. and Wilensky, R. (2006) A Framework for Distributed Digital Object Services. *International Journal on Digital Libraries,* Springer, **6** (2), 115–23, doi:10.1007/s00799-005-0128-x.

Lagoze, C. (1996) The Warwick Framework: a container architecture for diverse sets of metadata, *D-Lib Magazine,* July/August, www.dlib.org/dlib/july96/lagoze/07lagoze.html.

Lagoze, C. and Davis, J. R. (1995) Dienst: an architecture for distributed document libraries, *Communications of the ACM,* ACM, **38** (4), 47, doi:10.1145/205323.205331.

Lagoze, C. and Van de Sompel, H. (2001) The Open Archives Initiative: building a low-barrier interoperability framework. In Fox, E. A. and Borgman, C. L. (eds), *Proceedings of the 1st ACM/IEEE-CS Joint Conference on Digital Libraries,* ACM, 54–62, doi:10.1145/379437.379449.

Lagoze, C., Van de Sompel, H., Nelson, M. and Warner, S. (2002a) *The Open Archives Initiative Protocol for Metadata Harvesting, Version 2.0,* Open Archives Initiative, www.openarchives.org/OAI/2.0/openarchivesprotocol.htm.

Lagoze, C., Hoehn, W., Millman, D., Arms, W., Gan, S., Hillman, D., Ingram, C., Krafft, D., Marisa, R., Phipps, J., Saylor, J., Terrizzi, C., Allan, J., Guzman-Lara, S. and Kalt, T. (2002b) Core Services in the Architecture of the National Science Digital Library (NSDL). In Hersh, W. and Marchionini, G. (eds), *Proceedings of the 2nd ACM/IEEE-CS Joint Conference on Digital Libraries,* ACM, 201–9, doi:10.1145/544220.544264.

Lagoze, C., Krafft, D., Cornwell, T., Dushay, N., Eckstrom, D. and Saylor, J. (2006) Metadata Aggregation and 'Automated Digital Libraries': a retrospective on the NSDL experience. In Nelson, M. L. and Marshall, C. C. (eds), *Proceedings of the 6nd ACM/IEEE-CS Joint Conference on Digital Libraries,* ACM, 230–9, doi:10.1145/1141753.1141804

Mikhail, Y., Adly, N. and Nagi, M. (2011) DAR: Institutional Repository Integration in Action. In Gradmann, S., Borri, F., Meghini, C. and Schuldt, H. (eds), *Proceedings of Research and Advanced Technology for Digital Libraries, International Conference on Theory and Practice of Digital Libraries (TPDL 2007), 26–28 September, Budapest, Hungary,* Springer, LNCS 6966, 348–59, doi:10.1007/978-3-642-24469-8_36.

Nakashole, N. and Suleman, H. (2009) A Hybrid Distributed Architecture for Indexing. In Agosti, M., Borbinha, J., Kapidakis, S., Papatheodorou, C. and Tsakonas, G. (eds), *Research and Advanced Technology for Digital Libraries: Proceedings of 13th European Conference (ECDL 2009), 27 September–2 October, Corfu, Greece,* Springer, 250–60, doi:10.1007/978-3-642-04346-8_25.

Oomen, J. and Arroyo, L. (2011) Crowdsourcing in the Cultural Heritage Domain: opportunities and challenges. In *Proceedings of 5th International Conference on Communities and Technologies, 29 June–2 July, Brisbane, Australia.*

Payette, S. and Lagoze, C. (1998) Flexible and Extensible Digital Object and Repository Architecture (FEDORA). In Nicholaou, C. and Stephanidis, C. (eds), *Research and Advanced Technology for Digital Libraries,* Springer, LNCS 1513, doi:10.1007/3-540-49653-X_4.

Shokouhi, M. (2007) Segmentation of Search Engine Results for Effective Data-Fusion. In Amati, G., Carpineto, C. and Romano, G. (eds), *Advances in Information Retrieval,* Springer, LNCS 4425, 185–97, doi:10.1007/978-3-540-71496-5_19.

Suleman, H. (2007) Digital Libraries without Databases: the Bleek and Lloyd Collection. In Kovacs, L., Fuhr, N. and Meghini, C. (eds), *Proceedings of Research and Advanced Technology for Digital Libraries, 11th European Conference (ECDL 2007), 16–19 September, Budapest, Hungary,* 392–403.

Suleman, H. and Fox, E. A. (2001) A Framework for Building Open Digital Libraries, *D-Lib Magazine,* 7 (12), www.dlib.org/dlib/december01/suleman/12suleman.html.

Suleman, H. and Fox, E. A. (2003) Leveraging OAI Harvesting to Build a Union Catalog, *Library Hi-Tech,* 21 (2), 19–227, doi:10.1108/07378830310479857.

Suleman, H., Parker, C. and Omar, M. (2008) Lightweight Component-Based Scalability, *International Journal on Digital Libraries,* 9 (2), 115–28.

Suleman, H., Bowes, M., Hirst, M. and Subrun, S. (2010) Hybrid Online-Offline Collections. In *Proceedings of Annual Conference of the South African Institute for Computer Scientists and Information Technologists (SAICSIT 2010), Bela Bela, South Africa, 11–13 October,* ACM Press.

Webley, L., Chipeperekwa, T. and Suleman, H. (2011) Creating a National Electronic Thesis and Dissertation Portal in South Africa. In Olivier, E. and Suleman, H. (eds), *Proceedings of 14th International Symposium on Electronic Theses and Dissertations (ETD 2011), Cape Town, 13–15 September,* http://dl.cs.uct.ac.za/conferences/etd2011/papers/etd2011_webley.pdf.

Witten, I. H., Bainbridge, D. and Boddie, S. (2001) Power to the People: end-user building of digital library collections. In Fox, E. A. and Borgman, C. L. (eds), *Proceedings of the 1st ACM/IEEE-CS Joint Conference on Digital Libraries,* ACM, 94–103, doi:10.1145/379437.379458.

CHAPTER 3

Metadata and crowdsourced data for access and interaction in digital library user interfaces

Ali Shiri and Dinesh Rathi

Introduction

Metadata has remained a major area of research in information science for nearly two decades. The increasing number and variety of metadata formats and standards has given rise to a number of digital library projects and initiatives that have focused on semantic interoperability among various metadata formats and standards. Interoperability, like metadata, is a widely researched and discussed topic in the literature of digital libraries. However, this chapter does not discuss interoperability per se; rather, it focuses on the use of metadata in the search interfaces of digital libraries.

With the widespread use of metadata in digital libraries as access and retrieval points, it seems logical that they be used in user interfaces to support information seeking strategies. Shiri (2008) reported a study of metadata-enhanced visual interfaces and found that visual interfaces enhanced with metadata are an emerging category of visual interfaces. The growing number of digital libraries that create, maintain and support a variety of metadata provide ample opportunity for designers and developers of user interfaces.

This chapter evaluates and compares four digital library user interfaces from four different countries (Edmonton Public Library (EPL), Canada; Trove: National Library of Australia, Australia; the Ann Arbor District Library System, USA; and the British Library, UK) in order to identify new developments in the use of metadata and to explore the emerging trends and new features and functionalities, such as social tags, recommendations, reviews and ratings in digital library user interfaces.

The next section of the chapter introduces the definition, types and standards of metadata, followed by an introduction to digital libraries and user interfaces. Then the chapter presents the methodology used in the evaluation of the user interfaces of these four digital libraries, the findings and related discussion. Finally, the concluding section highlights some key trends and makes suggestions for future research.

Metadata: definition, types and standards

Numerous definitions of the term 'metadata' have been proposed by various research and development communities, including library and information science, archives, museums, computing, information technology, government organizations and educational institutions. This trend in itself points to the importance, popularity, usefulness and utility of metadata in various contexts, domains and disciplines. They all share the same philosophy that metadata aims to bring order to digital information and to support consistent and coherent description and discovery of digital objects. One of the most frequently used definitions is attributed to the National Information Standards Organization (NISO). NISO (2004) defines metadata as follows:

> Metadata is structured information that describes, explains, locates, or otherwise makes it easier to retrieve, use, or manage an information resource. Metadata is often called data about data or information about information.
>
> (see also Pope and Holley, 2011; Parandjuk, 2010; Ma, 2009; http://dublincore.org/metadata-basics/)

This definition provides a generally solid basis for delineating the uses, functions and purpose of metadata for resource description and discovery. Parandjuk (2010) argues that the creation of metadata standards is an example of best practices in information architecture in digital libraries because metadata makes interoperability easier between different digital libraries. The term 'metadata' is undoubtedly one of the most widely and frequently used terms in the literature of digital libraries. Table 3.1 shows the number of hits for the term in various databases, digital libraries and the Google search engine. These searches were conducted on 19 July 2011. This simple table shows the extent and scope of research and development activities associated with metadata and its application.

Table 3.1 *Number of hits for the term 'metadata'*		
Database	Type of search	Number of records
Library, Information Science and Technology Abstracts (LISTA)	Subject	2355
Library and Information Science Abstracts (LISA)	Subject	1363
Library Literature and Information Science Abstracts	Subject search	1009
ACM Digital Library	Title	1298
Google	Free-text search	4,550,000 pages

Categories and types of metadata can be defined based on the nature of the collection, type of digital objects involved, subject domain, functionality, user community and metadata generation methods or the agents and people involved in extracting or assigning metadata. Greenberg (2005) suggests a comprehensive typology of metadata that includes:

- identification and description metadata
- administrative metadata
- terms and conditions metadata
- content rating metadata
- provenance metadata
- linkage relationship metadata
- structural metadata.

There are several different metadata standards and formats: some focus on a particular subject domain, or on document type, others focus on organizational mission or community of users. Well known examples of metadata include Machine-Readable Cataloguing (MARC),[1] which is the most commonly used metadata schema, followed by the Dublin Core Metadata Initiative[2] (Jung-ran and Tosaka, 2010), Metadata Object Description Schema (MODS)[3], the Text Encoding Initiative (TEI)[4] and Encoded Archival Description (EAD)[5].

   Greenberg (2010) notes that the creation of metadata is crucial for digital libraries' success, as the metadata allow users to have multiple access points to the services and content provided by the digital library system. For example, the Dublin Core Metadata (DCM) Standard[6] has 15 basic elements (e.g., author, title, subject, date) that can be used to describe an information resource, so that a digital library using this standard may be able to provide up to 15 access points (Weagley, Gelches and Jung-Ran, 2010) to a resource. However, a range of problems are associated with the use of metadata and these include incorrect values, incorrect elements, missing information and misrepresentation (Yasser, 2011). As the quality of metadata is critical to accurate retrieval (Beall, 2005), the errors and problems in metadata should be taken care of in order to support both full-text search and its use in accessing and retrieving documents from digital libraries.

   Users can search the material in digital libraries through multiple access points (e.g. topics, media type, title, authors). As such, practically all the elements of metadata can be utilized as access points in digital libraries, as compared to limited known item search access points (e.g. author, subject and title) offered in a traditional physical library's OPAC (Online Public Access Catalogue) records. Many such access points in digital libraries are part of either the basic search or advanced search features (Morville and Rosenfeld, 2007 as cited in Parandjuk, 2010). In the following section, a discussion of the role and importance of user interfaces to digital libraries is presented.

Digital library user interfaces

Digital libraries provide access to digital collections of materials (Lesk, 1997) as cited in Zaphiris et al., 2004). They comprise collections of digital resources or objects and a suite of services that allow a community of users to access, use and reuse these resources or objects (Meghini, Spyratos and Yang, 2010). As discussed in Chapter 1, the Digital Library Federation (2004) provides a more comprehensive definition of digital libraries that focuses on content as well as services and emphasizes the need for present as well as future access to information. Digital libraries (e.g. Haathi Trust [www.hathitrust.org/], ACM Digital Library [http://dl.acm.org/] and so on) are becoming popular in use, and one of the reasons for their popularity is that they have been effective in reducing spatial and temporal barriers (Malizia, Bottoni and Levialdi, 2010). Users are able to search and browse collections with ease, anytime from anywhere, using the internet. Digital libraries are multifaceted and complex information structures that offer a wide range and variety of information-bearing objects. They vary in their content, subject matter, cultural characteristics, language and other parameters. The variety of digital objects and materials in a digital library poses challenges for the design of usable and easy-to-understand user interfaces. Arms (2000) notes that 'a digital library is only as good as the interface it provides to its users'. In order to design a convenient and effective digital library for users (e.g. patrons, librarians and system administrators), interface design and metadata should be taken into account as two key components working together.

Harper (2006) identified five key elements in the development of a good digital library: system architecture, digitization of content, metadata development, visual interface and preservation of digital objects. The author argued that the visual interfaces of digital libraries and good metadata elements for the digital objects are very important from the end-user's perspective. Wan (2006) also states that the designing of user-friendly interfaces is crucially important for the exploration (and retrieval) and management of content in digital libraries. Fox et al. (1993) suggest that digital libraries are becoming the main repository of mankind's knowledge and, as a result, the design of user-friendly interfaces to access, understand and manage digital library content has become an active and challenging field of study.

Social networking and crowdsourcing

While, traditionally, metadata is assigned to digital library objects by professionals, internet and social networking technologies have brought new opportunities for the tagging and indexing of digital resources by users rather than professionals. Harper (2006) argues that progress in enhancing or adding features in digital library interfaces is limited only by time, the functionality of digital asset management systems and the ingenuity of digital library developers. For example, the increasing popularity of social media or Web 2.0 tools and technologies (e.g. social networking, blogs, social tagging) has led to the addition of new features in digital library user interfaces so as to make effective use of crowdsourced data in order to improve access to digital content (Howe, 2006). According to Jeff Howe (n.d.), 'Crowdsourcing is the act of taking a job traditionally performed by a designated agent (usually an employee) and outsourcing it to an undefined, generally large group of people in the form of an open call.' Howe (2006) describes crowdsourced data as user-generated data where a large number of online users may contribute a wider variety of data, ranging from reviews, ratings and tags to relevance judgement and opinions. Many libraries have incorporated social media tools in their websites. For instance, Rubin, Gavin and Kamal (2011) found that 26% and 6% of the library websites that they examined had links to Facebook and Flickr, respectively. In addition, they found evidence of the use of Twitter, social tagging and other applications on library websites. Social tags, also commonly known as folksonomies, are generated by users (Smith, 2004; Sun, 2008) and are now seen as 'a form of emergent indexing' (Woolwine et al., 2011, 81). It is also described as a social indexing process (Hassan-Montero and Herrero-Solana, 2006). Folksonomies are a form of crowdsourced (meta)data that serve as an alternative mode of access to content in digital libraries, and the tag cloud generated from social tags is becoming an increasingly popular 'interface model for visual information retrieval' (Hassan-Montero and Herrero-Solana, 2006).

At the outset, the interface designers may not be able to think of or incorporate all the emerging features (e.g. social tagging) in digital library user interfaces that will be helpful to the user in resource discovery. For example, Na et al. (2011, 310) argued that 'sentiment-based browsing and searching would be a standard feature in future digital libraries of social media content (e.g., expert reviews, user reviews, blog postings and discussion board postings) as they enhance the usability of the digital library'. Therefore, it is critical to evaluate different digital library user interfaces in order to learn more about newly emerged features so that they 'compare well with other web destinations in appearance and in navigation. When users interact with intuitive interfaces and visually appealing sites elsewhere on the web, libraries feel challenged to offer interfaces that work just as well and look just as good' (Breeding, 2007, as cited in Yang and Hofmann, 2011).

Methodology
Selection of digital libraries
Four digital libraries were selected from four English-speaking countries, namely Canada, the USA, the UK and Australia, for analysis in this study. It was decided to choose two national and two public libraries so as to be able to compare the features and functionalities across different types of institutions. The rationale for this selection lies in our interest in international digital library developments and innovations. The two public and national digital libraries selected are listed in Table 3.2.

Table 3.2 Digital libraries selected for study	
Public libraries	**National libraries**
Edmonton Public Library (EPL) (Canada) [http://epl.bibliocommons.com/dashboard]	Trove: National Library of Australia [http://trove.nla.gov.au/]
Ann Arbor District Library System (United States) [www.aadl.org/]	The British Library (UK) [www.bl.uk/]

Grounded theory

The analytical categories of different features offered by digital libraries were developed by using grounded theory (Glaser and Strauss, 1967; Corbin and Strauss, 1990; Pandit, 1996). The advantages of grounded theory include the use of the theory in exploring a research domain that has limited literature, and it provides a strong theoretical foundation for discovering features and their properties from either single or multiple sources of data through an iterative process without having *a priori* categories (Pandit, 1996; Goulding, 1999). The feature list (as shown in Table 3.3) was not predetermined but was developed incrementally when researchers browsed in and interacted with the selected digital libraries. In our analysis, we took into account the notions of richness and variety of metadata elements used and the ways in which metadata elements were used to support searching, browsing and exploratory interaction. More specifically, we developed a set of analytical categories based on metadata elements. These elements include basic and advanced search functions, query formulation and reformulation, collection-level metadata, visual representations, as well as such emerging features as social bookmarking, social tagging and other types of user-generated content.

Findings

All four digital library user interfaces provided faceted views of metadata elements for browsing, navigation and query refinement. Table 3.3 shows a comparative view of the categories across the selected digital libraries. There follows a brief analysis of each digital library and its interesting and unique features.

The Ann Arbor District Library System

The Ann Arbor District Library (AADL) System interface makes use of metadata elements such as format, language, availability, series, age group, and publication by year and decade in order to provide query reformulation support. The user selection of metadata elements in query formulation and reformulation is visually represented on the interface. The interface provides access to both browsing and searching functions in its initial search user interface. Furthermore, it provides an option to use 'Google Translate' to automatically translate the page that is being viewed into six different languages.

One of the very useful features of the basic function is the inclusion of tags and reviews as filtering elements. User-generated tags and reviews are searchable within both basic and advanced search functions. Another interesting but rarely found interface feature in the AADL System search interfaces is the use of the 'age group' metadata element. The 'age group' metadata element is designed in such a way as to allow users to both browse and conduct (advanced) searches (Figure 3.1). The query refinement feature in the AADL System interface is particularly well designed, as it provides a number of filtering mechanisms, by means of which users are able to narrow down

Table 3.3 *Analytical categories developed for the examination of selected digital library user interfaces*

User interface	Library 1 Ann Arbor	Library 2 EPL	Library 3 NLA	Library 4 BL
Use of metadata in browsing searching query formulation and re-formulation	• Format • Language • Availability • Series • Age group • Publication by year and decade	• Availability • Format • Audience • Acquired date of the item • Topic • Language • Genre form • Published date • Content • Author • Region • Tags • LCSH (Library of Congress Subject Headings)	• Format • Decade • Language • Availability • Australian content • Other websites (e.g. Google, Amazon, Wikipedia, etc.)	• Author • Subject • Material type • Collection • Creation date • Language • Publisher • Journal title • Genre • Suggested authors • Suggested subjects
Search results (sort by)	• Relevance • Just added • Top rated • Most popular (this week this month this year)	• Relevance • Date acquired • Title • Author • Date published	• Books • Photos • Maps • Digitized • Newspapers • Journals • Articles • Archived • Websites • Videos, etc. • Relevance • Recency†	• Date_Oldest • Date_Newest • Title • Author
Collection level metadata (browse by)	• New items • Hot items • Format	• Format • Genre • Language • Age, etc.	• Collection type: — Newspapers — Books — Photos — Journals — Maps — Archived websites — Music sound and videos — Diaries, letters and archives — People and organizations	• General reference • Document supply • Sound archive • Music collection, etc.

Notes:
* Login and select some libraries to enable searching in my libraries.
† The sort by relevance and recency feature is available only after the selection of document type (e.g. books).

Continued on next page

Table 3.3 *Continued*

User interface	Library 1 Ann Arbor	Library 2 EPL	Library 3 NLA	Library 4 BL

Basic search function	• Keywords
	• Author
	• Title
	• Series
	• Tags
	• Reviews
	• Subjects
	• Call number
	• Location (availability)
		• Keywords
		• Author
		• Title
		• Subject
		• Tag
		• List
		• User
		• Search within catalogue website and articles
			• Keyword-based search with search limits for availability and Australian content	• Keyword search with three options:
				  – 'everything in the catalogue'
				  – 'newspaper library'
				  – 'remote supply'

Advanced search function	• Format • Publisher • Year • Age group	• Subject • Series • Award • Identifier • Geographic region • Genre • Publisher • Language • Locations • Availability • Audience • Category • Date	• Keyword • Title • Creator • Subject • ISBN • ISSN • Public tag • Year • Format • Availability • Language • Library • Australian content • In my libraries*	• Author • Main title • Other title • Subject description • Place name • Abstract • Map scale • Publication year • Material type • Search scope

Other features including social media tools	• Community reviews
	• Ratings
	• Tweet
	• Google +1
	• Facebook
	• Blogs
	• Social tagging
		• Recently reviewed items filtered by:
		  – format
		  – user comments
		  – ratings
		• Facebook
		• Twitter
		• Social tagging
		• List of other social bookmarking services
			• Twitter
			• Facebook
			• Delicious
			• Connotea
			• Digg
			• User comments or reviews including reviews from other resources (e.g. Amazon)
			• Ratings
			• Social tagging
				• Twitter
				• Facebook
				• Blogs
				• RSS
				• Delicious
				• Connotea
				• Social tagging

Visual re-presentations (e.g. tag clouds)	• Tag cloud	• Browse the shelf • Result display by list or cover • Tag list	• Tag cloud	• Tag cloud • Tag list

Notes:
* Login and select some libraries to enable searching in my libraries.
† The sort by relevance and recency feature is available only after the selection of document type (e.g. books).

their search or retrieved results. Figure 3.1 provides a snapshot of query refinement in the AADL System. The interface provides the user with the initial search term, the search strategy used and the sorting option selected. Users can then refine their initial search using such metadata elements as format, availability and the interesting feature 'age group'.

Tag clouds are becoming a popular user interface feature in many social media applications. Figure 3.2 shows a tag cloud for a search for 'Harry Potter' in the AADL System. This type of interface provides a different user interaction paradigm, where users can explore user-generated content visually and gain insight into the most frequently and most commonly used tags and terms. This type of tag presentation supports various information seeking strategies such as browsing, exploring and query (re)formulation.

Edmonton Public Library interface

The Edmonton Public Library (EPL) interface supports effective metadata-based searching and browsing. Within this interface both basic and advanced search functionalities are available for limiting the search to the library catalogue, the websites or licensed databases (labelled as 'articles'). One of the interesting features of the basic search interface is the 'recently reviewed items' history, where users can filter by format, namely music CDs, downloadable audiobooks, DVDs and books.

Among the advanced search features there are two metadata elements that refer to the location: one indicates whether a given library holds the item and the other indicates whether the item is available at a particular branch library. This metadata element is particularly useful for interlibrary or inter-branch loan services. An innovative feature in the advanced search interface is 'category', which lists categories that have been developed using a combination of such elements as language, community and genre. Examples of a category

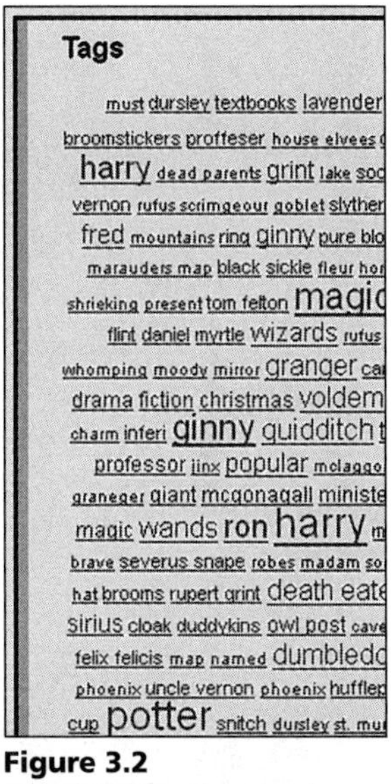

Figure 3.1
AADL search refinement interface (courtesy of Ann Arbor District Library)

Figure 3.2
Tag cloud for the search term 'Harry Potter' (courtesy of Ann Arbor District Library)

include 'Hindi nonfiction', 'Persian fiction', 'animal story' and 'aboriginal'. This feature allows users to make effective use of multiple metadata elements to narrow their search.

The query refinement feature uniquely classifies tags into 'tag tone', 'tag genre' and 'tag theme', as compared to a basic tag cloud or tag list, commonly found in other digital libraries. Another way of reformulating a query in this interface is supported by the use of the Library of Congress Subject Headings (LCSH), where users are able to view and choose a particular subject heading so as to retrieve items described using that subject heading. This feature is available only when the user selects to view details of an item.

The interface makes extensive use of emerging user interface features, such as social tags, social bookmarking and social networking functionalities. The interface has a sophisticated design to allow members of the library community to create, rate and comment on items. The 'community activity' is divided into the following categories: comments, age, summaries, notes, quotes and videos. For example, users can add quotes or videos related to the item here. Users can recommend the suitability of the item for various age groups. In addition, users can create a list of interesting items that can be shared with other users, similar to popular social bookmarking sites (e.g. Delicious and Connotea). Although the interface supports tagging for organization and retrieval of items, it does not provide a visual tag cloud; rather, it offers a tag list feature.

The interface also provides a link to a mobile user interface for small-screen devices. The EPL user interface has a shelf-browsing feature that provides users with the opportunity to browse books that are classified close to the item selected by the user. Figure 3.3 shows a screenshot of the shelf-browsing feature. Users can view the title, author and item format metadata for each item that they browse. Similar to the AADL digital library, the EPL interface allows users to search tags in the basic search mode.

Figure 3.3
EPL shelf browsing feature (courtesy of Edmonton Public Library)

The British Library

The British Library (BL) user interface provides basic and advanced search functionalities to allow users to search within the catalogue or the website. The main interface provides a facet-based search refinement feature where users can choose

Figure 3.4 *British Library query refinement interface (© British Library Board, P3)*

metadata elements to modify or reformulate their initial searches. Metadata elements are provided on the interface to refine the search results as well as to reformulate queries based on suggested authors and subjects (Figure 3.4).

For each retrieved item, a metadata record can be shown, upon the user's request, along with features that allow the user to add notes and assign tags to the item. One of the interesting features of the interface is that users can have an option to view (through hyperlinks) the metadata record in other catalogues like WorldCat, Amazon or COPAC, a union catalogue of a number of academic, research and special libraries in the UK. A useful feature of the interface is the provision of information about the number of versions of the same item, as well as the delivery information.

The collection-level metadata offered by the BL interface varies depending on the nature of the query. For instance, searches for 'India' and 'Harry Potter' will result in two different sets of collection-level metadata. Only the metadata elements for collections that contain the searched item will be shown to the user, as is shown in Table 3.4.

In addition to the above features, the catalogue has a list of electronic journals that can be browsed or searched using such elements as title or subject, or through advanced search. The advanced features for electronic journals provide such elements as subject, title, ISSN and vendor.

Table 3.4 *Collection-level metadata in the British Library catalogue user interface*

Search term 'India'	Search term 'Harry Potter'
Asia, Pacific and Africa (102,268)	Document Supply (8014)
General Reference Collection (49,772)	General Reference Collection (4422)
Document Supply (29,641)	Asia, Pacific and Africa (655)
Sound Archive (10,679)	Science, Technology and Business (449)
Cartographic Items (4544)	Sound Archive (267)
Science, Technology and Business (2639)	
On open access shelves (1405)	

The BL catalogue user interface supports social tagging and provides tag clouds and tag lists with additional information on the frequency of the assigned tags. It also presents information about the most popular and the most recent tags assigned to items, along with a function for searching within tags (Figure 3.5).

Trove: National Library of Australia

Trove is a repository of Australian material maintained by the National Library of Australia. It includes digitized newspapers, journals, articles and datasets, Australian theses, and other resources. Wikipedia defines Trove as 'a search engine to locate resources about Australia and Australians, which reaches many locations otherwise unavailable to external search engines. It is a centralized national service built with the collaboration of major libraries of Australia.'[7]

Similar to the digital library user interfaces above, Trove provides basic and advanced search functionalities. On the advanced search page there are links to various digital collections as identified in our collection-level metadata description in Table 3.1. Trove

Figure 3.5 *British Library tag-related features (© British Library Board, P3)*

Figure 3.6 *Trove social bookmarking/networking features (Courtesy of the National Library of Australia)*

provides a list of metadata elements for reformulating queries using format, language, decade, availability and Australian content. In addition, there is a 'From other websites' feature that provides links to such search systems and resources as Google Books, Amazon and Wikipedia. In addition, Trove provides users with reviews from external resources such as Amazon.

The refinement of queries takes place in two ways. First, with the results are displayed the query refinement features, and users can make use of such elements as format, language and availability to narrow down the search. Second, the user can also select a particular document type, like books, maps or others, and then narrow the search down using the same metadata elements as mentioned above. However, for certain document types, there are slight variations of metadata elements. For instance, when the user selects the 'Archived websites' document type, they will be able to narrow down their search using 'keywords' as a metadata element.

Trove provides a number of social bookmarking and social networking tools (Figure 3.6). These features are available only at the individual document level, meaning that the user has to choose one specific item to be able to use those features. All of the four digital library interfaces studied make use of collection-level metadata to support users' information interaction and exploration. Users are able to choose elements such as format, genre and recent. There is a 'tags' link from the home page of the National Library of Australia's Trove. The tags are searchable and can be narrowed by top tags or by date (Figure 3.7 overleaf). Among the interesting features of the tag cloud is that the user can bookmark the generated tag and can view the frequency of a given tag by hovering the mouse.

Discussion

Item-level metadata elements exist in all four digital libraries. However, not all the item-level metadata elements are available for browsing, searching or query refinement. For instance, the Trove digital repository has the Dewey Decimal Classification number as one of its item-level metadata elements, but the user interface does not provide any mechanism for searching this information in either the basic or advanced search. Another example is from

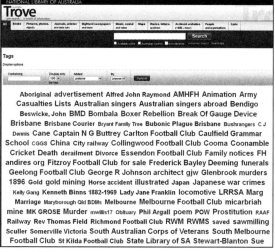

Figure 3.7
Trove tag cloud (courtesy of the National Library of Australia)

Edmonton Public Library, where some items have the Library of Congress Classification and Dewey Decimal Classification numbers. But, like Trove, the interface does not provide any basic or advanced search to support searching or browsing these classification metadata.

Emerging trends

The use of social media or Web 2.0 tools and technologies is one of the emerging trends in the visual interfaces of all four of the digital libraries evaluated in this study. Each library has different types of social media tools incorporated into its website (see Table 3.3). These include Twitter, social tagging and bookmarking sites (e.g. Delicious, Connotea), blogs and links to social networking sites like Facebook. The use of social media tools and technologies has a number of advantages for digital libraries. For example, social tagging helps in creating uncontrolled vocabulary through tags, which provide additional access points for retrieving material from digital collections. Tags enhance and expand standard metadata elements and controlled vocabulary terms. The tags could be used to organize the information based on users' collaborative perception, which would then support browsing, serendipitous discoveries (Twidale, Nichols and Paice, 1997; Mathes, 2004), navigation of the collection (Goh et al., 2009) and the search process (Sun, 2008).

Another interesting feature found on the visual interfaces of three of the libraries (excepting the British Library) is the inclusion of user ratings and comments. These features assist users to identify highly rated resources recommended by others, help them to learn more about the resource and assist in their search for related information.

These developments are in line with current trends in many e-commerce websites, where the systems use opinion-mining techniques to gather, index and present users' views, comments and ratings on various services and products.

Metadata and information interaction

As was shown in our examination of four digital library user interfaces, the use of metadata for information organization, representation and access is becoming more prevalent than ever before.

The digital libraries analysed in the study combined different types of metadata to facilitate users' interaction with information and to support faceted navigation (Yang and Hofmann, 2011). A noticeable development was observed in relation to the combined use of different metadata. All of the four digital library user interfaces make use of manually, automatically and user generated metadata to provide various ways of searching and browsing of digital collections. Another interesting development, with regard to the digital library interfaces examined, was the provision of support for query formulation and refinement based on metadata elements. For instance, AADL and the British Library provide a 'refine by' feature to allow users to narrow down their searches using such metadata elements as title, author, date and format. AADL shows a larger number of metadata elements for use in searching or query refinement. EPL makes use of the term 'Explore further' to help users narrow down their searches using such metadata elements as subject headings and user-generated tags. Trove offers users such metadata elements as format, language and availability to support their search reformulation.

With the growing number of multimedia digital collections, collection-level metadata becomes an important and useful component of multi-collection digital libraries. We found that all of the digital library interfaces we evaluated made use of collection-level metadata to allow users to explore and interact with collections of information. Users can choose such elements as format, genre or language to search for and browse through digital collections. Search-result displays in the digital library user interfaces make effective use of metadata. For instance, EPL and Trove provide relevance as an element for filtering retrieved results. EPL provides a feature called 'date acquired' to allow users to look at the displayed results based on that date. AADL has a number of interesting result-display filtering mechanisms, including 'most popular' (this week, this month, this year) and 'just added'.

Current digital library user interfaces have made attempts to incorporate new visual and graphical representations of digital collections. In this study we found a number of visual features, including visual shelf browsing, tag clouds and tag lists.

Summary

The findings of this study suggest that metadata-enhanced user interfaces to digital libraries represent varying levels of focus on stages of the search process. For instance, some interfaces put more emphasis on the query-formulation stage, some accommodate features and functionalities for query or search reformulation, while others focus on collection understanding. There is a trend towards the use of metadata elements for improving access to digital library collections. The digital libraries evaluated in this study made use of metadata not only at the initial search stage, but also at the search or query-reformulation stage. Some provided seamless access to the results retrieved, as well as metadata elements to provide alternative ways of interacting with the digital library.

Emerging social media applications have found their way into digital library user interfaces. It was found that all of the digital libraries evaluated had incorporated a wide range of socially contributed content and metadata in order to help users to make decisions and to remain engaged in their search and interaction process. Such features as social tags, user ratings, social bookmarks and recommendation functionalities are becoming increasingly popular in digital libraries.

In order to maximize the benefit of metadata for interface design, future research should explore the ways in which different types of metadata, including user-generated metadata, can be used to support all stages of the search and exploration process, including query formulation, query reformulation, results display and query-term recommendation. Further research should explore the ways in which people make use of and interact with these emerging socially created metadata elements to inform the design and development of digital library user interfaces that support users' experiences of interacting with information.

Notes

1   www.loc.gov/marc/.
2   http://dublincore.org/.
3   www.loc.gov/standards/mods/.
4   www.tei-c.org/index.xml.
5   www.archivists.org/saagroups/ead/aboutEAD.html.
6   http://dublincore.org/metadata-basics/.
7   http://en.wikipedia.org/wiki/National_Library_of_Australia#cite_note-32.

References

Arms, W. (2000) *Digital Libraries*, www.cs.cornell.edu/wya/DigLib/.

Beall, J. (2005) Metadata and Data Quality Problems in the Digital Library, *Journal of Digital Information*, **6** (3), http://jodi.tamu.edu/articles/v06/i03/beall.

Breeding, M. (2007) Introduction, *Library Technology Reports*, **43** (4), 5–14.

Corbin, J. and Strauss, A. (1990) Grounded Theory Research: procedures, canons, and evaluation criteria, *Qualitative Sociology*, **13**, 3–21.

Digital Library Federation (2004) *A Working Definition of Digital Library* (1998),
   http://old.diglib.org/about/dldefinition.htm.

Fox, E. A., Hix, D., Nowell, L., Brueni, D. J., Wake, W. and Heath, L. (1993) Users, User
   Interface, and Objects: Envision, a digital library, *Journal of the American Society for
   Information Science*, **44** (8), 480–91.

Glaser, B. G. and Strauss, A. L. (1967) *The Discovery of Grounded Theory: strategies for qualitative
   research*, Aldine.

Goh, D. H., Chua, A., Lee, C. S. and Razikin, K. (2009) Resource Discovery through Social
   Tagging: a classification and content analytic approach, *Online Information Review*, **33** (3),
   568–83.

Goulding, C. (1999) *Grounded Theory: some reflections on paradigm, procedures and misconceptions*,
   Technical Working Paper, University of Wolverhampton, UK.

Greenberg, J. (2005) Understanding Metadata and Metadata Schemes, *Cataloging & Classification
   Quarterly*, **40** (3/4), 17–36.

Greenberg, J. (2010) Metadata and Digital Information. In *Encyclopedia of Library and
   Information Science*, 3rd edn, Marcel Dekker, Inc., 3610–23.

Harper, C. A. (2006) Collaboration in User Interface Design, or Bringing the Public Service
   Perspective to Building a Digital Library, *Public Services Quarterly*, **2** (1), 115–28.

Hassan-Montero, Y. and Herrero-Solana, V. (2006) Improving Tag-Clouds as Visual
   Information Retrieval Interfaces. In *Proceedings of International Conference on Multidisciplinary
   Information Sciences and Technologies*,
   http://citeseerx.ist.psu.edu/viewdoc/download?doi=10.1.1.85.9998&rep...

Howe, J. (2006) The Rise of Crowdsourcing, *Wired Magazine*, **14** (14), 1–5.

Howe, J. (n.d.) *Crowdsourcing: a definition*, http://crowdsourcing.typepad.com/.

Jung-ran, P. and Tosaka, Y. (2010) Metadata Creation Practices in Digital Repositories and
   Collections: schemata, selection criteria, and interoperability, *Information Technology &
   Libraries*, **29** (3), 104–16.

Lesk, M. (1997) *Practical Digital Libraries: books, bytes and bucks*, Morgan Kaufman.

Ma, J. (2009) Metadata in ARL Libraries: a survey of metadata practices, *Journal of Library
   Metadata*, **9** (1/2), 1–14.

Malizia, A., Bottoni, P. and Levialdi, S. S. (2010) Generating Collaborative Systems for Digital
   Libraries: a model-driven approach, *Information Technology & Libraries*, **29** (4), 171–86.

Mathes, A. (2004) *Folksonomies – Cooperative Classification and Communication through Shared
   Metadata*, www.adammathes.com/academic/computer-mediated-
   communication/folksonomies-old.html.

Meghini, C., Spyratos, N. and Yang, J. (2010) A Data Model for Digital Libraries, *International
   Journal on Digital Libraries*, **11** (1), 41–56.

Morville, P. and Rosenfeld, L. (2007) Organization Systems. In St Laurent, S. (ed.) *Information
   Architecture for the World Wide Web*, O'Reilly, 53–81.

Na, J.-C., Thet, T. T., Nasution, A. H. and Hassan, F. M. (2011) A Sentiment-Based Digital
   Library of Movie Review Documents Using Fedora/Une bibliothèque numérique de
   documents critiques de films basée sur les sentiments en utilisant Fedora, *Canadian Journal*

of Information and Library Science, **35** (3), 307–37.

NISO (2004) *Understanding Metadata*, NISO Press,
www.niso.org/standards/resources/UnderstandingMetadata.pdf.

Pandit, N. R. (1996) The Creation of Theory: a recent application of the grounded theory methods, *The Qualitative Report*, **2** (4),
www.nova.edu/ssss/QR/QR2-4/pandit.html/pandit.html.

Parandjuk, J. C. (2010) Using Information Architecture to Evaluate Digital Libraries, *Reference Librarian*, **51** (2), 124–34.

Pope, J. T. and Holley, R. P. (2011) Google Book Search and Metadata, *Cataloging & Classification Quarterly*, **49** (1), 1–13.

Rubin, V. L., Gavin, P. T. and Kamal, A. M. (2011) Innovation in Public and Academic North American Libraries: examining white literature and website applications / L'innovation dans les bibliothèques publiques et académiques en Amérique du Nord: examen de la littérature blanche (livres et périodiques) et des applications pour sites web, *Canadian Journal of Information and Library Science*, **35** (4), 187–212.

Shiri, A. (2008) Metadata-Enhanced Visual Interfaces to Digital Libraries, *Journal of Information Science*, **34** (6), 763–75.

Smith, G. (2004) *Atomiq: Folksonomy: social classification*,
http://atomiq.org/archives/2004/08/folksonomy_social_classification.html.

Sun, B. D. (2008) Folksonomy and Health Information Access: how can social bookmarking assist seekers of online medical information? *Journal of Hospital Librarianship*, **8** (1), 119–26.

Twidale, M. B., Nichols, D. M. and Paice, C. D. (1997) Browsing is a Collaborative Process, *Information Processing & Management*, **33** (6), 761–83.

Wan, G. (2006) Visualizations for Digital Libraries, *Information Technology and Libraries*, **25** (2), 88–94.

Weagley, J., Gelches, E. and Jung-Ran, P. (2010) Interoperability and Metadata Quality in Digital Video Repositories: a study of Dublin Core, *Journal of Library Metadata*, **10** (1), 37–57.

Woolwine, D., Ferguson, M., Joy, E., Pickup, D. and Udma, C. M. (2011) Folksonomies, Social Tagging and Scholarly Articles / Les folksonomies, l'étiquetage social et les articles scientifiques, *Canadian Journal of Information and Library Science*, **35** (1), 77–92.

Yang, S. Q. and Hofmann, M. A. (2011) Next Generation or Current Generation? A study of the OPACs of 260 academic libraries in the USA and Canada, *Library Hi Tech*, **29** (2), 266–300.

Yasser, C. M. (2011) An Analysis of Problems in Metadata Records, *Journal of Library Metadata*, **11** (2), 51–62.

Zaphiris, P., Gill, K., Ma, T. Y., Wilson, S. and Petrie, H. (2004) Exploring the Use of Information Visualization for Digital Libraries, *New Review of Information Networking*, **10** (1), 51–69.

CHAPTER 4

Information access

Gobinda Chowdhury and Schubert Foo

Introduction
....

As discussed in Chapter 1, information access includes all the typical information retrieval processes and activities ranging from content and data selection, and processing and indexing, to search and retrieval, and use of information and data by a designated user community in order to meet their information requirements. Research in information access (information retrieval, to be precise) began in the 1950s and the emphasis in the early days was on building automated systems for indexing so as to facilitate retrieval of documents, rather than on the needs of users. Progress in information retrieval may be summarized as follows (Agosti, 2008; Chowdhury, 2010; Ruthven and Kelly, 2011):

- Stage 1 (from 1950s to mid-1970s): The focus was on document and text retrieval using small test collections, and the application areas included catalogue, bibliographic and full-text documents. The focus was more on designing retrieval systems than on users' needs and usability. A large number of remote online databases appeared, providing search and retrieval of abstracts and some full-text documents of scholarly information resources such as journal and conference papers.
- Stage 2 (mid-1970s to mid-1980s): The focus was still on systems rather than on users, but retrieval systems became more sophisticated and more advanced systems were built both for managing unstructured text in databases and for structured library management operations. Online Public Access Catalogues (OPACs) and more online databases appeared, facilitating remote access to information, but the systems were centralized and the focus was still on text.
- Stage 3 (mid-1980s to mid-1990s): During this period 'the attention of information management system researchers started to move from the collection of documents towards the user and the retrieval model, with the focus on the invention of models better able to support user–system interaction' (Agosti, 2008, 4). Alternative models, especially natural language processing and knowledge-based retrieval models, as well as hypertext and network-based

models, began to appear. There was also a major shift in research from systems to users and interactions, giving rise to various information seeking and retrieval models. This was also the early phase of digital library research, where the focus was on developing robust information retrieval models and systems that were capable of processing and retrieving large quantities of digital information of different kinds – text as well as multimedia. Free internet search engines began to appear that were several times more powerful than the conventional retrieval systems used in text databases.

- Stage 4 (mid-1990s to early 2010s): This phase saw several major changes in information access: many new and powerful search engines like Google; online question-answering systems like Ask; visual search engines like Kartoo and Vivisimo; meta search engines like Mamma. Several multimedia search engines appeared that were based on many old and newly developed information retrieval techniques and models. Large-scale research and evaluation of information retrieval became possible and a common platform for sharing of expertise in information retrieval at the international level was formed under the name of TREC (Text Retrieval Conference). Multilingual and multimedia information retrieval research became more powerful, and during this time the scope of digital library research was extended from building systems to user evaluation and impact studies, including the emergence of platforms similar to TREC in the form of CLEF (Cross Language Evaluation Forum) and NTCIR (NII Test Collection for IR Systems). Several large-scale digital libraries were created and information access, usability and impact studies became the focus of digital library research. A new open access movement (discussed in Chapter 10) began that gave birth to several open access repositories and open access journals.
- Stage 5 (the last few years): Information access in the web and large-scale digital libraries and distributed information systems became more challenging and diverse, due to the emergence of Web 2.0, semantic web and social networking technologies. New approaches for the creation and organization/tagging of information appeared through social media like YouTube, Facebook and Twitter, and were embraced and widely used. In parallel, there more robust and special search engine services appeared, such as Google Books and Google Scholar, and Microsoft Academic Search. Open access, e-scholarship, e-science, digital humanities and digital culture became new areas of research within digital libraries, posing new challenges for access to large volumes of digital information – free as well as fee-based, created by and available from a multitude of sources in a variety of forms, formats and languages.

User-centred design and usability became a major research area within information access. Of late, the scope of digital library research is being extended to both research data and research output, bringing more challenges as well as opportunities for information access, information and data analytics and visualization. The rest of this chapter provides examples of the information access features and facilities of some selected types of digital libraries and, on the basis of these, discusses different issues and challenges associated with information access in digital libraries.

Information access and digital libraries

Access to information in digital libraries may be influenced by a number of factors such as the following:

- content of the digital library
- target users, their characteristics and information requirements
- interface and retrieval features
- objectives and business plans of the organization providing the digital library service
- specific standards and regulations, such as the design and usability guidelines for information products and services, web accessibility guidelines, and so on.

While each of these factors plays an important part in the overall success of a digital library in terms of information access and use, they are not mutually exclusive and often need to be considered in conjunction with one another. Furthermore, with the recent developments in web and social-networking technologies, new approaches to information access and use are emerging. Such new access mechanisms and practices include: social information retrieval, social tagging, social review/evaluation/rating, and collaborative content creation and use.

Various issues related to information access in digital libraries, focusing particularly on the first three areas mentioned above, are discussed in this chapter using examples drawn from some large live digital libraries, including the ACM DL (American Computing Machinery Digital Library), Europeana, the NSDL (National Science Digital Library), PubMed, Music Australia and the NDLTD (Networked Digital Library of Theses and Dissertations), to point out how each of the three factors plays an important part in access to information. The two remaining factors will be elaborated in Chapter 12 in the context of usability and evaluation of digital libraries. Some new digital libraries and information services are also adopting new and emerging technologies, such as semantic and ontology-based access and visualization. Overall, access to information in digital libraries is becoming a fascinating area of study and research.

Sample digital libraries

Six digital libraries have been chosen as a basis for review and discussion. These are:

- PubMed (www.ncbi.nlm.nih.gov/pubmed/) – the US National Library of

Medicine and the Institute of National Health digital library of medical and biomedical research (Figure 4.1)

- ACM Digital Library (http://dl.acm.org/) – scholarly digital library of ACM publications (Figure 4.2)
- NDLTD (www.ndltd.org/) – the Networked Digital Library of Theses and Dissertations (Figure 4.3)
- NSDL (http://nsdl.org/) – the US National Science Digital Library (Figure 4.4)
- Europeana (www.europeana.eu) – Europe's digital library of cultural and scientific heritage information (Figure 4.5)
- Music Australia (www.musicaustralia.org/) – Australia's digital library of music (Figure 4.6).

Although these digital libraries are quite large and diverse in their content, users and services, and other features, their selection for the discussions in this chapter does not necessarily mean that they are the best or the most representative of today's digital library world. They have been chosen to illustrate different examples of information access facilities provided by some of today's digital libraries. As such, these libraries will have similarities and differences along the dimensions of the discussion.

Information access in digital libraries: content issues

The process of accessing information is fundamentally similar in most content databases or digital libraries: content is stored in one or more places (servers), one or more indexes are created for the content of the digital library, these indexes are searched by the users, and when a match is found the corresponding items are retrieved from their storage servers. Thus, the success of a digital library depends primarily on two factors: how effectively and efficiently the content items are indexed and how the searching and matching process takes place. The underlying processes of indexing and searching/matching may be simple or complex. In a simple system, an index is created based on some simple metadata created for each item, such as author, title, date, descriptors or keywords, and a simple Boolean search – that is, combining search terms with 'AND', 'OR', 'NOT' (for details of Boolean search principles and techniques, see Chowdhury, 2010; Chu, 2010; Goker and Davies, 2009) – may be used to search for and retrieve items from a digital library. Also, some digital libraries provide navigation facilities through a variety of predefined categories or through visual interfaces. However, the process may be very complex for full-text retrieval systems, where every word or phrase in every item in a digital library may be a potential index term, and complexity increases when more advanced retrieval and matching and filtration or relevance-assessment techniques are used, e.g. retrieval systems based on term weighting and relevance assessment based on a combination of techniques such as link analysis or semantic analysis (for details of these techniques see Chowdhury, 2010; Chu, 2010; Goker and Davies, 2009). These complex information-access systems involve several

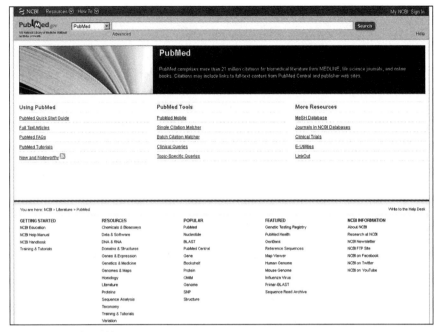

Figure 4.1 *PubMed home page*

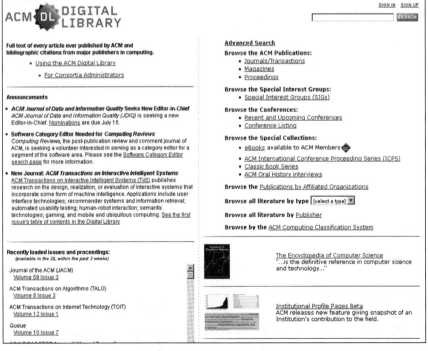

Figure 4.2 *ACM Digital Library home page*

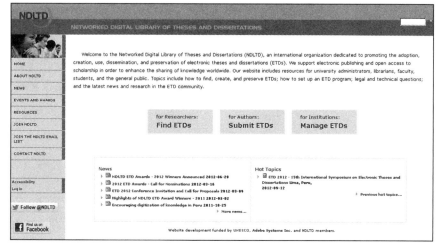

Figure 4.3 *NDLTD home page*

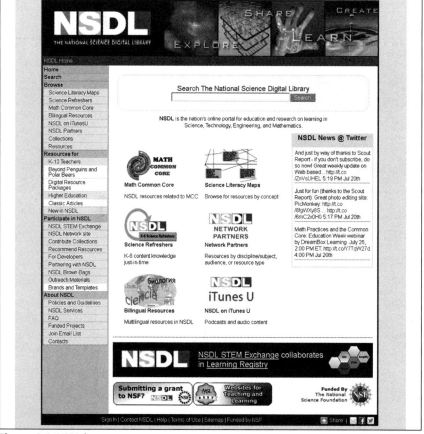

Figure 4.4 *NSDL home page*

Figure 4.5 *Europeana home page*

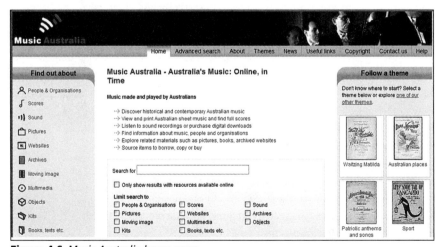

Figure 4.6 *Music Australia home page*

sophisticated indexing and retrieval techniques that allow users to search in a natural language, as opposed to a structured search using typical Boolean search operators (e.g. AND, OR, NOT) and they aim to generate an output list where every retrieved item has a different value or weight and therefore the output list is ranked. Link-analysis technique, which is based on the principles of citation analysis, i.e. how frequently a given information resource is cited or referenced (often though hyperlinks), is often used in determining the importance or weighting of retrieved items.

The process of retrieval becomes even more complex when multimedia items like image, audio or video materials are involved. This complexity arises because of the differences in nature between text and multimedia items. In the case of textual items, the content of an item can be segmented into words and phrases that can be easily matched with the search terms: the individual units of the content, i.e. words or phrases, are similar in nature to those that represent user queries, i.e. search terms or phrases. However, multimedia items cannot be segmented into such units that can be matched directly with the search terms. In simpler multimedia systems, the retrieval can be based on term matching where some terms used to describe the content, such as the singer or composer of a piece of music, or the actors or producer of a film, are matched with the search terms entered by the user. However, more complex multimedia retrieval systems use content-based retrieval, where the retrieval takes place based on the digital representation of the items and sample multimedia content provided by the user as a search criterion (for details see Chowdhury, 2010; Chu, 2010; Goker and Davies, 2009).

Indexing and representation of content in a digital library are therefore some important criteria for success of a digital library. However, one of the challenges here is how best to describe the content – at the collection, document and content levels – so that users can find the required content easily. A variety of metadata standards, encoding schema, vocabulary control tools and, most importantly, indexing techniques and algorithms are used for the selection of search terms, their weighting, retrieval mechanisms, etc. (for details, see Chowdhury, 2010; Chu, 2010; Goker and Davies, 2009).

By looking at the six digital libraries chosen for this chapter, it may be noted that they offer a variety of information access facilities. For example, Music Australia provides access to music made and played by Australians. Through Music Australia (www.musicaustralia.org), users can:

- discover historical and contemporary Australian music
- view and print Australian sheet music and find full scores
- listen to sound recordings or purchase digital downloads
- find information about music, people and organizations
- explore related materials such as pictures, books, archived websites
- source items to borrow, copy or buy.

At the time of writing, Music Australia provides access to 276,931 resources on music, of which 60,820 are available in digital form. Users can access information about people, music scores, sound recordings, music-related websites, books, journals and theses, pictures and videos, and so on.

Like Music Australia, Europeana also has a geographical boundary in terms of its content, and this is, obviously, Europe. Similarly, NSDL also has a boundary, but focuses on its target or most immediate users, i.e. school students and teachers. The chosen digital libraries have significant differences in terms of their content and target users. For example, NSDL, NDLTD, PubMed and ACM Digital Library deal primarily with scholarly information and their primary goal is to provide access to digital information in order to promote education and research, while for Europeana the primary content is cultural heritage information on Europe that may be of interest to anyone, and the content of Music Australia is music or music-related information produced in Australia and by Australians. These differences obviously result in differences in the features and facilities for information access provided by these digital libraries.

Information access in digital libraries: user issues

A digital library may have one or more designated user communities, and the information access features and facilities are governed by the nature and characteristics of the target user communities. Some of the chosen digital libraries have designated users from one or more specific disciplines, for example for NSDL, PubMed and ACM Digital Library; in some cases users come primarily from a specific community, for example, school students and teachers for NSDL, research students and academics for NDLTD, and so on. These designated user communities and their characteristics have a significant influence on the design and the overall information access features of the digital libraries concerned. 'Know thy user' is the mantra of a user-centred design and, in order to be successful, a digital library should try to build information-access features, i.e. the search and retrieval features, and facilities, i.e. the options that the search interface provides to the user in order to perform search and retrieval operations, in line with the user characteristics and requirements (for details of user-centred design see Albert, Tullis and Tedesco, 2010; Chowdhury and Chowdhury, 2011; ISO, 2010). The examples provided in the following sections justify this argument.

However, although this means additional work, sometimes having a designated user community is better than having to build a digital library that aims to meet the information needs and characteristics of every possible category and type of user. This was noted in a recent study on the usability of Europeana, in which Dobreva and Chowdhury (2010) noted that the information access facilities of Europeana were perceived differently by different categories of users, and the expectations of the younger users (the so-called digital natives), especially, were quite different from those of older users.

Information access in digital libraries: interface and access features

A quick look at the home pages of the six digital libraries shows some significant differences in their design, look and feel, search options and other details. It is difficult to ascertain whether these differences are indeed due to the differences among the chosen digital libraries in terms of their objectives, content, target users or other factors. Ideally, if these digital libraries had followed the user-centred design principles (for details see, ISO, 2010; Pearrow, 2007) and usability guidelines (for details, see Chowdhury and Chowdhury, 2011), then the features of these digital libraries would reflect the designated user communities and their requirements. While more usability research is needed in order to find this out, some differences among these digital libraries' interface features and information-access facilities are quite distinct.

PubMed

The PubMed digital library has a number of access features that are particularly suitable for expert users, in this case the designated user community in health and biomedical sciences. Its home page (see Figure 4.1) provides a brief introduction to PubMed, pointing out that it provides access to over 21 million items of biomedical literature. It also provides links to various specific collections and services. From the home page a user can choose a specific collection from a drop-down box and enter search terms in a simple search box to conduct a search, choose options to 'limit' the search, click on the 'Help' button or go to the advanced search option. Thus, the home page of this digital library is very simple and yet very rich in content and options. By clicking on the 'limit' option, the user can limit a simple search by various parameters, like the type of article, language, species, specific subsets of the collection/discipline, and specific age groups (an important characteristic of the health and biomedical domain because some treatments and applications etc. are applicable only to some specific age groups of patients/people). This clearly indicates that the options for information access are specifically related to the discipline and the target users. This is also reflected in the advanced search page. From the home page of PubMed, users can also choose to conduct specific searches, for example for 'clinical trials' (a registry and results database of clinical trials conducted in the USA and elsewhere in the world). Users can use the MeSH (Medical List of Subject Headings) controlled vocabulary to choose specific terms for searching. Another novel feature of PubMed is that it shows how a query is translated and executed. For example, a search on 'HIV and children and Africa' entered in the simple search screen is translated and executed as:

("hiv"[MeSH Terms] OR "hiv"[All Fields]) AND ("africa"[MeSH Terms] OR "africa"[All Fields]) AND ("child"[MeSH Terms] OR "child"[All Fields] OR "children"[All Fields])

This is useful for an expert searcher, who, from this query translation, can find out how the actual search is executed and thus can modify the query appropriately, if necessary. Thus the PubMed digital library provides a good mix of traditional tools like MeSH and several modern and unique information-access features and facilities that are suitable for specialist users.

ACM Digital Library

Like PubMed, ACM Digital Library (ACM DL) is a digital library of scholarly information for a designated user community that has domain knowledge in computer science and related disciplines. The home page of ACM DL provides very brief but useful information about the service. It provides a simple search box and an 'Advanced Search' option, and also options for browsing specific collections, like journals, conferences, books and interviews. The home page also provides several announcements (see Figure 4.2). ACM DL is basically a membership fee-based service, although the public can search and browse its catalogue. One of the unique features of ACM DL is that if a user from a subscribing institution goes to the home page it automatically recognizes the user (as shown on the top of Figure 4.2) and provides access to the digital versions of publications accordingly. This is a very useful feature because it means that the user does not need to log in personally to obtain access. There are a number of useful search and retrieval features, too. For example, by entering search terms in the simple search box, the user not only gets a list of hits with bibliographic details of the retrieved items, linked PDF files etc., but can also refine the search results by various parameters, like authors, institutions, editors, reviewers, publication year, publication name, conference sponsors and proceedings series. The user can also go to the advanced search screen from the search results page or from the home page (see Figure 4.2). The advanced search screen provides several search boxes where the user can enter search terms and various other criteria for making the search more specific. This screen appears to be suitable for expert users. The target user community for this digital library is academics and scholars in computer science and related disciplines and therefore the user can search by computing classification system (CCS), conference sponsor name, DOI (digital object identifier) etc. There are some other advanced features that are particularly useful for advanced users (as opposed to just one-time casual users). For example, by clicking on a retrieved item, the user can get such additional data as the number of downloads, citation counts and others, which are some useful bibliometric indicators for the item.

NDLTD

Like PubMed and ACM Digital Library, NDLTD also deals with scholarly information and has a designated user community primarily comprising academics, scholars and students of higher education. However, unlike the two other digital libraries, NDLTD covers every discipline and subject, but it is limited to one specific type of information resource: theses and dissertations. NDLTD not only allows users to access digital theses and dissertations, but from the same interface it also allows them to submit theses (see Figure 4.3). Users can access this digital library through the 'Find ETDs' button, which provides access to a union catalogue of more than one million digital theses and dissertations. Access to the union catalogue is provided through two search tools: the Scirus ETD search tool from Elsevier, or a search tool known as VTLS Visualizer. The Scirus ETD search tool provides access to the union catalogue of theses and dissertations hosted by OCLC, which includes a simple and an advanced search option. The advanced search option allows users to conduct a search in specific fields, like author, title, keywords, description, item type and review status. In VTLS Visualizer users can search by language, continent, country, date, format and source institution and can sort results by relevance, title and date.

NSDL

Like the three other digital libraries discussed so far, NSDL also deals with scholarly information, but unlike the others its target users are school teachers and kindergarten to high school students in the USA, and the content covers the disciplines of science, technology, mathematics and engineering. The first screen of NSDL (see Figure 4.4) provides a simple search option; and it also provides browse options for specific collections. NSDL also provides some unique access options. For example:

- NSDL Science Literacy Maps is a tool designed for students and teachers to find resources that relate to specific science and mathematics concepts. For each science topic there is a separate map of concepts that can be used to find specific information on aspects of the chosen subject.
- For the 'Math Common Core' users can find information relevant to a specific year in school education and the corresponding topics, as illustrated in Figure 4.7. Likewise, the search output also shows the specific group of users for which the output is suitable. An example of a typical output is shown in Figure 4.8.

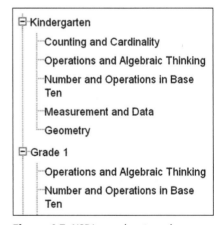

Figure 4.7 *NSDL search categories*

Some collections are also available in multimedia and multilingual form. Specific search results take the user to specific course materials. Figure 4.9 is a typical search result.

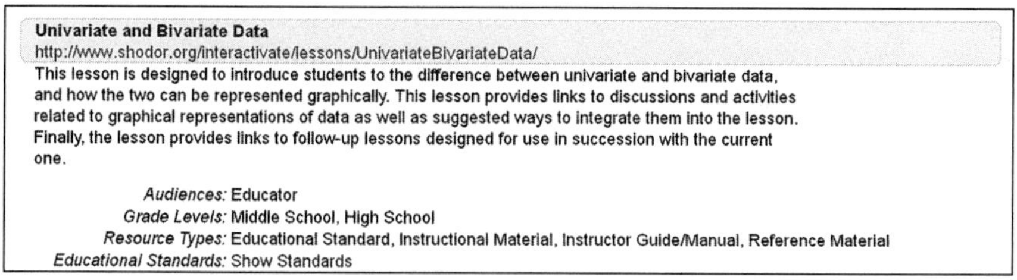

Univariate and Bivariate Data
http://www.shodor.org/interactivate/lessons/UnivariateBivariateData/
This lesson is designed to introduce students to the difference between univariate and bivariate data,
and how the two can be represented graphically. This lesson provides links to discussions and activities
related to graphical representations of data as well as suggested ways to integrate them into the lesson.
Finally, the lesson provides links to follow-up lessons designed for use in succession with the current
one.

Audiences: Educator
Grade Levels: Middle School, High School
Resource Types: Educational Standard, Instructional Material, Instructor Guide/Manual, Reference Material
Educational Standards: Show Standards

Figure 4.8 *NDSL search results*

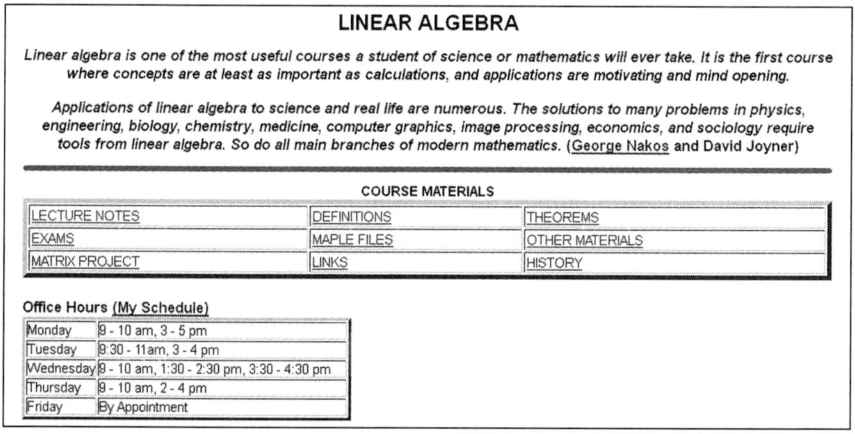

LINEAR ALGEBRA

*Linear algebra is one of the most useful courses a student of science or mathematics will ever take. It is the first course
where concepts are at least as important as calculations, and applications are motivating and mind opening.*

*Applications of linear algebra to science and real life are numerous. The solutions to many problems in physics,
engineering, biology, chemistry, medicine, computer graphics, image processing, economics, and sociology require
tools from linear algebra. So do all main branches of modern mathematics.* (George Nakos and David Joyner)

COURSE MATERIALS

LECTURE NOTES	DEFINITIONS	THEOREMS
EXAMS	MAPLE FILES	OTHER MATERIALS
MATRIX PROJECT	LINKS	HISTORY

Office Hours (My Schedule)

Monday	9 - 10 am, 3 - 5 pm
Tuesday	9:30 - 11am, 3 - 4 pm
Wednesday	9 - 10 am, 1:30 - 2:30 pm, 3:30 - 4:30 pm
Thursday	9 - 10 am, 2 - 4 pm
Friday	By Appointment

Figure 4.9 *NDSL specific search results*

Europeana

As discussed earlier in this chapter, Europeana is one of the largest digital libraries of
cultural heritage information. Unlike the four other digital libraries discussed so far,
Europeana provides access to cultural heritage information and the users can be anyon
anywhere in Europe, and virtually anyone anywhere in the world. The home page of
Europeana (see Figure 4.5) provides a simple search box along with some images with
links to some specific collections – online exhibitions. Users can click on any exhibition
and they will be taken to a specific page providing information about the collections
and a button for starting the exhibition. The exhibitions are organized according to
specific themes (that appear on a new page). Users can choose a specific language for
the exhibition from a drop-down menu. The organization of items in the exhibition
and the browse options are very simple to use. Along with the text and images that
represent the exhibition, there is a button for discovering the music archive that takes
users to a new page for playing audio. A search using the search box on the home page
not only produces a list of hits with thumbnail images and some brief description of
the retrieved items, but also allows the user to filter the search results by media type
(such as image, text, video and sound), by language, date, country, copyright and
provider. Again, the design of the search output page is very simple, and with each

retrieved item there is a symbol that indicates whether it is an image, text, audio or video. The digital library can be explored through a timeline or on a map, and more information about the retrieved items, such as copyright and licence information, and other details, can be obtained.

Music Australia

Music Australia has a single focus on music and music-related information in Australia. Its home page (see Figure 4.6) provides a simple search box and users can limit their search by several parameters, such as scores, picture, people, archives and others. From this page users can also choose to access a specific collection, like scores, sound, pictures or multimedia. The advanced search screen provides options for searching on many specific fields, such as title, genre, notes or artist. The search results can be limited by various parameters, like scores, sound, objects, pictures, books, time, and location of the collections. Finally, the collection is organized by themes such as popular music, children's music, opera, musical theatres and indigenous music.

Some emerging research directions

The discussion so far in this chapter provides a snapshot of different types of information-access facilities available from various digital libraries. As mentioned earlier in the chapter, these are just some examples, and there are many other digital libraries that offer many more unique search and retrieval features. For example, the Variations music digital library (http://variations.sourceforge.net/) provides a variety of facilities for access to audio and score images, and a variety of analysis and annotation tools that are useful for the teaching and learning of music. Similarly, as discussed in Chapter 3, Trove (http://trove.nla.gov.au) provides access to a large digital library of books, journal articles, newspapers, letters, maps, music, sound, video and so on through a very simple interface. At the same time, Trove provides a variety of options for searching, browsing, refining searches and viewing digital objects retrieved by the system.

While the discussion so far has focused on the practical aspects of information access in digital libraries and examples have been drawn from some chosen digital libraries to show the different approaches and facilities for information access, this section addresses some – in particular, emerging – research issues in the area.

Social information retrieval

Information seeking is becoming more social and collaborative in nature. Increasingly, we work as a group in the workplace, and tap into our social networks, like our friends, colleagues and librarians, to seek information. Utilizing the concept of the collective wisdom of the crowd, social information retrieval is evidenced by many examples on the web. These include hyperlinking of web pages, creation of subject directories, Google's Page Rank algorithm, user annotations of resources, social tagging, collaborative querying, social network analysis and collaborative filtering. Social information retrieval provides many opportunities for the research, design and implementation of a new generation of digital libraries and information systems (for a detailed treatise of these emerging technologies and applications, see Goh and Foo, 2008; see also Chapter 5 in this book). Research studies in schools and in the classroom; academic research and collaboration; seeking information in the medical world; and the use of collaborative filtering in the tourism industry – all clearly demonstrate the need to better represent the social context that at present is generally lacking in digital library systems (Buchanan and Hinze, 2008). The generic digital library architecture can be augmented with additional recommendation, alerting and communication services so as to provide and support social context as a means to closing the gap between human communication and the digital library. In order to support this, there will be a need to provide a user registration service and corresponding creation of user-profile and alert-profile databases to support alerting and recommender services for users of the digital library. Social media tools to support peer discussion, reviews and other forms of information-sharing activity will subsequently be created to support group work and information seeking in the digital library.

When we examine the six sample digital libraries in this chapter, it becomes apparent that they are largely designed and operate in typical generic digital library architectures. For instance, PubMed, ACM DL, Europeana and Music Australia are large repositories that support individual information seeking with links to external resources for users. NLDTD, while similar to these digital libraries, has the added functionality of an e-mail listserv to support members' general discussions.

NSDL is perhaps the exception, in that it provides support for more social and collaborative work through the recent development of the STEM (Science, Technology, Engineering and Mathematics) Exchange, in collaboration with other STEM education partners, as a web service to capture and share social media-generated information and other networked associations of educational resources in these subject areas. STEM support for such work comes from the three areas of resource access, resource data and usage data. In terms of resource access, STEM aims to support customizable feeds and widgets within teachers' networks and portals to allow users to discover and collaborate around resources in context. In terms of resource data, STEM supports the generation of paradata in order to blend expert- and user-generated information so as to describe resources and how they are being utilized by communities of educators at different teaching settings. Social-networking styles and widgets will support the generation and use of paradata. Finally, in terms of usage data, STEM will attempt to capture usage patterns when resources are selected, downloaded, embedded and used in various settings. In this instance, the paradata will be aggregated accumulatively at the community-platform level without personal identification information about individual users (NSDL, 2011). Thus, it can be seen that NSDL is moving in the direction of supporting social and collaborative work in the 'new' digital library environment.

The digital divide

The digital divide can be broadly defined as a gap that exists between groups of people who have and who do not have access to ICT (information and communication technology). Such a division can be caused by several factors (as discussed in Chowdhury and Chowdhury, 2011), from technological to socio-economic and human-related. Furthermore, a gap in terms of access to and use of ICT is also observed between younger people, who have been born into the digital world and therefore are called 'digital natives', and those who were born before the internet era and have learnt their use of ICT through training and practice ('digital migrants'). We need to be mindful of the challenges of meeting the needs of the digital native versus the digital migrant, and the real problem of the digital divide that still exists. A study of digital library trends in the Asia-Pacific region noted the dire statistics and the large digital-divide problem facing this heterogeneous region of underdeveloped, developing and developed countries (Foo and Theng, 2004, 2005). While we can recognize that constant efforts have been directed to solving this and other, related problems since the first UN World Summit on Information Society (WSIS) in 2003, it is highly likely that it will continue to be a major challenge to provide connectivity and free access to the global population for a long time to come. The impact of the digital divide on usability of digital libraries is discussed in Chapter 12.

Cloud computing

From the digital library point of view, there is a need to consider providing a range of services and applications at different levels of sophistication and functionality to meet different user needs and expectations. These can range from 'simple is beautiful' solutions to highly intelligent semantic access to digital resources. In parallel with this, technological advances such as cloud computing promise to be an important development for making information access more flexible and affordable.

Simply stated, cloud computing is a shared computing service (see also Chapter 10) that can be classified as either the Public Cloud (a pay-as-you-go service to the public offered, for example, by AmazonWeb Service, Google AppEngine and Microsoft Azure) or the Private Cloud (the fee-paying internal data centres of businesses or other organizations, not made available to the public). The main benefits of using cloud computing include the possibility of having access to infinite computing resources available on demand, the elimination of up-front set-up commitment and costs, and flexible payment methods for the use of computing resources needed in the short term (Armbrust et al., 2009). New application opportunities have been identified, through the adoption of cloud computing, that include the provision of mobile interactive applications that may require multiple data sources and access to large datasets in different data centres, parallel batch processing and analytics of information resources and user-generated information (for example, through social media). In other words, cloud computing fuels the possibility of new functionalities and capabilities in digital libraries to be envisaged and delivered on such a platform in the future (for further details see Chapter 10).

Semantic web technologies

While we journey towards Semantic Web 3.0 and, in parallel, aim to provide semantic access to digital libraries in order to facilitate better information and knowledge discovery, the key to development hinges on the successful development and deployment of metadata and ontologies, and the ability to support interoperability among different schemas across information systems. The generation, mapping, evolving and maintenance of ontology continue to draw research interest as we attempt to close the gap between human and computing understanding and communication (Ding and Foo, 2002a, 2002b). There are two aspects of ontologies that need to be considered – the more well defined metadata that supports logical reasoning, and socially generated metadata that supports sharing and recommendations. The Semantic Web layers (comprising components and concepts like URIs [Uniform Resource Identifiers], RDF [Resource Description Framework], ontologies/linked data, logical languages) support reuse and intelligent search facilities to enable greater granularity and return resources of higher relevance in result lists. At the same time, we need to cater for the socially generated metadata, like tags for sharing and linking related information resources, to provide the extra dimension of connectivity. For example, the work in Upper Tag Ontology (UTO) can be used to model the structure of social tagging behaviours and align such metadata with any other social metadata scheme that may exist. The scheme was derived by modelling, harvesting, integrating, searching and analysing metadata harvested from three major social tagging systems, namely, Delicious, Flickr and YouTube (Ding et al., 2010). Social tagging can thus be considered as value-added metadata that will further define and support the semantics of related information.

User interfaces

An often overlooked issue of information access to digital libraries is the user interface – the key component that intercedes between the user and the system. This is often less understood than the other components of digital libraries, as we are dealing with humans with different characteristics, familiarity and preferences. An important related area is visualization, which is concerned with using various forms of information representation to aid users to understand and use information more effectively. It enables users to make discoveries and decisions, or to make connections between patterns (such as trends, clusters, gaps and outliners), groups of items or individual items. This is even more important when we move into larger datasets of research data made available through digital libraries, since these add a new requirement to support interactive manipulation and exploration of such datasets.

Nonetheless, the basic tenet remains, and it is to find appropriate and useful displays and ways for users to understand or manipulate information. An information display can be a single entity (for example, a classical textual result list) or multiple entities combined in context to provide more information (for example, a multi-frame interface to support views of a textual result list, document content, references and related links). Information can be displayed in 1D, 2D (such as a hierarchical tree map or map view) and 3D (such as a cluster or cone view). Many alternatives and combinations are thereby possible.

Arising from this, we have seen researchers proposing different forms of visualization technique to support users' interaction with digital libraries at different stages of information seeking. These include the provision of overviews of collections at the commencement of the search task; query previews, query recommendations, topic overviews to support query formulations; and a host of visualizations for result display and processing, such as text, image cover flow views, timeline views, cluster views and tag clouds. While many of such techniques are research driven and have been subjected only to small-scale user evaluation, in the last few years we have also seen some innovative interfaces offered by visual web search engines. For example, the Ujiko.com search interface uses topic maps, icons and highlights to group related retrieved information for users (Figure 4.10). Kartoo.com uses a contoured map view with links to show relationships between documents, keywords and types of resources (Figure 4.11). Grokker.com uses an outline and map view to show clusters of domain-related information so as to aid exploration and discovery (Figure 4.12). These examples suggest the potential of their adoption in new digital library interface designs.

However, and somewhat surprisingly, one thing exists in common today among these

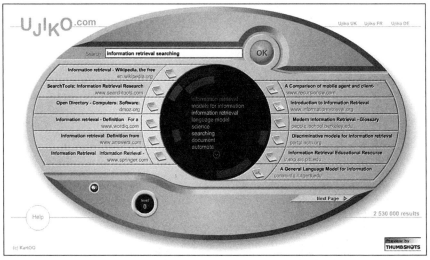

Figure 4.10 *Ujiko.com uses classification, categorization and highlighting for result preview and processing*

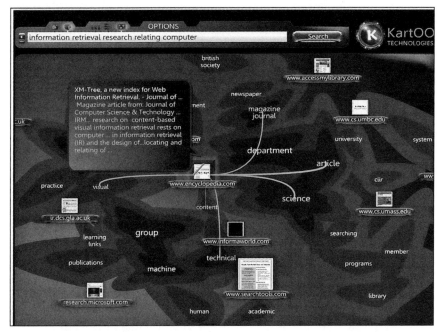

Figure 4.11 *Kartoo.com supports a map contour view to display and link related information along with retrieved documents*

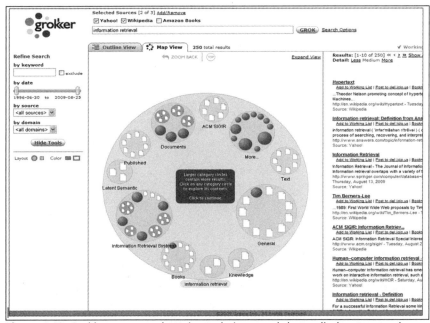

Figure 4.12 *Grokker.com uses clustering techniques and cluster displays to organize retrieved documents into layers of group and sub-groups of information*

search engines – they have basically ceased to exist or their sites have been put up for sale! Likewise, a check and hands-on review on the compilation of 16 visual search engines, carried out in 2009 at Robin Good's Master New Media website (Good and Bazzanov, 2009), reveals that the majority of these highly visual search interfaces (including the three search engines mentioned above) have experienced a similar fate. While we cannot ascertain the real reasons why this has happened, a plausible explanation and contributing factor could be related to the usability of the interfaces, which may turn out to be less effective and useful than was at first envisaged. However, as there are no reported direct evaluation studies on these specific interfaces, nor any possibility to carry out one at present, we can only draw on related evaluation studies to gain some insights into this observation. For example, in an evaluation of an integrated visual desktop search engine that encompasses different views such as the hierarchical tree, bubble, map, tile and word cloud views for search results processing, it was found that many of these views are novel and have the potential to increase usefulness and ease of use and to aid information display and processing. Nonetheless, they can also become very crowded, with an increasing number of data elements being displayed, and confusing to users when they do not understand them (Foo and Hendry, 2007a, 2007b). Other studies suggest that visualization seems to be particularly effective where the complexity of the task and volume of data are at their highest (Morse, Lewis and Olsen, 2002; Wingyan, Chen and Nunamaker, 2005); that visualization works best when the interface is kept as simple as possible (Chen and Yu, 2000); and that, while complex interfaces summarizing lots of data in comparison with simple interfaces will invariably initially fall short of users' satisfaction metrics, they have the potential to become gradually accepted when used over longer periods of time (Shneiderman and Plaisant, 2006). These collective studies suggest that visualization and user interfaces will continue to be important areas for development. The ability to design appropriate interfaces, even multiple interfaces so as to tailor to different user groups, the provision of filtering mechanisms, contextual support for processing information, and associated user studies, are important considerations for future digital library interface designs.

Summary

This chapter has traced the development of information access to digital libraries. Drawing upon a sample of six different digital libraries and other examples, it has discussed the various factors that play a role in determining the success of information access and use: target users and requirements, content, retrieval features, interface, visualization and others.

A few research and development fronts are worth noting. The continued progress made in the development of the Semantic Web and semantic access to digital resources through the support of rich linked metadata provides new possibilities for enhanced information browsing and knowledge discovery. The advent of the cloud computing model offers a new business model and platform for delivering alternative forms of digital library architecture and service offerings. While we are expanding the scope of digital library content, providing new intelligence and functionalities, the pervasive nature and take-off rate of social media, linking users to users, users to information and information to information, implies that the traditional, individualistic model of the digital library needs to shift into a more social and collaborative mode in order to cater for this landscape of change and new user requirements. At the same time, we need to be mindful that the issue of information divide remains, even in today's highly networked world, and so efforts need to be devoted to reaching out and providing information access to relevant population groups. Finally, the basic aspect of the user interface and visualization, which seems to have made limited progress in the last decade, needs further attention and research so that these solutions can be collectively harnessed and integrated in order to deliver a new generation of digital libraries.

References

Agosti, M. (2008) Information Access Using the Guide of User Requirements. In Agosti, M. (ed.), *Access Through Search Engines and Digital Libraries*, Springer, 1–12.

Albert, B., Tullis, T. and Tedesco, T. (2010) *Beyond the Usability Lab: conducting large-scale online user experience studies*, Morgan Kaufmann Pub.

Armbrust, M., Fox, A., Griffith, R., Joseph, A. D., Katz, R. H., Konwinski, A., Lee, G., Patterson, D. A., Rabkin, A., Stoica, I. and Zaharia, M. (2009) *Above the Clouds: a Berkeley view of cloud computing*. Technical Report No. UCB/EECS-2009-28, www.eecs.berkeley.edu/Pubs/TechRpts/2009/EECS-2009-28.html.

Buchanan, G. and Hinze, A. (2008) Social Information Seeking in Digital Libraries. In Goh, D. and Foo, S. (eds), *Social Information Retrieval Systems: emerging technologies and applications for searching the web effectively*, IGI Global. Information Science Reference.

Chen, C. and Yu, Y. (2000) Empirical Studies of Information Visualization: a meta-analysis. *International Journal of Human–Computer Studies*, **53** (5), 851–66.

Chowdhury, G. G. (2010) *Introduction to Modern Information Retrieval*, 3rd edn. Facet Publishing.

Chowdhury, G. G. and Chowdhury, S. (2011) *Information Users and Usability in the Digital Age*. Facet Publishing.

Chu, H. (2010) *Information Representation and Retrieval in the Digital Age*, 2nd edn, Information Today.

Ding, Y. and Foo, S. (2002a) Ontology Research and Development – Part 1: A review of ontology generation, *Journal of Information Science*, **28** (2), 123–36.

Ding, Y. and Foo, S. (2002b) Ontology Research and Development – Part 2: A review of ontology mapping and evolving, *Journal of Information Science*, **28** (5), 375–88.

Ding, Y., Jacob, E., Fried, M., Toma, I., Yan, E., Foo, S. and Milojevic, S. (2010) Upper Tag Ontology (UTO) for Integrating Social Tagging Data, *Journal of the American Society for Information Science and Technology*, **61** (3), 505–21.

Dobreva, M. and Chowdhury, S. (2010) A User-centric Evaluation of the Europeana Digital Library. In Chowdhury, G., Khoo, C. and Hunter, J. (eds), *The Role of Digital Libraries in a*

Time of Global Change, 12th International Conference on Asia-Pacific Digital Libraries, ICADL 2010, Gold Coast, Australia, June 21–25, 2010, Proceedings, 148–57.

Foo, S. and Hendry, D. (2007a) Evaluation of Visual Aid Suite for Desktop Searching, *Proceedings of the 11th European Conference on Research and Advanced Technology for Digital Libraries (ECDL2007), Budapest, Hungary, September 16–21*, Lecture Notes in Computer Science (LNCS) 4675, 333–44.

Foo, S. and Hendry, D. (2007b) Desktop Search Engine Visualization and Evaluation, *Proceedings of the 10th International Conference of Asian Digital Libraries (ICADL2007), Hanoi, Vietnam, December 10–13*, Lecture Notes in Computer Science (LNCS) 4822, 372–82.

Foo, S. and Theng, Y. L. (2004) Digital Library Trends in the Asia Pacific, *Proceedings of the Asian Libraries and Information Conference (ALIC 2004), Bangkok, November 22–24*.

Foo, S. and Theng, Y. L. (2005) A Snapshot of Digital Library Development: the way forward in the Asia Pacific. In Theng, Y. L. and Foo, S. (eds), *Design and Usability of Digital Libraries: Case Studies in the Asia Pacific*, Idea Group Publishing, 351–70.

Goh, D. and Foo, S. (2008) *Social Information Retrieval Systems: emerging technologies and applications for searching the web effectively*, IGI Global, Information Science Reference.

Goker, A. and Davies, J. (2009) *Information Retrieval: searching in the 21st century*, John Wiley & Sons.

Good, R. and Bazzanov, D. (2009) *Top Visual Search Engines: the most interesting ways to visually explore search engine results*, www.masternewmedia.org/top-visual-search-engines-the-most-interesting-ways-to-visually-explore-search-engine-results/.

ISO (2010) *Ergonomics of Human–system Interaction – Part 210: human-centred design for interactive systems*, ISO 9241-210:2010, International Organization for Standardization.

Morse, E., Lewis, M. and Olsen, K. A. (2002) Testing Visual Information Retrieval Methodologies Case Study: comparative analysis of textual, icon, graphical, and 'spring' displays, *Journal of the American Society for Information Science and Technology*, **53** (1), 28–40.

NSDL (2011) *Reconceptualizing the Impact of Digital Learning Resources in a Networked World*, http://nsdlnetwork.org/stemexchange.

Pearrow, M. (2007) *Web Usability Handbook*, 2nd edn, Charles River Media.

Ruthven, I. and Kelly, D. (eds) (2011) *Interactive Information-seeking Behaviour and Retrieval*, Facet Publishing.

Shneiderman, B. and Plaisant, C. (2006) Strategies for Evaluating Information Visualization Tools: multi-dimensional in-depth long-term case studies, *AVI Workshop on Beyond Time and Errors: novel evaluation methods for information visualisation, Venice, Italy*, ACM Press.

Wingyan, C., Chen, H. and Nunamaker Jr, J. F. (2005) A Visual Framework for Knowledge Discovery on the Web: an empirical study of business intelligence exploration, *Journal of Management Information Systems*, **21** (4), 57–84.

....

CHAPTER 5

Collaborative search and retrieval in digital libraries

Dion Hoe-Lian Goh

Introduction
....

Information retrieval may be considered as the quest for content relevant to a given information need. This is typically expressed by query terms submitted to a search engine. However, the performance of existing search engines has been shown to be far from users' satisfaction in their precision and recall. For example, a search engine often returns thousands of results in response to a query, but the results contain information irrelevant to the user's information needs. This phenomenon can be attributed to a few causes. First, errors may be introduced during query formulation. Such errors may include lexical/spelling errors and syntactic errors in which the query is expressed in a form not compatible with the query language (Willson and Given, 2010). This could be because users are unfamiliar with the syntax and semantics associated with the particular search interface (Belkin, 2000). Second, users may not be able to adequately express their information needs as query terms. Here, there may be a disparity between users' query terms that express their information needs and those used in the system to describe the information sources (Furnas et al., 1987). Additionally, users could fail to choose terms at a proper conceptual level to specify their information needs.

Ensuring that information needs are met efficiently and effectively is critical, given the increasing popularity of social computing applications, which has empowered users to create and share content on the web. Such user-generated content may include text (e.g. blogs, wikis), multimedia (e.g. YouTube) and even organizational/navigational structures providing personalized access to web content (e.g. social tags). The result is that people have now come to depend more on the web in searching for information. However, the amount of information and its growth is a double-edged sword, due to the problem of information overload, leading to a situation where users are swamped with too much information, resulting in the difficulty of sifting through the materials in search of relevant content.

Some may argue that the above problems may be less complex in digital libraries, especially when a collection is more focused and, typically, there are stakeholders who ensure the quality and the relevancy of the collection. However, for large digital libraries the problem of information overload is still present (Kim and Abbas, 2010). Further, there may be novices or infrequent users who do not know much about the digital library, its collection or how to best search it so as to get the information they need. Many approaches have been used to address these issues, drawing mainly from the fields of information retrieval, text mining, human–computer interaction and information seeking behaviour.

Among these, two of the major categories are the user-interface approach and the algorithmic approach. For the former, researchers have developed novel user interfaces to visualize content or the query-formulation process, in order to alleviate the difficulties faced by users in specifying their information needs (Ahmed, McKnight and Oppenheim, 2009). This approach relies on diagrammatic presentation of concepts or data schemas. A second approach that helps users in retrieving content is to use query reformulation, which aims to detect users' interests through their submitted queries and to select terms related to the given query. The related terms are obtained by parsing the list of results documents, the entire collection of documents or sources that are independent of the searched document collection, and extracting the most relevant terms by using various term-selection techniques (Boldi et al., 2011). The selected terms can then either be automatically added to the original query (also known as automatic query expansion) or be recommended to users for selection in reformulating their information needs (also known as interactive query expansion).

Both the above approaches can alleviate the problems faced by users in the process of query formulation, to some extent. However, the study of information seeking behaviour has shown that interaction and collaboration with other people is an important part of the process of information seeking and use, thus yielding another possible approach to retrieving relevant content. For example, Taylor's (1968) model highlights the importance of the interaction between the enquirer and the librarian. Dervin and Dewdney's (1986) Sense-Making Model focuses on how individuals use the observations of others as their own observations to construct pictures of reality, and how they use these pictures to guide their search behaviours. Finally, Ellis (1993) argues that communication with colleagues is a key component in the initial search for information. In sum, successful information seeking may be said to rely on collaboration with others, and it is not uncommon that, in searching for information, people tap into their social networks – colleagues, librarians and so on – to better locate what they need.

The remainder of this chapter expands on the idea of collaborative search and retrieval, that is, helping users to retrieve relevant content by leveraging the expertise and experiences of other users.

Collaboration in information seeking

The rationale for collaborative search and retrieval may be found in the information-seeking literature. Information seeking is a broad term encompassing the ways in which individuals articulate their information needs, seek, evaluate, select and use information. Stated differently, information seeking behaviour is a purposeful seeking for information in consequence of a need to satisfy some goal. In the course of seeking, the individual may interact with manual information systems such as newspapers or libraries, with computer-based information systems or with other people (Wilson, 1997, 2000).

A major theme inherent in various information seeking models is that collaboration with other people plays an important role in ensuring that relevant content is retrieved. Taylor (1968) developed a question-negotiation model of information seeking in physical libraries, commencing from how people express a question to a librarian and moving on to the ensuing negotiation process with the librarian in order to obtain the needed information. In Taylor's model, information seeking may undergo several steps. At each step, the information seeker may perform searches alone or consult others, such as colleagues and librarians. Taylor's research thus demonstrates that interaction with others is a very important step during the information seeking process. Stated differently, how one harnesses other people's knowledge is an essential factor that will determine the outcome of the information seeking process. Dervin and Dewdney's (1986) Sense-Making Model reinforces Taylor's work and focuses on how individuals use the observations of others to construct images of reality that guide their search behaviours. The term 'sense-making' refers to a set of concepts and methods to describe how people perceive their world. Thus, sense-making behaviour is communicating behaviour, and information seeking and use is central to sense-making. People communicate and collaborate with others within a certain context in order to meet their own information needs and then make use of the retrieved information for different purposes.

Further, Ellis's (1993) work demonstrates the importance of other people as a valuable information source for information seeking. Ellis's research resulted in a pattern of information seeking behaviour that includes eight generic features or research activities: starting, chaining, browsing, differentiating, monitoring, extracting, verifying and ending. As each activity is performed, interaction with other people, such as colleagues, may occur. Kuhlthau (1993, 1996) defined a model of the information-search process from the cognitive and affective perspectives. This involves six stages: initiation, selection, exploration, formulation, collection and presentation. Again, inherent in this model is the importance of other people in the information seeking process, especially in the selection stage, where typical actions are to consult others, for example, librarians.

In a later work, Ingwersen and Jarvelin (2005) proposed a model that combines both information seeking and retrieval. The model contains various contexts centred around the information seeker. One of the contexts is known as the social context, where information seekers may obtain help from others to carry out their retrieval tasks. More specifically, information seekers will interact with their colleagues and rely on other social contacts to facilitate their information seeking. This, in turn, will affect the results of the information seeking. This model highlights the importance of social factors inherent in the information seeking process. Evans and Chi (2010) argue that social interactions are important during the process of searching. By integrating original research with sense-making and information seeking models, they developed a model that describes social search in three phases: before, during and after search. The before-search phase is characterized by the definition of information needs stemming from oneself or from others. Once established, search requirements are refined, and again these may be specified by others. The during-search phase involves three different search types, of which one, informational (exploratory) search, may be improved through social interactions. In the after-search phase the results are organized and/or distributed, in which the latter action involves other people.

Despite the differences between the various information seeking models reviewed, they share some commonalities. First, collaboration with others is a key component in the search for information, especially in the initial stage of information seeking, as demonstrated by Kuhlthau (1993, 1996), Ellis (1993) and Ingwersen and Jarvelin (2005), among many other examples. Second, people almost always require help before their information needs can be expressed explicitly or formulated as query terms (Belkin, 2000; Marchionini, 1995), and often such help can again be obtained from other people (Evans and Chi, 2010; Shah and Marchionini, 2010).

Collaborative querying

As described, information seeking typically relies on collaboration with others to ensure proper query formulation. It is typical that, in searching for information, people tap into their social networks – colleagues, librarians and so on – to better locate what they need. Collaborative querying refers to a suite of tools and technologies that aim to assist users in formulating queries to an information retrieval system by sharing expert knowledge or other users' search experiences. The term 'collaborative' refers to formulating queries with the assistance of others.

A review of the literature suggests two major approaches for supporting collaborative querying: manual and automatic. The manual approach refers to techniques that need significant amounts of human effort to support query formulation collaboratively. Here, collaboration usually occurs between users and librarians or domain experts. Digital reference services provide a good example of such an approach. A digital reference service provides online support and resources for users seeking answers (Buckland, 2008). Such services can be divided into asynchronous and synchronous types. Asynchronous digital reference services may be defined as professional question-and-answer services using asynchronous communication media, such as web-based forms, e-mail or discussion forums. Such services are common and may be found in many library websites. For example, the Sims Memorial Library at Southeastern Louisiana University offers reference services not only via e-mail and chat, but also through Short Messaging Service (Hill, Hill and Sherman, 2007). In contrast, synchronous digital reference services provide online, real-time personal assistance. Many of these services utilize a chat software component to deliver instruction, bibliographic records or actual answers. AskMac, offered at the McGoogan Library of Medicine, University of Nebraska (Bobal, Schmidt and Cox, 2005), is one such example. The system provides a real-time, internet chat service and includes a co-browsing feature that allows the librarian to direct the user to appropriate electronic resources.

The manual approach via digital reference services provides reliable, quality information to users anytime, anywhere through expert intermediaries. The typical usage scenario involves many users depending only on several experts. Consequently, this approach has the inherent limitation of overloading, especially if too many users ask questions at the same time. In such cases, users may experience poor service, such as long waiting times or answers that are inadequate. Furthermore, phone, e-mail and chat, which are techniques commonly adopted, usually limit experts and users to one-on-one communication, making the sharing of information more difficult (Stover, 2004).

In contrast, the automatic approach provides an information system acting as an intelligent agent that handles users' queries and provides guidance automatically. Stated differently, human intervention is not required, and this overcomes the limitation of human involvement inherent in the manual approach. One way of accomplishing this is to mine the query logs of search engines and utilize these queries as resources for meeting a user's information needs. This can be done by clustering related queries and then recommending these clusters to users. Wen, Nie and Zhang (2002) clustered similar queries based on their term vectors by varying similarity thresholds. Respectable precision values of up to 96% were obtained. However, this method may not be appropriate when submitted queries are short. A recent study suggests that the mean length of queries on the Dogpile meta-search engine was 2.79 words (Jansen, Booth and Spink, 2009). The implication here is that query terms are not able to convey much information. Further, they may not be able to help to detect the semantics behind them, since the same term may represent different semantic meanings, while, on the other hand, different terms may refer to the same semantic meaning (Raghavan and Sever, 1995).

Another method of clustering queries is to utilize a user's selections from the search results listings as the similarity measure (Teevan et al., 2007). This method analyses query logs that contain query terms and the corresponding documents that users clicked on. It assumes that two queries are similar if they lead to the selection of a similar document. This method was also used by Wen, Nie and Zhang (2002). However, the drawback is that it may be unreliable if users select too many irrelevant documents.

Thus, yet another method that has been proposed is to determine the similarity between queries by parsing and comparing the results returned by the search engine to a submitted query. Here, feature vectors are typically constructed using the terms found in the clicked-on URLs of the respective query. These vectors are then clustered according to their similarity, and the resulting clusters thus contain the corresponding queries. Both Baeza-Yates, Hurtado and Mendoza (2005) and Li, Otsuka and Kitsuregawa (2010) employed variations of this method. Glance (2001) used a simpler variation by considering the overlap of result URLs as the similarity measure instead of the document content. Queries are posted to a reference search engine (Google) and the similarity between two queries is measured using the number of common URLs in the top-50 results list returned from the reference search engine. The generated query clusters are employed to help users formulate queries. A potential shortcoming of a purely results-based approach ignores the original query terms, which could provide useful clues for determining similarity between queries. Finally, given the strengths and weaknesses of each method reviewed above, Goh, Fu and Foo (2005) experimented with a weighted combination of the three methods. They found that a linear combination of the term-based and results-based approaches produced the best query clusters in terms of F-measure (used to compare how similar two clustering results are) and cluster size.

Collaborative filtering

Recommender systems have become popular both in academic research and in commercial software applications because they represent an enabling technology for helping people to evaluate and retrieve relevant content automatically (Resnick and Varian, 1997). They act as personalized decision guides, aiding users in decisions on matters related to personal taste or needs. Collaborative filtering is one of the approaches used in recommender systems and will be the focus of the following discussion, in line with the theme of this chapter.

Collaborative filtering is a technique for recommending items to a user based on similarities between the past behaviour of the user and that of people who have similar 'tastes'. It assumes that human preferences are correlated, and hence if a group of users prefer an item, then the present user may also prefer it (McDonald and Ackerman, 2000; Shardanand and Maes, 1995). A profile is usually created on the basis of the user's past behaviour and similarity functions are used to find similar items or similar users. Amazon.com is a commercial example that has successfully employed collaborative filtering to recommend books and other products (Linden, Smith and York, 2003).

Collaborative filtering systems that recommend similar items do so based on a small set of previously selected items in which users have expressed an interest. GroupLens (Konstan et al., 1997), one of the earlier and more influential collaborative filtering systems, is a Usenet news-reading client that lets readers rate each message as they read it. The system aggregates these ratings and uses them to predict how much a user will like a certain article, as well as disseminate the ratings on request. While GroupLens requires users to provide ratings in order to make recommendations, other work has adopted an automatic approach. For example, Liao et al. (2010) implemented a collaborative filtering system for recommending documents in a digital library's English collection. The system builds individual user profiles by examining loan records and extracting keywords found in the borrowed documents. These profiles are then matched against other users to recommend documents of interest. Another example, described by Kim et al. (2010), employs user-generated social tags to determine neighbourhoods of like-minded users. Documents recommended are based on the preferences of these neighbourhoods.

With the increasing connectedness facilitated by the emergence of social media and, in particular, social-networking services, collaborative filtering systems are now being used to recommend similar users. For example, Hannon, Bennett and Smyth (2010) describe a collaborative filtering approach to recommend Twitter users based on, among other attributes, a user's followees as well as followers. Cai et al. (2011) argue that recommending people is different from recommending items, due to bilateral interactions that are not found in item recommendation, that is, the actions between the initiator of an interaction and the recipient. They thus proposed a neighbourhood-based collaborative filtering algorithm that considers successful interactions, that is, those that evoke positive responses between initiator and recipient. More specifically, one possible application is in expertise location, or finding experts who can help to solve a problem (Becerra-Fernandez, 2006). Here, Zhang, Ackerman and Adamic (2007) proposed a number of algorithms for determining Java programming expertise within a discussion forum using post/reply threads on topics or questions. Further, Lopes et al. (2010) employed publication patterns such as co-authorships and topic interests in a digital library to determine potential research collaborators.

Collaborative tagging

Collaborative tagging, also known as social tagging, is another approach to sharing and managing content. Collaborative tagging systems allow users to annotate useful content by assigning keywords (tags), and possibly other metadata, facilitating their future access by the tag creator (Macgregor and McCulloch, 2006). These tags may further be shared by other users of the collaborative tagging system, creating a community where users can create and share tags pointing to useful resources (Goh et al., 2009). Stated differently, the collection of tags may be considered as an organizational structure that supports access to resources via browsing or searching. However, tags are 'flat', lacking a predefined taxonomic structure, and their use relies on shared, emergent social structures and behaviours, as well as on a common conceptual and linguistic understanding within the community (Marlow et al., 2006; Razikin et al., 2008). Tags are therefore also known as 'folksonomies', short for 'folk taxonomies', suggesting that they are created by ordinary users, as opposed to domain experts or information professionals such as librarians. The use of tags has been popularized in social media applications such as Delicious, CiteULike, Flickr and YouTube.

Collaborative tagging as a means of organizing content has been compared favourably against conventional methods of categorization based on taxonomies, controlled vocabularies, faceted classification and ontology. Proponents of collaborative tagging argue that creating organizational structures utilizing the latter methods requires experts with domain knowledge, and often adds to the costs of implementing them. Conventional categorization methods require rules to make their classification schemes work (Morville, 2005). A complex rule system, in turn, potentially contributes to possible maintenance and accessibility issues. In contrast, classifications made by ordinary people are driven by tacit knowledge that is dependent on a person's language and culture (Lakoff, 1987). Given this argument, a conventional categorization system suffers from a lack of precision, as it may not be able to supply relevant information needed by a user (Macgregor and McCulloch, 2006). Collaborative tagging, in contrast, makes use of the knowledge from a (possibly large) community of users instead of relying on (a few) experts. Such systems do not have prescribed rules for defining tags that should be used with a resource. Taken together, the knowledge harnessed from the community of users should be a reliable means of discovering resources when compared to the knowledge that comes from an individual.

However, collaborative tagging is not without its detractors. The lack of a controlled vocabulary, stemming from the freely assigned keywords, contributes to the problem of vocabulary mismatch (Furnas et al., 1987). The mismatch in vocabulary between tag creators and tag consumers is caused by the inherent polysemic and synonymous aspects of natural language. Further, the selection of tags by the tag creator might be motivated by their own agenda, which may not be congruent with the needs of the community (Chua, 2003). This may lead to spamming (Koutrika et al., 2007), where tag creators with malicious intent steers tag consumers to sites that have no relation to the tag assigned. Altogether, these factors may impede the value of tags as an effective means of sharing and organizing resources.

Despite its limitations, people do see value in collaborative tagging, and its use continues to grow in popularity. In parallel, there exists extensive research conducted from various perspectives. These include the architecture and implementation of social tagging systems (Benz et al., 2010; Puspitasari et al., 2007), usage patterns in these systems (Golder and Huberman, 2006; Santos-Neto et al., 2009), visualization of tags (Sinclair and Cardew-Hall, 2008), user interfaces in tagging systems (Shiri, 2009) and the use of tags in search systems (Heymann, Koutrika and Garcia-Molina, 2008; Zheng and Li, 2011).

Beyond these, there is also an emerging body of research that explores the effectiveness of tags for resource organization and sharing. This may be divided into two approaches. The first employs machine-learning techniques. Zubiaga, Martinez and Fresno (2009) examined the use of social annotations (tags and comments) to determine which resulted in a better performance for classifying web documents. Of the two, the authors found that tags performed best, thus suggesting the effectiveness of tags over other annotation types. In contrast, a study of tag effectiveness for content discovery, conducted on a dataset drawn from Delicious, yielded an opposite result

(Razikin et al., 2011). Using a text-categorization approach, the study found that using document terms alone resulted in better classifier performance than using both terms and tags.

The second approach to investigating tag effectiveness is taken from the user's perspective. research has been conducted to compare tags with controlled vocabularies in order to determine their potential for describing and, hence, discovering relevant content. For example, Lin et al. (2006) evaluated tags from Connotea and Medical Subject Heading (MeSH) terms and found that there was only an 11% overlap between MeSH terms and tags. This was because MeSH terms served as descriptors, while tags focused primarily on areas that are of interest to users. Similarly, Lu, Park and Hu (2010) compared user-created tags from LibraryThing, an online service for cataloguing books, with Library of Congress Subject Headings (LCSH) terms assigned by experts. Their study showed that 50.1% of the terms in LCSH were found in LibraryThing tags. Conversely, the overlapping terms constituted only 2.2% of the tag vocabulary of LibraryThing users. Taken together, these plus other findings suggest that expert indexers and tag creators employ different vocabularies, but the two could be complementary in the search for relevant content.

Summary

This chapter has reviewed research in collaborative search and retrieval methods that are applicable to digital libraries, the web and information-rich systems in general. The basis for these methods may be traced to a number of information seeking models which argue that collaboration with other people is critical to success in retrieving relevant content.

Each of the methods reviewed supports access to relevant content differently. In collaborative querying, the focus is on query formulation. Here, various techniques are used to help users craft their queries in a search system by harnessing domain experts or the experience of others who have previously conducted searches. More specifically, the reliance on experts is akin to digital reference services, while the utilization of past searches typically involves the mining of related queries and recommendation to users. Next, collaborative filtering aims to recommend relevant content to a user, based on his/her interests. Such recommendations are performed automatically and are dependent on a user's similarity to other users. Collaborative filtering systems may recommend either items (e.g. documents) or users. Finally, the goal of collaborative indexing, also known as social tagging, is to generate keywords or tags that are useful descriptors of documents. These tags are created by a community of users and can be shared with others to retrieve content associated with them.

The collaborative search and retrieval methods reviewed have broad applicability to digital libraries, and ideas implemented in other information systems may be adapted. Collaborative querying techniques could be embedded within a digital library's search interface to improve its users' retrieval experience. In a typical scenario of use, after entering a query and obtaining the corresponding results, previously submitted queries relevant to the current one are recommended. The user may then refine his/her search using these recommendations. Thus, for example, if a query for 'data mining' is executed, recommendations such as 'knowledge discovery in databases', 'classification' and 'text mining' may be returned. Besides recommending related queries, collaborative filtering could be employed to suggest documents that potentially relate to those that have already been accessed by a user. Hence, while reading an article about usability issues in digital libraries, a user might also be pointed to other resources within the repository that had been accessed in conjunction with the current document. In this way a user would be introduced to new content that he/she might not otherwise have accessed. Finally, digital libraries could support collaborative tagging by allowing users to contribute keywords to documents that they have read. Such keywords might then be visualized in tag cloud, as is now commonly found on the web. By selecting a particular tag, a user would be able to view other documents that had been similarly associated with it. Again, this opens new pathways for exploring a digital library's collection, hence increasing the likelihood of a user's discovering relevant content.

To conclude, collaborative search and retrieval is a rich and multidisciplinary field, and the work covered in this chapter represents a fraction of the research that has been conducted. Nevertheless, there exist various opportunities for conducting further research by drawing on disciplines such as information science, human–computer interaction, information retrieval, machine learning, computer–supported collaborative work and the social sciences.

References

Ahmed, S. M. Z., McKnight, C. and Oppenheim, C. (2009) A Review of Research on Human–computer Iinterfaces for Online Information Retrieval Systems, *The Electronic Library*, **27** (1), 96–116.

Baeza-Yates, R., Hurtado, C. and Mendoza, M. (2005) Query Recommendation Using Query Logs in Search Engines, *Current Trends in Database Technology – EDBT 2004 Workshops, (14–18 March, 2004, Crete, Greece)*, Lecture Notes in Computer Science 3268, Springer, 588–96.

Becerra-Fernandez, I. (2006) Searching for Experts on the Web: a review of contemporary expertise locator systems, *ACM Transactions on Internet Technology*, **6** (4), 333–55.

Belkin, N. J. (2000) Helping People Find What They Don't Know, *Communications of the ACM*, **43** (8), 58–61.

Benz, D., Hotho, A., Jäschke, R., Krause, B., Mitzlaff, F., Schmitz, C. and Stumme, G. (2010) The Social Bookmark and Publication Management System Bibsonomy, *The VLDB Journal*, **19** (6), 849–75.

Bobal, A. M., Schmidt, C. M. and Cox, R. (2005) One Library's Experience with Live, Virtual Reference, *Journal of the Medical Library Association*, **93** (1), 123–25.

Boldi, P., Bonchi, F., Castillo, C. and Vigna, S. (2011) Query Reformulation Mining: models, patterns, and applications, *Information Retrieval*, **14** (3), 257–89.

Buckland, M. K. (2008) Reference Library Service in the Digital Environment, *Library & Information Science Research*, **30** (2), 81–5.

Cai, X., Bain, M., Krzywicki, A., Wobcke, W., Kim, Y. S., Compton, P. and Mahidadia, A. (2011) Collaborative Filtering for People to People Recommendation in Social Networks, *Proceedings of AI 2010: Advances in Artificial Intelligence (7–10 December 2010, Adelaide, Australia)*, Lecture Notes in Computer Science 6464, Springer, 476–85.

Chua, A. Y. K. (2003) Knowledge Sharing: a game people play, *Aslib Proceedings*, **55** (3), 117–29.

Dervin, B. and Dewdney, P. (1986) Neutral Questioning: a new approach to the reference interview, *Reference Quarterly*, **25** (4), 506–13.

Ellis, D. (1993) A Comparison of the Information Seeking Patterns of Researchers in the Physical and Social Sciences, *Journal of Documentation*, **49** (4), 356–69.

Evans, B. M. and Chi, E. H. (2010) An Elaborated Model of Social Search, *Information Processing & Management*, **46** (6), 656–78.

Furnas, G. W., Landauer, T. K., Gomez, L. M. and Dumais, S. T. (1987) The Vocabulary Problem in Human–System Communication, *Communications of the ACM*, **30** (11), 964–71.

Goh, D. H., Fu, L. and Foo, S. S. B. (2005) Collaborative Querying Using the Query Graph Visualizer, *Online Information Review*, **29** (3), 266–82.

Goh, D. H., Chua, A., Lee, C. S. and Razikin, K. (2009) Resource Discovery Through Social Tagging: a classification and content analytic approach, *Online Information Review*, **33** (3), 568–83.

Golder, S. A. and Huberman, B. A. (2006) Usage Patterns of Collaborative Tagging Systems, *Journal of Information Science*, **32** (2), 198–208.

Glance, N. S. (2001) Community Search Assistant, *Proceedings of the 6th ACM International Conference on Intelligent User Interfaces (14–17 January 2001, Santa Fe, NM, USA)*, ACM Press, 91–6.

Hannon, J., Bennett, M. and Smyth, B. (2010) Recommending Twitter Users to Follow Using Content and Collaborative Filtering Approaches, *Proceedings of the 4th ACM Conference on Recommender Systems (26–30 September 2010, Barcelona, Spain)*, 199–206.

Heymann, P., Koutrika, G. and Garcia-Molina, H. (2008) Can Social Bookmarking Improve Web Search? *Proceedings of the 2008 International Conference on Web Search and Web Data Mining (11–12 February 2008, Stanford, CA, USA)*, ACM Press, 195–205.

Hill, J. B., Hill, C. M. and Sherman, D. (2007) Text Messaging in an Academic Library: integrating SMS into digital reference, *The Reference Librarian*, **47** (1), 17–29.

Ingwersen, P. and Jarvelin, K. (2005) *The Turn: integration of information seeking and retrieval in context*, Springer.

Jansen, B. J., Booth, D. L. and Spink, A. (2009) Patterns of Query Reformulation During Web Searching, *Journal of the American Society for Information Science and Technology*, **60** (7), 1358–71.

Kim, Y. M. and Abbas, J. (2010) Adoption of Library 2.0 Functionalities by Academic Libraries and Users: a knowledge management perspective, *Journal of Academic Librarianship*, **36** (3), 211–18.

Kim, H. N., Ji, A. T., Ha, I. and Jo, G. S. (2010) Collaborative Filtering Based on Collaborative Tagging for Enhancing the Quality of Recommendation, *Electronic Commerce Research and Applications*, **9** (1), 73–83.

Konstan, J. A., Miller, B. N., Maltz, D., Herlocker, J., Gordon, L. R. and Riedl, J. (1997) GroupLens: applying collaborative filtering to Usenet news, *Communications of the ACM*, **40** (3), 77–87.

Koutrika, G., Effendi, F. A., Gyöngyi, Z., Heymann, P. and Garcia-Molina, H. (2007) Combating Spam in Tagging Systems, *Proceedings of the 3rd International Workshop on Adversarial Information Retrieval on the Web (8 May 2007, Banff, Alberta, Canada)*, ACM Press, 57–64.

Kuhlthau, C. C. (1993) *Seeking Meaning: a process approach to library and information services*, Ablex Publishing Corporation.

Kuhlthau, C. C. (1996) *The Virtual School Library: gateway to the information superhighway*, Libraries Unlimited, Inc.

Lakoff, G. (1987) *Women, Fire, and Dangerous Things: what categories reveal about the mind*, University of Chicago Press.

Li, L., Otsuka, S. and Kitsuregawa, M. (2010) Finding Related Search Engine Queries by Web Community Based Query Enrichment, *World Wide Web*, **13** (1–2), 121–42.

Liao, I. E., Hsu, W. C., Cheng, M. S. and Chen, L. P. (2010) A Library Recommender System Based on a Personal Ontology Model and Collaborative Filtering Technique for English Collections, *The Electronic Library*, **28** (3), 386–400.

Lin, X., Beaudoin, J. E., Bui, Y. and Desai, K. (2006) Exploring Characteristics of Social Classification, *Proceedings of the 17th Workshop of the American Society for Information Science and Technology Special Interest Group in Classification Research (4 November 2006, Austin, TX, USA)*, http://dlist.sir.arizona.edu/1790/.

Linden, G., Smith, B. and York, J. (2003) Amazon.com Recommendations: item-to-item collaborative filtering, *IEEE Internet Computing*, **7** (1), 76–80.

Lopes, G. R., Moro, M. M., Wives, L. K. and de Oliveira, J. P. M. (2010) Collaboration Recommendation on Academic Social Networks, *Proceedings of Advances in Conceptual Modeling – Applications and Challenges, ER 2010 Workshops, (1–4 November 2010, Vancouver, BC, Canada)*, Lecture Notes in Computer Science 6413, Springer, 190–9.

Lu, C., Park, J.-R. and Hu, X. (2010) User Tags Versus Expert-assigned Subject Terms: a comparison of LibraryThing tags and Library of Congress Subject Headings, *Journal of Information Science*, **36** (6), 763–79.

Macgregor, G. and McCulloch, E. (2006) Collaborative Tagging as a Knowledge Organisation and Resource Discovery Tool, *Library Review*, **55** (5), 291–300.

Marchionini, G. N. (1995) *Information Seeking in Electronic Environments*, Cambridge University Press.

Marlow, C., Naaman, M., Boyd, D. and Davis, M. (2006) HT06, Tagging Paper, Taxonomy, Flickr, Academic Article, to Read, *Proceedings of the 17th Conference on Hypertext and Hypermedia (22–25 August 2006, Odense, Denmark)*, ACM Press, 31–9.

McDonald, D. W. and Ackerman, M. S. (2000) Expertise Recommender: a flexible recommendation system and architecture, *Proceedings of the 8th ACM Conference on Computer Supported Cooperative Work (2–6 December 2000, Philadelphia, PA, USA)*, ACM Press, 12–22.

Morville, P. (2005) *Ambient Findability*, O'Reilly.

Puspitasari, F., Lim, E. P., Goh, D. H., Chang, C. H., Zhang, J., Sun, A., Theng, Y. L., Chatterjea, K. and Li, Y. Y. (2007) Social Navigation in Digital Libraries by Bookmarking, *Proceedings of the 10th International Conference on Asian Digital Libraries (10–13 December 2007, Hanoi, Vietnam)*, Lecture Notes in Computer Science 4822, Springer, 297–306.

Raghavan, V. V. and Sever, H. (1995) On the Reuse of Past Optimal Queries, *Proceedings of the 18th Annual International ACM SIGIR Conference on Research and Development in Information Retrieval (9–13 July 1995, Seattle, WA, USA)*, 344–50.

Razikin, K., Goh, D. H., Chua, A. Y. K. and Lee, C. S. (2008) Can Social Tags Help you Find What you Want?, *Proceedings of the Research and Advanced Technology for Digital Libraries 12th European Conference (14–19 September 2008, Aarhus, Denmark)*, Lecture Notes in Computer Science 5173, Springer, 50–61.

Razikin, K., Goh, D. H., Chua, A. Y. K. and Lee, C. S. (2011) Social Tags for Resource Discovery: a comparison between machine learning and user-centric approaches, *Journal of Information Science*, **37** (4), 391–404.

Resnick, P. and Varian, H. R. (1997) Recommender Systems, *Communications of the ACM*, **10** (3), 56–8.

Santos-Neto, E., Condon, D., Andrade, N., Iamnitchi, A. and Ripeanu, M. (2009) Individual and Social Behavior in Tagging Systems, *Proceedings of the 20th ACM Conference on Hypertext and Hypermedia (29 June-1 July 2009, Torino, Italy)*, ACM Press, 183–92.

Shah, C. and Marchionini, G. N. (2010) Awareness in Collaborative Information Seeking, *Journal of the American Society for Information Science and Technology*, **61** (10), 1970–86.

Shardanand, U. and Maes, P. (1995) Social Information Filtering: algorithms for automating 'word of mouth', *Proceedings of the 13th ACM Conference on Human Factors in Computing Systems (7–11 May 1995, Denver, CO, USA)*, ACM Press, 210–17.

Shiri, A. (2009) An Examination of Social Tagging Interface Features and Functionalities, *Online Information Review*, **33** (5), 901–19.

Sinclair, J. and Cardew-Hall, M. (2008) The Folksonomy Tag Gloud: when is it useful? *Journal of Information Science*, **34** (1), 15–29.

Stover, M. (2004) Making Tacit Knowledge Explicit: the Ready Reference Database as codified knowledge, *Reference Services Review*, **32** (2), 164–73.

Taylor, R. (1968) Question-negotiation and Information Seeking in Libraries, *College & Research Libraries*, **29** (3), 178–94.

Teevan, J., Adar, E., Jones, R. and Potts, M. A. S. (2007) Information Re-retrieval: repeat queries in Yahoo's logs, *Proceedings of the Proceedings of the 30th Annual International ACM SIGIR Conference on Research and Development in Information Retrieval (23–27 July 2007, Amsterdam, The Netherlands)*, ACM Press, 151–8.

Wen, J. R., Nie, J. Y. and Zhang, H. J. (2002) Query Clustering Using User Logs, *ACM Transactions on Information Systems*, **20** (1), 59–81.

Willson, R. and Given, L. M. (2010) The Effect of Spelling and Retrieval System Familiarity on Search Behavior in Online Public Access Catalogs: a mixed methods study, *Journal of the American Society for Information Science and Technology*, **61** (12), 2461–76.

Wilson, T. D. (1997) Information Behavior: an interdisciplinary perspective, *Information*

Processing & Management, **33** (4), 551–72.

Wilson, T. D. (2000) Human Information Behavior, *Informing Science*, **3** (2), 49–55.

Zhang, J., Ackerman, M. S. and Adamic, L. (2007) Expertise Networks in Online Communities: structure and algorithms, *Proceedings of the 16th International Conference on World Wide Web (8–12 May 2007, Banff, Alberta, Canada)*, ACM Press, 221–30.

Zheng, N. and Li, Q. (2011) A Recommender System Based on Tag and Time Information for Social Tagging Systems, *Expert Systems with Applications*, **38** (4), 4575–87.

Zubiaga, A., Martinez, R. and Fresno, V. (2009) Getting the Most out of Social Annotations for Web Page Classification, *Proceedings of the 9th Symposium on Document Engineering (16–18 September 2009, Munich, Germany)*, ACM Press, 74–83.

CHAPTER 6

The social element of digital libraries

Natalie Pang

Introduction

Since the 1990s much interest has been generated in digital libraries. This has led to several digital libraries conferences and journals, such as the International Conference of Asian Digital Libraries, the Joint Conference on Digital Libraries and the *International Journal on Digital Libraries*. Other than researchers, library practitioners have also shown much enthusiasm in digital libraries, with various initiatives by libraries to make digital libraries widely accessible, digitization projects and the development of document management systems. Over the years, digital libraries have broadened in their conceptualization and offer different connotations for both practitioners and researchers, although these meanings may not always be mutually exclusive.

Such a broad conceptualization of digital libraries is not accidental, according to Borgman (1999). She offered the explanation that research on digital libraries had attracted a large number of scholars from various disciplines, such as information retrieval, library studies, archives and computer science. This community, consisting of practitioners and researchers, has worked at different stages of the life cycle of digital libraries, in both theoretical and applied aspects. This has further led to the emergence of several definitions of digital libraries, as shown in Table 6.1. In Borgman's (1999) paper, more sources discussing each definition can be found, but for the purposes of this chapter only those that are the most encompassing of the core elements of each definition are selected.

In addition to the definitions provided by communities of both researchers and practitioners, Borgman (1999) also pointed out that none of these definitions recognizes the many digital databases that exist on the world wide web, CD-ROMs and the hidden web such as LexisNexis. Some of these databases may be viewed as 'incomplete' content collections, given that they may not be organized around the information needs of specific communities, and lack standards and cataloguing. Moreover, the world wide web is not an institution and therefore would not fit in with the definition of library practitioners. However, since Borgman's paper, various institutions have initiated projects to carry out large-scale digitization and made the results available on the world wide web. One such example is the Million Book Project,

Table 6.1		*Summary of definitions (adapted from Borgman, 1999)*	
	Definition	**Elements**	**Source**
Research	Digital libraries as content, collections and communities	a. Set of electronic resources, with associated technical capabilities for creating, searching and using information. b. Content includes data, metadata. c. Constructed by (and for) a community of users. d. In meeting the needs of user communities, they are key drivers of interactions between individuals and groups (234).	Borgman et al. (1996)
		a. Some sense of a collection, with some kind of organization, with content that may be electronic, or partly physical and electronic. b. Must contain full-text materials and not a bibliographic collection or merely a reference to other materials. c. Goal oriented, to link a community with attributes of the collection (235).	Bishop and Star (1996)
Practice	Digital libraries as institutions or services	a. Organizations that provide the resources (including specialized staff) to select, structure, offer intellectual access to, interpret, distribute, preserve the integrity of and ensure the persistence over time of collections of digital works so that they are readily and economically available for use by a defined community or set of communities (236).	Waters (1998)
		b. An integrated service of a library, made possible via collaborative partnerships with other libraries, publishers and academic staff (237).	Rusbridge (1998)

led by Carnegie Mellon University in collaboration with research partners in the USA, India and China. Such institution-led initiatives add to the volume of digital databases available on the world wide web.

Where are we going with these definitions? This author would like to put forward two propositions. First, the internet has since penetrated both definitions of digital libraries, leading to digital libraries' being much more integrated with the digital databases of the world wide web than before. Many libraries have included resources from the world wide web as part of their digital library services. With social media the notion of user communities has also become much more apparent in the world wide web, and in such online communities content is organized around them. Second, this has also resulted in a blurring of boundaries between the research and practice definitions of digital libraries. These two propositions suggest a re-examination of digital libraries addressing the role of the internet (and more specifically, social media – the rationale for which will be explained below). This may also imply that there is a need to revisit these definitions, working in both research and practice – but that is not the aim of this chapter and is beyond its scope.

The adoption of the internet in various societies, together with associated tools such as internet forums, blogs, wikis, podcasts and social bookmarking sites, has resulted in a growing interest in what has become known today as social media. Throughout the literature, one can find incidences of the term being associated with the somewhat related concepts of Web 2.0, user-generated content and participatory media. Towards this loose conceptualization, Kaplan and Haenlein (2010, 61) have attempted to make clarifications, resulting in a definition of social media as 'a group of Internet-based applications that build on the ideological and technological foundations of Web 2.0, and that allow the creation and exchange of User Generated Content'. This perspective stems from a close examination of the historical roots of social media, thereby also differentiating it from Web 2.0 and user-generated content, both of which are characterized by mass participation. In this sense, while Web 2.0 is considered as the platform of social media, user-generated content is facilitated and produced by interactions on Web 2.0. In other words, user-generated content can be considered as a core product of social media. The terms 'social media,' 'Web 2.0', 'participation' and 'user-generated content' will be used in the chapter as explained in this context.

That said, none of what is now known as user-generated content and social media would be possible without Web 2.0. In 2005, Tim O'Reilly attempted to define Web 2.0 by coming up with a meme map in a seminal paper (Figure 6.1).

O'Reilly (2005b) further defined Web 2.0 as 'the network as platform, spanning all connected devices; Web 2.0 applications are those that make the most of the intrinsic advantages of that platform: delivering software as a continually-updated service that gets better the more people use it, consuming and remixing data from multiple sources, including individual users, while providing their own data and services in a form that allows remixing by others, creating network effects through an "architecture of participation," and going beyond the page metaphor of Web 1.0 to deliver rich user experiences.'

Web 2.0, as a networked platform, facilitates the production of user-generated content and leads to an increase in unstructured and emergent content. In other words, while social media can present unprecedented opportunities as enriched forms of digital libraries, they can also present certain challenges. Against this background in understanding digital libraries and the development of social media, several questions arise. What is the role of social media in information access in the digital libraries conceptualized by research and practice? What opportunities and pitfalls does it present in terms of information access? This chapter will attempt to address them.

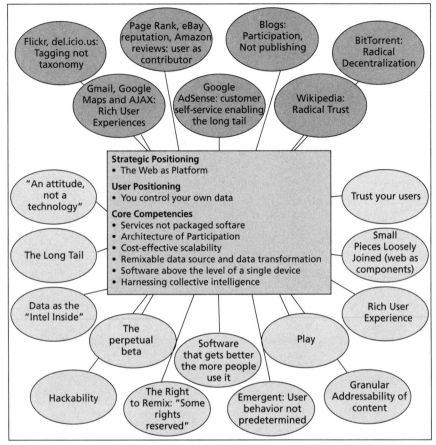

Figure 6.1 *Meme map of Web 2.0 (O'Reilly, 2005a)*

Digital libraries as an ecosystem

Although there are differences in the conceptualizations of digital libraries coming from researchers and practitioners, it is this author's view that digital libraries are essentially social in nature. One cannot fathom a digital library without considering the social interactions driving its development, sustainability and use. The social interactions underlying digital libraries are what make them similar in concept. As an ecosystem, digital libraries can also provide new opportunities for social learning. This was demonstrated in an earlier study involving youths using digital libraries (Pang, 2005). Before we can examine social media's role in shaping information access in digital libraries, it is necessary to first recognize the social aspects of digital libraries.

That digital libraries have a social element was well recognized from the beginning of research on digital libraries, and first formalized in a workshop jointly organized by the National Science Foundation and University of California, Los Angeles, in February 1996 (Borgman, 1996). The workshop brought together many scholars, practitioners and researchers – all working on various fields of digital libraries – and was concerned about the social aspects of digital libraries. The workshop resulted in a research framework consisting of three components, each with associated research issues. As the report of the workshop reads:

> *Human-centered research issues*: a focus on people, both as individual users and as members of groups and communities, communicators, creators, users, learners, or managers of information. We are concerned with groups and communities as units of analysis as well as with individual users. *Artifact-centered research issues*: a focus on creating, organizing, representing, storing, and retrieving the artifacts of human communication. *Systems-centered research issues*: a focus on digital libraries as systems that enable interaction with these artifacts and that support related communication processes.

From this historical underpinning one can see that the community of researchers and practitioners of digital libraries has long ago recognized the social value and potential that digital libraries bring about, even before Web 2.0 and social media. Research on each of these components has made much progress since the workshop. Studies have also shown that components in this research framework are not mutually exclusive. For example, Hong et al. (2002) have demonstrated the significance of the technology-acceptance model, which looks at both individual and system characteristics in predicting acceptance of digital libraries.

Levy and Marhsal (1995) also identified three common characteristics of digital libraries: their collections contain fixed, permanent documents (78), are based on digital technologies (79) and are to be used by individuals working alone (79). In their paper, they questioned the sustainability and future of digital libraries based on these characteristics. As they rightfully pointed out, the construction of digital libraries based on the assumption that they are meant to be used only by 'individual[s] working alone' is impractical and unrealistic. Even in actual libraries it is rare that users seek and access information without involving some form of social interaction, collaboration or communication, either with other users or with librarians.

The recognition that information access is highly collaborative is even more essential in the context of using digital libraries for knowledge production. From the time when the study of knowledge and hermeneutics began, scholars have always acknowledged the application of knowledge in human pursuits, and the collaborative nature of developing, using and evaluating such knowledge. Confucius once stated: 'I have finished my greatest work and I am proud to say that not a single idea in it is mine' (quoted in Liang, 2004, 13). This reflection by Confucius crystallizes the notion that knowledge is rarely developed independently. Users typically seek information by tapping into their trusted personal and professional networks for recommendations. Scholars build on existing knowledge to develop new knowledge.

Additionally, Drucker (1993) argued that knowledge as a resource does not degrade when used but, rather, increases in value the more it is used. As such, knowledge resources cannot be treated like natural resources in terms of scarcity. The validity of Drucker's argument has been reinforced in many examples of social media, where the higher the usage of a resource, the better its value. A good contemporary example is Wikipedia, whose value and quality depend on the increasing use of the resource – and especially on the continuous critiquing by the readers/creators of its coverage and accuracy (Wilkinson and Huberman, 2007).

With social media, the potential value of information resources in digital libraries is heightened, as social media brings users together to create, use, evaluate and share information resources. Beyond the almost instantaneous connections to a community of like-minded users is access to a vast resource of highly emergent, dynamic, remixed and unstructured content.

Web 2.0 and its impacts on information access in digital libraries

Social media is characterized by active users who contribute and produce content. Content is thus dynamic and constantly updated with new material. Miller (2005) described the key principles that govern Web 2.0 today. Table 6.2 provides a summary of these principles.

Table 6.2 Key principles of Web 2.0 and social media (Miller, 2005)	
Principle	Description
Freeing of data	Data can be discovered and accessed, independently of its original form and the application used to gain access to it.
Permitting the building of virtual applications	Allows for different data and applications to be deployed.
Participative	Users are transformed from passive to active users.
'Work for the user'	Content and applications are highly customizable for individual users.
Modular	Enables users to 'build' solutions for themselves, from an array of interoperating components.
Sharing	A community of users that is highly collaborative and receptive to sharing content.
Communication and facilitating community	Web 2.0 is characterized by communication between users.
Remix	Content can now be 'remixed' freely by users – into a form comprised of content from others and their own.
Smart	The technologies driving Web 2.0 are also able to make use of what users access, and their information behaviour, to deliver timely and relevant services. They gather intelligence over time to provide compelling services, such as Amazon's 'recommended books' function.
Long tail	Achieves economies of scale – by making it possible to serve the needs of large numbers of small groups of people.
Trust	Based on trust – in communities of users or data.

It should be noted that these principles are not mutually exclusive. Many of these principles are possible only because of the highly collaborative and communicative function and modality of the community. Unlike users of the preceding generation of the web, users of Web 2.0 participate in building the value of any website or database. That said, the community of users driving the production of content at each site therefore becomes important in the Web 2.0 generation.

Social media, which comes with communication technologies and networks enabled by the internet, has made the social networks that operate within and between communities much more transparent. Information and communication technologies enable social-networking activities to have greater breadth and speed, and lower costs of co-ordination (Pang and Schauder, 2006).

Researchers such as Bimber, Flanagin and Stohl (2005), Wellman and Haythornthwaite (2000), Castells (2003) and Lessig (2004) have also collectively identified the following features of social media's impact on communities:

- portals and applications that facilitate non-commercial publishing
- communication technologies that facilitate interactions between people
- media devices that increase the capability of people to share knowledge and exchange resources
- peer-to-peer networks, interactive forums and other participative technologies that support decentralized collective action
- communication technologies and efficient transfers of resources that help to redefine the concepts of time and space
- virtual communities that fundamentally re-pattern social networks through transformations of bonding (strong) and bridging (weak) ties.

Bridging ties, especially those between rather than within communities, are multiplied by communication technologies. For example, the social application Facebook makes recommendations for users to add other users, based on the number of mutual contacts two people have. In that way, individuals are connected to one another and their communities – even though they may not have immediate or strong ties.

People are enabled to share content and, in some cases, build on the efforts of others. For example, an essay by one person can easily be forwarded to another for further additions; context can be provided in documents by embedding links and rich multimedia objects in a message.

The scenario of a community of active participants contributing and shaping resources in a digital library is enticing. It resolves many dilemmas of the everyday librarian: how can we ensure that the resources provided to users are useful? How do we gather timely feedback from users? How can we keep track of changing user needs, so as to stay relevant? How can users gain access to resources quickly, as and when they need them?

Social bookmarking: Delicious

In the world of Web 2.0 and social media, these issues are almost non-existent. Users are adept at giving feedback, and take an active role in shaping what they want in a digital library, how they want to access information resources and stay informed. With participatory technologies, it has also become easier for people to create and contribute knowledge, even though they may not be consciously aware that they are doing so (Bimber, Flanagin and Stohl, 2005). To illustrate this we will use the example of the popular social bookmarking tool Delicious. Although it was acquired by Yahoo! in 2005 and later resold to AVOS Systems in 2011, Delicious represents one of the first few applications epitomizing the principles and features of Web 2.0 and social media. Delicious (delicious.com) uses a non-hierarchical classification system where users can save their bookmarked URLs with tags – terms and keywords of any form. Users can view not only their own bookmarks, but also everyone's bookmarks with the same tag, or everyone's tags in the same bookmark. This tool allows users to manage and make sense of their personal bookmarks, and aggregates the collective knowledge created around bookmarks by individuals into one integrated repository. On the individual's Delicious page, individual knowledge is contextualized within the knowledge of the community that identified with a resource, i.e. a bookmark. This is best explained by using an example. Figure 6.2 shows a page of a bookmark saved by a user, after a user logs in to Delicious in which:

1   The location of the bookmark is shown as well as the popularity of the bookmark within the community. The greater the number of people who have saved the bookmark, the more popular it is. This provides the user with a sense of how many in the Delicious community are sharing and using the bookmark together. In the context of a digital library, such functions also provide a sense of how popular a resource is, and its degree of use.

2   The highlighted box reflects how the user made sense of the bookmark. For the individual user, it helps to capture individual knowledge – and, in the long run, is a form of personal archive. This is shown by the tags and notes accompanying the bookmark, as well as the date when the bookmark was saved.

3   All of the notes created by users who have saved this bookmark are shown. Individual knowledge is contributed as a collective pool of knowledge around a bookmark. Digital libraries can utilize such collective knowledge and intelligence to understand how information resources are used.

4   The most popular tags created for the resource (i.e. bookmark) are shown. This enables the user to see the most popular ways in which others in the community (who have saved this resource) interpret the resource. For digital libraries, such intelligence provides important information on how different resources are interpreted and accessed by their community of users.

5   The history of posts provides further context for the user to see how the resource has been shared and made sense of within the community. The value of

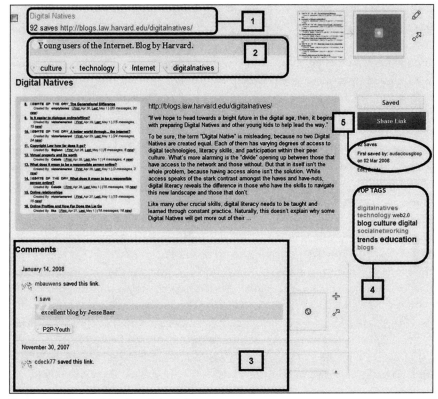

Figure 6.2 *A saved bookmark in Delicious*

such history as an archive is perhaps less talked about in the discourse concerning Web 2.0, although scholars like Gehl (2011) have acknowledged and highlighted the synthesized value of Web 2.0 and social media as archived memory.

Wikipedia

The example of Delicious has provided explanations of how elements of social media may impact on information access in digital libraries. There are many more examples of social media today, such as Wikipedia, the popular online encyclopaedia. Wikipedia is, in many ways, a digital library, especially in terms of Borgman's (1999) research definition of digital libraries 'as content, collections and communities'. Since its inception, Wikipedia has also grown a lot, with packets of content being organized around certain user communities. Users on the internet can freely contribute and edit any article in Wikipedia. Despite the seemingly undirected, haphazard and chaotic structure, Wilkinson and Huberman (2007) argued that Wikipedia in fact follows certain general regularities, and the greater the number of edits to an article, the greater its perceived quality. In other words, the larger the number in the community that is actively shaping and contributing to a resource, the greater is the value of the resource. This characteristic places much importance on the community behind each page of information resource in Wikipedia – which can also lead to great diversity and variances in quality and structure between pages of content in Wikipedia.

A less apparent feature of Wikipedia lies in its capacity as 'institutions or services' (Borgman, 1999). The value of Wikipedia has been much talked about in terms of its ability to offer dynamic and rich content, and the communities driving the production and reproduction of its user-generated content. Wikipedia as a digital library offering services to help select, structure, distribute, preserve and offer interpretations of its resources for users seem to be less evident (Voss, 2005). However, Wikipedia does provide services to accompany its voluminous collections of content The number of editors involved in Wikipedia has grown exponentially, although not in the traditional form of a library with specialized staff or collaborations with other information institutions. Editors in Wikipedia are also users, reflecting an era of the 'prosumer': the consumer who is also a producer (Tapscott and Williams, 2006). Wikipedia did not start off with this design. Before the development of its participative design and collaborative community, it began as an expert-driven online encyclopedia, Nupedia. By 2003, Nupedia was taken down, and its content incorporated into Wikipedia (Wikipedia, 2011). This history demonstrates the potential and power of community collaboration to produce and sustain an online encyclopedia. None of this would have been possible, however, without the social-network-enabling platform of Web 2.0 facilitating the communication, production and sharing of content between users.

The discussion so far has focused on the benefits of Web 2.0 and social media for information access. Wikipedia and Delicious can be seen as modern-day digital libraries providing users with not just informational resources, but also collective intelligence regarding how such resources are being used by others. Managers of digital libraries can integrate some of these functionalities and envisage further development of digital libraries by tapping into the participation of their users – transforming passive users into 'prosumers'.

Challenges and pitfalls

Yet social media is not without its challenges and pitfalls. The same collaborative and participative communities also present certain pitfalls and challenges. Keen (2007) found examples that rely on user communities of the internet disturbing. As he argued, the problem is with mass participation in the production of knowledge via user-generated content. With contemporary technologies and the internet, participation is easily made possible – and knowledge resources in such forms are also characterized by mass 'amateurization', which can easily lead to misinformation. Keen (2007) quoted Marshall Poe, who recognized that resources in Wikipedia are:

not exactly expert knowledge; it's common knowledge … when you go to nuclear reactor on Wikipedia you're not getting an encyclopedia entry, so much as you're getting what people who know a little about nuclear reactors know about nuclear reactors and what they think common people can understand. Wikipedia constantly throws people off and they think, well, if it's an encyclopedia why can't I cite it; why can't I … rely on it? And you can't; you just can't rely on it like that.

(Keen, 2007, 39–40)

In addition to the commonness of knowledge, Keen (2007) also highlighted that:

while the professionals – the editors, the scholars, the publishers – are certainly the victims of an Internet that diminishes their value and takes away their jobs, the greater victims of all this are us, the readers of Wikipedia and of the blogs and all the 'free' content that is insistently reaching out for our attention.

(Keen, 2007, 45)

In other words, Keen's concern is that the 'amateur'-produced quantity of information is eliminating professionally produced quality of information. Yet Wikipedia's history, beginning as the expert-driven project Nupedia, seems to address this concern already. Although there was a considerable amount of resources created by the time Nupedia was shut down, the difference in quality between expert-contributed articles and user-generated articles was never found to be a major issue. Regarding quantity, Keen's (2007) critique of the amateur's trajectory on the internet seems, paradoxically, to have made a positive point for the peer-produced, user-generated content without realizing it. The problem of scarcity of information resources – which exist in a physical library where a resource is available only to a single user at any point in time – is eliminated. This is because the amount of resources that is freely accessible continually increases on the internet. Thus the abundance of informational resources existing as collections and packets of digital content presents itself as an opportunity to resolve global literacy divides, which perhaps explains the increase in the number of projects to bring technologies and the internet to developing countries in recent years. Some examples are the One Laptop Per Child project in the USA, the Telecentre project in Belgium and the Swedish Program for ICT in Developing Regions (SPIDER).

Keen (2007) is not the only one who is critical of user-generated content brought about by Web 2.0 and social media. Petersen (2009), while recognizing the benefits of information that is accumulating online, highlighted the pitfall of having to process 'an endless stream of articles, news, pictures, websites, products, updates, comments of updates and comments to these comments' – so much so that people might have become 'slaves of the feed'. In his thought-provoking article, he presented the argument that the need to filter for quality information, instead of quantity, has become more important than before.

Regarding the quality of information, Keen's (2007) and Petersen's (2009) arguments elucidate a key role for digital libraries as institutions and service providers. Problems such as misinformation and a lack of coherence are significant implications for digital libraries to consider. The issues of control and allocation therefore become central to the sustainability of good digital libraries. The challenge in the current and modern context is not so much in digitize or trying to provide as many resources as possible in digital form. It is not that these are not important, but recognizing the changing needs and participatory forms of user communities requires digital libraries to provide their communities with some level of quality control amid the plethora of good, bad or indifferent information resources that are co-produced by the same users. Thus, key functions for digital libraries, in this era of social media, Web 2.0 and user-generated content, are prioritization and allocation of information resources.

As Bradley (2006, 84) puts it,

> Twenty-five years ago, at a time when ICT (information and communication technologies) was known as EDP (electronic data processing), I used to close my speeches by arguing that computerisation is really an issue of allocation.

The immediate challenge ahead for digital libraries in the context of contemporary computing technologies with social media is to move beyond content provision and consider themselves more as digital libraries with integrated services. Although Borgman's (1999) definitions of digital libraries date from more than a decade ago, it is worthwhile revisiting them to reconsider the ways by which the challenges of today, as presented by social media, may be addressed.

Summary

Borgman's (1999) paper, titled 'What are Digital Libraries?', reflects a need to conceptualize the different definitions arising from various communities of researchers and practitioners back in the 1990s. In fact, since the development of ICT, the concept of digital libraries has been broadening and there is a need to construct and reconstruct them in the context of contemporary technologies. The contemporary technological environment facing us today is social media, with Web 2.0 as an enabling platform and user-generated content as a product of mass user participation. While there are many potential benefits and much added value for digital libraries, as shown in the examples of Delicious and Wikipedia, social media is not without its challenges and pitfalls. A critical element to address is the user community – harnessing the community towards quality participation and use of information resources is key to sustaining a good digital library.

With the accumulation of online content, certain gaps are created, especially with regard to the quality of information. This is where digital libraries must examine their roles as 'institutions and services' – a definition of digital libraries that arose from the community of practitioners (Borgman, 1999). Digital libraries need to design for quality and to assist users to select and interpret relevant resources. At the same time, they need also to recognize themselves as archives and to be able to tap into the technologies of Web 2.0 to provide collective intelligence regarding information resources in a timely manner. Such developments are still underdeveloped and provide immediate opportunities for further research concerning digital libraries.

References

Bimber, B., Flanagin, A. J. and Stohl, C. (2005) Reconceptualizing Collective Action in the Contemporary Media Environment, *Communication Theory*, **15** (4), 365–88.

Bishop, A. P. and Star, S. L. (1996) Social Informatics for Digital Library Use and Infrastructure. In Williams, M. E. (ed.), *Annual Review of Information Science and Technology* Information Today, 301-401.

Borgman, C. L. (1999) What are Digital Libraries? Competing visions, *Information Processing and Management*, **35**, 227–43.

Borgman, C. L., Bates, M., Cloonan, M. V., Efthimiadis, E. N., Gilliland-Swetland, A., Kafai, Y., Leazer, G. L. and Maddox, A. (1996) *Social Aspects of Digital Libraries*, University of California, Los Angeles–National Science Foundation, http://is.gseis.ucla.edu/research/dig_libraries/UCLA_DL_Report.html.

Bradley, G. (2006) *Social and Community Informatics: humans on the new*, Routledge.

Castells, M. (2003) *The Power of Identity*, 2nd edn, Blackwell Publishing.

Drucker, P. (1993) *Post-capitalist Society*, Harper-Collins Publishers.

Gehl, R. W. (2011) The Archive and the Processor: the internal logic of Web 2.0, *New Media and Society*, **13** (8), 1228–44.

Hong, W., Thong, J. Y. L., Wong, W. M. and Tam, K. Y. (2002) Determinants of User Acceptance of Digital Libraries: an empirical examination of individual differences and system characteristics, *Journal of Management Information Systems*, **18** (3), 97–124.

Kaplan, A. M. and Haenlein, M. (2010) Users of the World, Unite! The challenges and opportunities of social media, *Business Horizons*, **53** (1), 59–68.

Keen, A. (2007) *The Cult of the Amateur: how today's internet is killing our culture*, Broadway Publishing Group.

Lessig, L. (2004) *Free Culture: the nature and future of creativity*, Penguin Books.

Levy, D. M. and Marshall, C. C. (1995) Going Digital: a look at assumptions underlying digital libraries, *Communications of the ACM*, **38** (4), 77–84.

Liang, L. (2004) *A Guide to Open Content Licenses*, Piet Zwart Institute.

Miller, P. (2005) Web 2.0: building the new library, *Ariadne*, **45**, www.ariadne.ac.uk/issue45/miller/intro.html.

O'Reilly, T. (2005a) *What is Web 2.0*, www.oreilly.com/go/web2 .

O'Reilly, T. (2005b) *Web 2.0: compact definition?* http://radar.oreilly.com/archives/2005/10/web_20_compact_definition.html.

Pang, N. (2005) Digital Libraries as Learning Environments for Youths. In Theng, Y. L. and Foo, S. (eds), *Design and Usability of Digital Libraries*, Information Science Publishing.

Pang, N. and Schauder, D. (2006) User-centred Design and the Culture of Knowledge

Creating Communities: a theoretical reassessment. In Burstein, F. and Linger, H. (eds), *The Local and Global in Knowledge Management – Why Culture Matters*, Australian Scholarly Publishing.

Petersen, T. (2009) *Slaves of the Feed – this is not the realtime we've been looking for*, http://000fff.org/slaves-of-the-feed-this-is-not-the-realtime-weve-been-looking-for/.

Rusbridge, C. (1998) Electronic Libraries Programme, Talk presented at *IEEE International Forum on Research and Technology Advances in Digital Libraries (ADL '98), April 22–24, Santa Barbara, CA.*, IEEE Computer Society.

Tapscott, D. and Williams, A. D. (2006) *Wikinomics: how mass collaboration changes everything*, Portfolio Publishing.

Voss, J. (2005) Measuring Wikipedia, *International Conference of the International Society for Scientometrics and Informetrics (Stockholm)*, http://eprints.rclis.org/archive/00003610/01/MeasuringWikipedia2005.pdf.

Waters, D. J. (1998) What are Digital Libraries?, *CLIR (Council on Library and Information Resources) Issues*, **4**, www.clir.org/pubs/issues/issues04.html#dlf.

Wellman, B. and Haythornthwaite, C. (2000) *The Internet in Everyday Life*, Blackwell Publishing.

Wikipedia (2011) *Wikipedia – Wikipedia, the free encyclopedia*, http://en.wikipedia.org/wiki/Wikipedia.

Wilkinson, D. M. and Huberman, B. A. (2007) Assessing the Value of Cooperation in Wikipedia, *First Monday*, **12** (4), www.firstmonday.org/issues/issue12_4/wilkinson/index.html.

CHAPTER 7

Towards socially inclusive digital libraries

Chern Li Liew

Introduction

Many digital libraries (DLs) are designed to appeal to a much broader community than are physical libraries, and to provide an extension of the resources that are found inside physical libraries, thus transcending spatial limitations (Pomerantz and Marchionini, 2007). However, the potential of the DL to address the limitations of the physical library is only useful if, at the same time, access and usability issues can be addressed.

At times, in the midst of reading about the recent innovation and developments of digital technologies and DLs, one gets the feeling that the current situation with digital initiatives appears to be that a *big digital information party* is being planned but somehow, in the excitement, someone is being left out. Joseph Licklider and Robert Taylor (1968) foresaw two of the challenges faced today: 'In a few years, men will be able to communicate more effectively through a machine than face to face' and 'For the society, the impact will be good or bad, depending mainly on the question, "Will, to be on line, be a privilege or a right?"' (52).

As digital information and technologies encroach further and into more areas of our life and endeavours, processes of social exclusion are reproduced in the digital realm. Digital technologies have no doubt revolutionized the lives of much of the world's population. It would be a mistake, however, to assume that the impact of information and communication technologies (ICTs) has been wholly positive. The implication of ICT for economies, locally, nationally or globally, can at times be divisive. The information divide is not limited to the 'technology insiders' and 'technology outsiders' of cyberspace (Floridi, 2001). Discussions regarding the accessibility of information and digital content have moved on from a focus on digital divide to a focus on social exclusion, which is a much more complex phenomenon.

The concepts of social inclusion and social exclusion can be said to be the two ends of a continuum that relates to how much disadvantage an individual or group suffers in the society in which they live (Hayes, Gray and Edwards, 2009). Social exclusion is not always the result of an intentional act or of intentional policy. Often, it is an accumulation of isolating factors denying an individual or a group of people a means of inclusion within society in terms of resources, rights, goods and services, and the ability to participate in the normal relationships and activities available to the majority of people in that society.

While social exclusion overlaps with concerns about poverty and deprivation, it is a much broader concept that encompasses not just a lack of material means, but also an inability to participate fully and effectively in economic, political, social and cultural life. It can include forms of exclusion due to, for instance, mental and physical disabilities, age, ethnic, gender, class, occupation, sexuality, lifestyle, geographical location, political or religious affiliation, and family or legal circumstances (Percy-Smith, 2000).

Whereas notions of a digital divide are concerned primarily with the unavailability of ICTs, discussions around social exclusion attempt to identify and address access to information in the context of wider social concerns.

The increasing pace of technology innovation is likely to make it impossible to eliminate social exclusion altogether. Realistically, some sectors of society will always have more access to and benefits from DLs than others. While differences will remain, social exclusion needs to be addressed, not only as a matter of social justice but also as a matter of long-term collaborative survival for the 'DL community', which relies on the use and sharing of information to grow, to evolve and to be sustainable (Tanner, 2009).

The DL community has long had the *vision* and *passion* to build DLs that benefit societies and humanity. Vision and passion are no doubt critical parts of any worthwhile ambition. However, to make a real impact – not just for ourselves and for our own communities, but for a more encompassing community around the world, we need not only the vision and the passion: we need also *compassion* – compassion that extends our vision and passion to benefit all fellow human beings.

Overview

Birdi, Wilson and Cocker (2008) pointed out that public libraries have for a long time provided social inclusion services by providing information resources to communities and encouraging civic engagement by providing a public space. DLs could play a similar role in providing resources and facilitating engagement. However, without proper forethought, DLs can easily become another barrier to social inclusion, due to insufficient understanding of users who could benefit from them.

The DL community has invented new technologies and developed DLs that aim to empower users and communities through a range of activities, such as those aimed at education and economic developments. However, has the potential use of DLs to empower and to transform been all encompassing?

At times, researchers and policy makers hold ambiguous views on the diffusion of ICT and its role in economic development and sustainable development. Some consider ICT to be the fundamental means of achieving development, global interaction and learning that will lead to improvement in standards of living and social welfare

(Morawczynski and Ngwenyama, 2007; Ngwenyama et al., 2006; Dewan and Riggins, 2005), while others believe ICT to be of no great value, or even unfavourable, to the less developed nations (Avgerou, 2008; Bollou and Ngwenyama, 2008; Alampay, 2006).

DLs and other digital initiatives have the potential to enrich and empower communities and individuals, but they will not do so by simply existing. Lack of access, affordability and computer literacy, for instance, are just some of the obstacles that stand in the way of potential users and beneficiaries. The value of a DL may also depend on the appropriateness of its content and application, on the effective use of technologies and on investment in complementary factors. DLs can be democratic institutions. However, some cultures are not inherently democratic. In such a circumstance, this begs the question of who controls the creation and use of memory.

Mere digitization of the cultural heritage of a community does not necessarily lead to social inclusion. Merely providing ICT tools without understanding the social and situational contexts of the target users cannot adequately address social exclusion concerns. This chapter sets out to explore and seek some answers to the following questions:

1   What are the current barriers to a socially inclusive use of DLs?
2   What initiatives towards overcoming exclusion can be incorporated and implemented in DL projects?

Barriers to and roles of DLs

An attempt to answer the question of what current barriers exist to the socially inclusive use of DLs requires an examination of the factors that hinder and/or discourage individuals and societies from accessing ICT and fully utilizing DLs. This section examines a number of the main barriers. The roles that DLs and the DL community can play in addressing them are also explored.

Costs and accessibility

There are numerous barriers to the socially inclusive use of DLs. Lack of access and skills are the factors most often discussed in depth in examinations of the digital divide (Chowdhury and Chowdhury, 2011; Kinney, 2010; Warschauer, 2004).

It may be that the creators of a DL have every intention of broadening the community that can access its content. However, given that some communities are excluded from ready access to digital technology (either restricted in access to the technology or restricted in ability to use the technology), these communities are consequently and inadvertently excluded from obtaining the information that DLs and other digital information resources disseminate and preserve (Baker and Evans, 2009).

In research carried out about a decade ago, it was noted that 'people on low incomes, people with few educational qualifications or with low literacy levels, the unemployed, elderly people, people in isolated or rural areas, people with disabilities, sole parents, women and girls', along with 'many indigenous peoples, and some migrant and minority ethnic groups' (Cullen, 2001, 312), are some of the groups that are disadvantaged in their uptake of ICTs and that thus are often found on the 'wrong side' of the digital divide. Since most DLs nowadays use ICTs and the internet as the medium of delivery, they can be used only by those with access to such resources and those with sufficient levels of computer and information literacy (Tedd and Large, 2004). These are known to be neither globally available nor universally affordable. Without internet access, people who are prone to marginalization are likely to have the least access. Warren (2007) describes this as the 'vicious cycle: social exclusion leads to digital exclusion, which in turn perpetuates and exacerbates that social exclusion' (379).

Geography can be a barrier. Limited network infrastructure in rural areas means that alternative delivery mechanisms may be better than internet delivery. There are various ways for DL teams to work around the lack of access and connectivity. About ten years ago, Witten and Bainbridge (2003) used the Greenstone software to develop the Humanity Development Library for Human Info (1200 books and journals on a CD-ROM). The software made available a wealth of information to people throughout the developing world without internet connection, at a tiny fraction of the cost of the equivalent printed books. A few years ago, Bainbridge et al. (2007) adapted Greenstone to make DLs available on iPods so as to allow aid workers to take DLs into remote areas.

Key roles for the DL community here include collaborating with appropriate agencies and lobbying for policies that support equal opportunities and increasing public access to the internet and open learning spaces; adopting and developing open access tools; improving the usability and accessibility of DL sites; organizing funding; and supporting information literacy programmes. In New Zealand, programmes such as Aotearoa People's Network (APN), Digital New Zealand and NetSafe are aimed at enhancing the use of and access to information technology for all sectors of society; and the government's Digital Strategy places great emphasis on the role of not only the government but also the relevant sectors, including the information profession, communities and businesses, and states emphatically that the strategy alone is useless without effective collaboration.

Another useful place to start thinking about the issues is by considering the position of people with special needs. Theoretically, people with disabilities should have gained a greater degree of social inclusion from the ICT revolution, with the invention of technologies and devices that cater for their needs. However, surveys consistently show that levels of computer use and internet connectivity among people with disabilities are considerably lower than among the rest of the population. In part, this reflects general socio-economic issues, with disability and poverty being significantly correlated (Vicente and Lopez, 2010; Adams and Kreps, 2009). As well as having to afford standard ICT costs, people with disabilities face the added costs of adaptive technologies. People living with visual, auditory, learning and/or physical impairments may find themselves underrepresented and marginalized. While DLs cannot directly resolve this situation, they can come up with specific measures to support users with special needs. This issue highlights a priority area for policy action. Currently, there is a lack of legislative or other co-ordination measures that address either public assistive technology services or the assistive technology equipment sector.

Lower levels of ICT use among people with disabilities also appear to be due, in large part, to technical barriers to accessibility. This is one area where the designers of DLs can contribute to social inclusiveness by taking more care over the manner in which DL websites are designed. Among the issues that need to be considered is the necessity to ensure compatibility with the assistive technology that, for example, the visually impaired use to convert texts into audio input. Most websites are not compatible in this way (Nomensa, 2006). Taking more responsibility and being more compassionate in considering people with special needs when designing DLs will be a move forward.

Projects, such as Non-Visual Access to the DL (NoVA), that investigate different ways in which electronic information can be accessed and make recommendations for DL system designs should be encouraged (Golub, 2002). Access considerations should include acceptable levels of service for users with special needs. Abascal and Nicolle (2005) emphasize the importance of inclusive design guidelines in order to minimize social exclusion, and advocate a 'universal accessibility philosophy' of designing interfaces that are 'suitable, or capable of being easily adapted, for all people'. Resources should also be created in appropriate formats, as well as be interoperable across a range of platforms, including those that cater for those with special needs. Endeavouring to include people with special needs when conducting evaluations of DLs will also assist in identifying and addressing potential issues (Vicente and Lopez, 2010).

Skills, abilities, knowledge and language

One of the most significant factors contributing to social exclusion in relation to digital information is illiteracy and language homogeneity. The majority of the world's illiterate live in the developing nations. Furthermore, information that exists in either print or digital forms is preserved predominantly in English and other 'principal' languages. Thus indigenous cultures and developing nations are significantly disadvantaged by content that exists currently, including that in DLs.

Socio-economic issues such as illiteracy, lack of computer skills and lack of integration into social networks where digital technologies are used and valued also prevent some groups from taking advantage of available resources. Adams, Blanford and Lunt (2005) pointed out that 'DLs, like many technologies are often designed and implemented on the basis of assumptions which can result in users being excluded' (198). Some assume that, by placing free computers and making DLs available in public places, we are removing several barriers to social inclusion, when in fact we could still be leaving an obvious one in place – absence of understanding of the target users' needs and lack of guidance for them. Every effort is made to make the resources accessible, easy to use and relevant, but without an intermediary they may not reach the section of society they would most benefit. Intermediaries need to connect with the communities concerned. For instance, they can attend local tribal meetings to demonstrate the benefits of using DLs and how to use them effectively. Their roles need also to be two-way. They need to learn and to thoroughly understand the needs of the communities they serve, and to relay these to the people responsible for creating and maintaining the DLs. Similar efforts can be adopted for other marginalized groups, such as those with special needs and the elderly.

DLs should also take advantage of new forms of media to capture oral histories in a form that is more appropriate to the societies that they serve. In the context of Máori resources in New Zealand, for instance, DLs could focus on particular *iwi* (Máori nations) and serve their unique cultural interests. DLs could incorporate audio recordings with digital photos or video recordings in order to illustrate ancestral links and unique content associated with a particular *iwi*. Such an approach would make an effort towards being culturally appropriate and socially inclusive because it could represent the way indigenous people regard their respective identities, and could allow *iwi* to work collaboratively with institutions to preserve their culture in sustainable formats. Written language is not as universal as those from a technologically privileged background are inclined to believe, and DLs, as social institutions, need to serve their user communities in ways that are most suitable to those communities.

When DLs are to serve a global population, they need also to take into account the diverse linguistic backgrounds from which their users come (Tedd and Large, 2004). An important expression of a culture's identity is its language. Hence, if DLs aim to be culturally inclusive, it is important to respect the cultures concerned and to operate in local languages, where appropriate, and to aim to strengthen individual cultures, promote diversity and reduce the overwhelming dominance of English and other majority languages in the global information structure (De Souza, Laffon and Leitao, 2008; Nichols et al., 2005).

A study in South Africa (Constable, Mabena and Minishi-Mjanja, 2007) revealed that 100% of the library staff interviewed indicated that they did not provide information in indigenous South African languages, despite English not being the main language of the majority of people. As a result, many intended users are excluded from receiving information that could improve their lives in their mother tongue, and most of the valuable digital contents remain accessible only to those who are able to read English (Ngcobo, 2009).

DLs need to work towards initiatives that aim to extend their interfaces so as to allow for bilingual or multilingual interfaces, whichever is appropriate. This is especially important in cases where the target users are, or the content of the DLs relate to, a group whose language is different from the dominant language of the country, or where the country has more than one official language. EuropeanaConnect provides an example, taking a multilingual and multicultural approach so that people across Europe will be able to use the resources (Kaiser, Nikolov-Ramirez Gaviria and Prandl-Zika, 2009).

Concept, identity and relevance; participation and protection; cultural divide

The problem of social exclusion is also a matter of the political, institutional and cultural contexts that affect people's ability to use technologies effectively (Tavani, 2007; Madon et al., 2006). As Salinas (2003) pointed out, until the internet offers content that has actual value, significance and relevance to all its potential users, it will remain a place for the selected few.

Certain groups, such as cultural and ethnic minorities, may have cultural needs and interests that are not met by available digitized content (Salinas, 2003) and hence may choose not to access the internet and use DLs because they do not find the content relevant or interesting. Lack of relevant content for low-income users is also a barrier to DL use and to members of this group getting information that they need so as to improve their lives. A survey of low-income and under-served Americans (Lazarus and Mora, 2000) found four content-related barriers to inclusion in digital society: lack of local information, lack of content for low-literacy users, language barriers and lack of culturally diverse content.

Interface design is another aspect that needs to be considered with regard to the social exclusion of ethnic and cultural minorities. An inclusive design will no doubt be more complex and expensive. As with most aspects of DLs, cost is likely to be a factor in the level of inclusive design features that a project can incorporate. In any case, social inclusion of ethnic and cultural minorities will occur when the creators of DLs are respectful of these minorities' traditions, involve appropriate consultation with relevant stakeholder groups, take care to avoid the kind of appropriation that occurred in the past with physical cultural resources, and create an environment that supports the diffusion of the community's knowledge in a manner that helps to strengthen its identity and reinforce its self-esteem, while staying true to its values.

Design features, colours and symbols may be confusing, or, worse, be offensive in some contexts (Chowdhury, Landoni and Gibb, 2006; Hutchinson et al., 2005; Bishop et al., 2000). Cultural sensitivity is hence necessary when designing a DL, including considering the cultural meaning of symbols, colours and metaphors and whether the material is even culturally appropriate for digital display. Also, while there is potential to increase visibility and inclusion, when creating DLs of indigenous content it is important to be aware of the potential for 'theft, misuse or dilution of respect for cultural tradition' (National Library of New Zealand, 2007, 21).

Ritchie and Hermanus (2004) explored the concept of collections in relation to the power relations that influence the exclusion of materials from national collections. They argued that certain documents are privileged over others and that the resulting collection thus reflects exclusion of the 'marginalised and silenced' (6). This is a serious concern indeed. Information is not an end in itself and will be useful only if it is of the appropriate quality, timely, relevant and usable to the specific needs of the target users. The contents of DLs need to be collated on the basis of needs analyses to determine the requirements of the users (Dorner, Liew and Yeo, 2007) and, where necessary, they need to reflect the aspirations of the communities concerned. Politics, attitudes and content are sometimes termed 'the new digital divide' and are prevalent where socio-economic status is not a barrier (Gzehoviak et al., 2009).

Particular attention must be paid when the digital collection is itself aimed at a cultural minority. It is easy to make assumptions that unconsciously draw on prevailing norms. The result can be alienating and, worse, offensive to those whom the DL is intended to serve. An excellent example of a socially inclusive approach to DL design is that taken by a group of Texan Library and Information Studies graduate students who designed a DL for a local tribal college. The DL collection was structured in accordance with the traditional concept of 'Oksale', a cycle of experience on which to build a fulfilled life. The architecture of the site, the terminology used and the colours and imagery of the interface drew on the belief system of the indigenous culture in ways that instilled a sense of belonging that made it accessible to its target users (Roy and Larsen, 2002). Another example is the digitization of the book *Moko* (Máori tattooing). Before embarking on the digitization, the New Zealand Electronic Text Centre (NZETC) consulted stakeholder groups. An outcome of the consultation revealed the sensitive nature of certain content and led to the decision to withhold some pictures depicting *mokamokai* (preserved human skulls) (New Zealand Electronic Text Centre, 2008).

It is also important that marginalized groups be equipped to create their own content (Greyling and Zulu, 2009; Salinas, 2003; Worcman, 2002; Witten et al., 2001). Worcman (2002) argues that it is important for the community itself to have control of the DL creation process, and cautions against repeating the colonization and appropriation and mistreatment of a group's culture. This ties in with Pymm's view that collections are not 'neutral' (Pymm, 2006). To be socially inclusive, DL creators need to be aware of the subjectivity of collection decisions and to include a diverse range of views. Examples of projects that allow users and stakeholders themselves to participate in the creation of DLs include the Afya project to create a DL on health for African American women (Bishop et al., 2000) and the Coromandel Community Digital Storytelling Project of New Zealand.[1]

These examples show that DLs can support community engagement and empowerment. If DLs are designed with and for socially excluded groups, they may become the impetus or means for communities to learn and to engage with the literacy, skills and technologies required to create, access and maintain the DLs. Such DLs may also offer the potential of a collaborative, community-empowering process that can be used as a tool for social development and community regeneration.

At the same time, nevertheless, it is important to be mindful that the Western notion of intellectual freedom and the library and information science value of equitable access may not fit with the desires of certain indigenous groups concerning the guardianship and use of their cultural heritage. Hence, when developing DLs for traditional cultural resources it is important that research and work is carried out *with* the indigenous people rather than on or about them, and that direct indigenous involvement and collaboration is present at all levels and phases of the work. Steps should be taken to ensure that sensitive information gathered during the research is handled appropriately, that the project has relevant goals and the ownership of the DL is clearly defined.

Initiatives towards overcoming social exclusion

Librarians have been long-time advocates for basic human rights such as freedom of the press and freedom to access and to share information. Whatever we call ourselves, be it the DL community or another name, we can be instrumental in making the vision of social inclusiveness in the use and development of DLs a reality. Peace (2001) identifies three aspects of living in a society that need to be addressed so as to achieve social inclusion: 'opportunity, reciprocity and participation' (33). DLs hold great promise to contribute to each of these facets. DLs cannot, however, simply exist and expect to be useful.

Songhui (2007) pointed out that the DL community can play a role in the digital age as 'advisor and navigator'. The community can indeed play an advocacy role for the development of standards, for collaborative management initiatives and to strive to create DLs that provide a 'safe and trusted virtual community space' (Tise, Raju and Masango, 2009). The responsibility for making DLs socially inclusive will require consideration beyond the focused vision of a particular DL project, to include also the wider contexts of other information access initiatives.

There are various ways in which DLs can contribute to social inclusiveness, in addition to addressing barriers such as those discussed in the previous section. DL managers and research communities can lobby their country's government for equal access to ICTs and for information literacy, which is a serious concern, even among digital natives. Many researchers have found that even though digital natives have grown up using the internet and mobile technologies, they do not all have the skills and knowledge to make effective use of information (Cunningham, 2010; Hargittai, 2010; Bennett, Maton and Kervin, 2008; Rowlands et al., 2008).

Adams, Blanford and Lunt (2005) and Worcman (2002), writing in different contexts, have also pointed out that any DLs or other digital initiatives that seek to be inclusive must engage with and be meaningful to their target user community. Engaging with communities attends not only to access to technologies and the DL, but also to cultural, ability, class and ethnic differences. It also means creating ongoing relationships with the communities in question, as in the case of the DLESE (Digital Library of Earth System Education in the USA, www.dlese.org). This DL is built through an iterative process involving communities of users, and feedback mechanisms are in place from the assembly of the first-cut collection to the subsequent evaluations. DLESE continues to foster mechanisms for understanding what users want and desire in the collection, and to pay attention to their needs (Kastens et al., 2005). Where possible, DLs should also be implemented within the communities concerned. This might mean using community centres as access points, implementing the technologies in their workplaces, drop-in centres, meeting and prayer houses (if allowed).

Klecun (2008) and Worcman (2002) noted that the key to sustainable projects is community ownership, which requires involving those concerned in content creation and placing a 'partner' within the community at least prior to and during the implementation of a DL project. This kind of involvement and partnership can help to ensure forms of content structure that make cultural sense to indigenous and migrant groups. Phipps (2000) also identifies community network as a method of promoting inclusion – a 'deep involvement with the community, application of ICTs as a means to achieve wider social and economic objectives, developing community confidence, and linking social inclusion to economic regeneration' (62).

As sources of information, DLs play a key role in social inclusion initiatives that recognize the importance of information in empowering people (Hamilton and Ole Pors, 2003). Collaborative community-oriented projects offer some of the best examples of current DL initiatives to address social inclusion. These projects take advantage of digital technology's capacity to break down traditional divisions between those who make information available, those who use it and those who object to it. Shilton and Srinivasan (2008) describe a project that involved creating a digital archive for a Los Angeles South Asian community by way of iterative consultation with the community concerned. Community members were invited to contribute content and to take part in the construction of a community-derived ontology for arrangement and description of the content.

Social inclusion initiatives, while informed by the grassroots community, must, of course, also be supported from the top levels of the project, otherwise they are not likely to be sustainable. DLs may begin with their local communities, particularly with potential users or those already marginalized or excluded from society, and explicitly aim to lower the barriers to these groups' use of DLs. DLs may aim to prioritize certain communities, depending on their mission and contexts. For instance, the NZETC (www.nzetc.org) has special note of Máori needs for information and content, and of the need to care about cultural rights when digitizing material. Hukilau (www.dahukilau.com) is another example, where the main aim is to provide online resources of the Hawaiian language and culture.

As discussed previously, focusing on incorporating usability features and interfaces targeted at a community, such as adaptive technologies for people with special needs, should also not be overlooked. A few years ago a study of web-based library databases (Byerley, Chambers and Thohira, 2007) concluded that, while some aspects of accessibility were addressed, 'accessibility' itself was not a major selling point, and most products were not tested with people with disabilities. The study concluded that neither the vendors nor the subscribing libraries considered accessibility by the disabled community to be a significant issue. This situation needs to be rectified.

Summary

DLs need to be accessible, both intellectually and in tangible terms. They will not fulfil their potential until they become inviting places to all sections of society. More than a decade ago, Capurro (1999) asserted the need to consider cyberspace in general, and DLs in particular, as belonging to people's life-space. The management of information and knowledge becomes 'an ethical imperative in a world of growing inequity and, at the same time, of growing superabundance of digital information and knowledge resources'. Capurro insisted that knowledge and information must be managed in order to reduce inequity of access and to support cultural diversity.

The European Union designated 2010 as the 'European Year for Combating Poverty and Social Exclusion' (European Commission, 2010) and brought together the two concepts of poverty and social exclusion. The Globethics Foundation Board, which governs the Globethics.net DL (Globethics.net, 2008), provides free access to multilingual content from subscription-based scholarly journals (Sage and Gale Group), open access repositories, e-books, theses and dissertations and encyclopedias. This is a project that hopes to provoke ethical reflection and action and to empower people from developing countries to become a part of the global discourse on ethics.

As evidenced in many projects, the DL community has long had the vision and passion for the development and use of DLs. Perhaps it is time to emphasize another element: compassion. Maybe then we will see signs of the maturity needed for the possibilities of the DL community to become reality.

The policies and initiatives promoted for DLs to foster the information society should not be only about 'wiring the country and attaching a computer at the end of the wires', but also about gathering, storing and disseminating information, with the goal of social inclusion (Pena-Lopez, 2009). As DLs develop, how we as communities and as a global society address digital and social exclusion will be an indication of our compassion and the maturity of our contributions.

It is not likely that the DL community will alone solve all the problems of digital and social exclusion. It is also not likely that any DL can be all inclusive. Indeed, it might be essential to respect the choices of certain groups and communities not to be part of a DL initiative. Nevertheless, DLs and technologies should be seen neither as irrelevant to those disempowered or at the margins of society, nor as a panacea for social ills. Instead, DL projects must capitalize on the potential of digital technologies to reduce social exclusion, and seek to create and maintain DLs that are truly accessible to those can and who want to benefit from them. There are great opportunities for DLs to contribute to an inclusive society. How DLs are prepared for and respond to the many opportunities for social empowerment, and their implications, will also be likely to have an effect on their values and long-term sustainability.

Note

1   www. Harakeke.co.nz/DST_CCDSP_index.html.

References

Abascal, L. and Nicolle, C. (2005) Moving Towards Inclusive Design Guidelines for Socially and Ethically Aware HCI, *Interacting with Computers*, **17**, 484–505.

Adams, A. and Kreps, D. (2009) Disability and Discourses of Web Accessibility, *Information, Communication and Society*, **12** (7), 1041–58.

Adams, A., Blanford, A. and Lunt, P. (2005) Social Empowerment and Exclusion: a case study on DLs, *ACM Transactions on CHI*, **12** (2), 174–200.

Alampay, E. A. (2006) Beyond Access to ICTs: measuring capabilities in the information society, *International Journal of Education and Development Using Information and Communication Technology* **2** (3). ijedict.dec.uwi.edu/viewarticle.php?id=196.

Avgerou, C. (2008) Information Systems in Developing Countries: a critical research review, *Journal of Information Technology*, **23**, 133–46.

Bainbridge, D., Jones, S., McIntosh, S. and Jones, M. (2007) *Digital Libraries on iPod: beyond the client-server model*, Working Paper 06/2007, University of Waikato (NZ): Department of Computer Science.

Baker, D. and Evans, W. (2009) Digital Library Economics: the environment. In Baker, D. and Evans, W. (eds), *Digital Library Economics: an academic perspective*, Chandos, 1–30.

Bennett, S., Maton, K. and Kervin, L. (2008) The 'Digital Natives' Debate: a critical review of the evidence, *British Journal of Educational Technology*, **39**(5), 775–86.

Birdi, B., Wilson, K. and Cocker, J. (2008) The Public Library, Exclusion and Empathy: a literature review, *Library Review*, **57** (8), 576–92.

Bishop, A., Mehra, B., Bazzell, I. and Smith, C. (2000) Socially Grounded User Studies in Digital Library Development, *First Monday*, **4** (6), firstmonday.org/htbin/cgiwrap/bin/ojs/index.php/fm/article/view/760/669.

Bollou, F. and Ngwenyama, O. (2008) Are ICT Investments Paying Off in Africa? An analysis of total factor productivity in six West African countries from 1995 to 2002, *Information Technology for Development*, **14** (4), 294–307.

Byerley, S. L., Chambers, M. B. and Thohira, M. (2007) Accessibility of Web-based Library Databases: the vendors' perspectives in 2007, *Library Hi-tech*, **25** (4), 509–27.

Capurro, R. (1999) Ethical Aspects of Digital Libraries, Paper presented at *CoLIS3 – Digital Libraries: Interdisciplinary Concepts, Challenges and Opportunities*, www.capurro.de/diglib.htm.

Chowdhury, G. and Chowdhury, S. (2011) *Information Users and Usability in the Digital Age*, Facet Publishing.

Chowdhury, S., Landoni, M. and Gibb, F. (2006) Usability and Impact of Digital Libraries, *Online Information Review*, **30** (6), 656–80.

Constable, T. F., Mabena, M. C. and Minishi-Mjanja, M. (2007) South African Government Library Services and the *Batho Pele* Principles: how the eleven official languages impact on service delivery. Paper presented at *73rd IFLA: Libraries for the Future: Progress, Development and Partnerships, 19–23 August*, archive.ifla.org/IV/ifla73/papers/097-Constable_Mabena_Minishi-Mjanja-en.pdf.

Cullen, R. (2001) Addressing the Digital Divide, *Online Information Review*, **25** (5), 311–20.

Cunningham, J. (2010) New Workers, New Workplace? Getting the balance right, *Strategic*

Direction, **26** (1), 5–6.

De Souza, C. S., Laffon, R. F. and Leitao, C. F. (2008) Communicability in Multicultural Contexts: a study with the International Children's DL. In *Proceedings of Information Federation for Information Processing – Human Computer Interaction Symposium,* **272,** 129–42.

Dewan, S. and F. J. Riggins (2005) The Digital Divide: current and future research directions. *Journal of Association for Information Systems,* **6** (2), 298–337.

Dorner, D., Liew, C. L. and Yeo, Y. P. (2007) A Textured Sculpture: an examination of the information needs of users of digitised New Zealand cultural heritage resources, *Online Information Review,* **31** (2), 166–84.

European Commission (2010) *Employment, Social Affairs and Equal Opportunity,* www.2010againstpoverty.eu/?langid=en.

Floridi, L. (2001) Information Ethics: an environmental approach to the digital divide. *Philosophy in the Contemporary World,* **9** (1), 1–4.

Globethics.net (2008) *Join Ethical Reflection + Action for Responsible Leadership,* www.globethics.net/c/document_library/get_file?p_1_id=14538&folderId= 1083734&name=DLFE-817.pdf.

Golub, K. (2002) DLs and the Blind and Visually Impaired, Paper presented at *4th CARNet Users Conference 2002, 25–27 September 2002,* www.it.lth.se/koraljka/Lund/publ/ Golub-CuC-2002-eng.pdf.

Greyling, E. and Zulu, S. (2009) *Content Development in an Indigenous Digital Library: a case study in community participation,* www.ifla.org/files/hq/papers/ifla75/191-greyling-en.pdf.

Gzehoviak, T., Grawbowska, K., McPhilips, D. and Cody, S. (2009) The New Digital Divide: LS769 Group Project, www.slideshare.net/newdigitaldivide/the-new-digital-divide-2707247.

Hamilton, S. and Ole Pors, N. (2003) Freedom of Access to Information and Freedom of Expression: the internet as a tool for global social inclusion, *Library Management,* **24** (8/9), 407–16.

Hargittai, E. (2010) Digital Na(t)ives? Variation in internet skills and uses among members of the 'net generation', *Sociological Inquiry,* **80** (1), 92–113.

Hayes, A., Gray, M. and Edwards, B. (2009) *Social Inclusion: origins, concept and key themes,* www.socialinclusion.gov.au/Documents/AIFS_SI_concepts_report_20April09.pdf.

Hutchinson, H., Rose, A., Bederson, B., Weeks, A. and Druin, A. (2005) The International Children's Digital Library: a case study in designing for a multi-lingual, multi-cultural, multi-generational audience, *Information Technology and Libraries,* **24** (1), 4–12.

Kaiser, M., Nikolov-Ramirez Gaviria, L. and Prandl-Zika, V. (2009) EuropeanaConnect: enhancing user access to European digital heritage. In *Proceedings of Cultural Heritage Online. Empowering Users: an active role for user communities,* www.rinascimwnto-digitale.it/eventi/conference2009/proceeidngs-2009/kaiser-gaviria.pdf.

Kastens, K., DeFelice, B., Devaul, H., DiLeonardo, C., Ginger, K., Larsen, S. et al. (2005) Questions and Challenges Arising in Building the Collection of a Digital Library for Education, *D-Lib Magazine,* **11** (11), www.dlib.org/dlib/november05/kastens/11kastens.html.

Kinney, B. (2010) The Internet, Public Libraries, and the Digital Divide, *Public Library Quarterly*, **29** (2), 104–61.

Klecun, E. (2008) Bringing Lost Sheep into the Fold: questioning the discourse of the digital divide, *Information, Technology & People*, **21** (3), 267–82.

Lazarus, W. and Mora, F. (2000) *Online Content for Low-income and Underserved Americans: the digital divide's new frontier*, www.markle.org.

Licklider, J. C. R. and Taylor, R. (1968) The Computer as a Communication Device, *Science and Technology*, **76**, 21–31.

Madon, S., Reinhart, N., Roode, D. and Walsham, G. (2006) Digital Inclusion Projects in Developing Countries: value, sustainability and scalability. In Trauth, E. M., Howcroft, D., Butler, T., Fitzgerald, B. and J. I. DeGross (eds), *Social Inclusion: societal and organizational implications for information systems*, Springer, 67–78.

Morawczynski, O. and Ngwenyama, O. (2007) Unraveling the Impact of Investments in ICT, Education and Health of Development: an analysis of archival data of five West African countries using regression splines, *Electronic Journal of Information Systems in Developing Countries*, **29** (5), 1–15.

National Library of New Zealand (2007) *Creating a Digital New Zealand*, www.digitalstrategy.govt.nz/upload/Main%20Sections/Content/ NATLIBDigitalContentStrategy.pdf.

New Zealand Electronic Text Centre (2008) *Moko; Máori Tattooing Project: a report on consultation*, www.nzetc.org/tm/scholarly/tei-MokoDiscussionPaper.html.

Ngcobo, M. N. (2009) A Strategic Promotion of Language Use in Multilingual South Africa: information and communication, *Southern African Linguistics and Applied Language Studies*, **27** (1), 113–20.

Ngwenyama, O., Andoh-Baidoo, K. F., Bollou, F. and Morawczynski, O. (2006) Is There a Relationship Between ICT, Health, Education and Development? An empirical analysis of five West African countries from 1997–2003, *The Electronic Journal on Information Systems in Developing Countries*, **23** (5), 1–11.

Nichols, D. M., Witten, I. H., Keegan, T. T., Bainbridge, B. and Dewsnip, M. (2005) Digital Libraries and Minority Languages, *New Review of Hypermedia and Multimedia*, **11** (2), 139–55.

Nomensa (2006) *United Nations global audit of web accessibility*, www.un.org/esa/socdev/enable/gawanomensa.htm.

Peace, R. (2001) Social Exclusion: a concept in need of definition?, *Social Policy Journal of New Zealand*, **16**, 17–36.

Pena-Lopez, I. (2009) *Digital Divide and Social Inclusion (III): organizations and institutions before the digital divide: model development and good practice*, http://ictlogy.net/20091029-digital-divide-and-social-inclusion-iii-organizations-and-institutions-before-the-digital-divide-model-development-and-good-practices.

Percy-Smith, J. (2000) Introduction: the contours of social exclusion. In Percy-Smith, J. (ed.), *Policy Responses to Social Exclusion: towards inclusion?*, Open University Press, 1–21.

Phipps, L. (2000) A Conduit for Social Inclusion, *Information, Communication & Society*, **3** (1), 39–68.

Pomerantz, J. and Marchionini, G. (2007) The Digital Library as Place, *Journal of Documentation*, **63** (4), 505–33.

Pymm, B. (2006) Building Collections for All Time: the issue of significance, *AARL*, **37** (1), 61–73.

Ritchie, G. and Hermanus, M. (2004) Challenging Neutrality: investigating the National Library of South Africa. Paper presented at *7th Annual LIASA Conference, Polokwane, 27 September – 1 October*, www.nlsa.ac.za/NLSA/.../LIASA_Conference_2004_Ritchie_Hermanus.pdf.

Rowlands, I., Nicholas, D., Williams, P., Huntington, P., Fieldhouse, M., Gunter, B. et al. (2008) The Google Generation: the information behaviour of the researcher of the future, *Aslib Proceedings*, **60** (4), 290–310.

Roy, L. and Larsen, P. (2002) Oksale: an indigenous approach to creating a library of education resources, *D-Lib Magazine*, **8** (3), www.dlib.org/dlib/march02/roy/03roy.html.

Salinas, R. (2003) Addressing the Digital Divide through Collection Development, *Collection Building*, **22** (3), 131–6.

Shilton, K. and Srinivasan, R. (2008) Participatory Appraisal and Arrangement for Multicultural Archival Collections, *Archivaria*, **63**, 87–101.

Songhui, Z. (2007) The Influence of Traditional Reading Habits on the Construction of DLs in Developing Countries, *The Electronic Library*, **26**, 46–64.

Tanner, S. (2009) The Economic Future of Digital Libraries: a 2020 vision. In Baker, D. and Evans, W. (eds), *Digital Library Economics: an academic perspective*, Chandos Publishing, 291–309.

Tavani, H. (2007) *Ethics and Technology: ethical issues in an age of information and communication technology*, John Wiley & Sons.

Tedd, L. A. and Large, A. J. (2004) *Digital Libraries: principles and practice in a global environment*, K. G. Saur.

Tise, E. R., Raju, R. and Masango, C. (2009) *Libraries Driving Access to Knowledge: a discussion paper*, ifl.sagepub.com/content/34/4/341.abstract.

Vicente, M. and Lopez, J. (2010) A Multidimensional Analysis of the Disability Digital Divide: some evidence for internet use, *The Information Society: an international journal*, **13** (5), 407–24, doi: 10.1080/01615440903423245.

Warren, M. (2007) The Digital Vicious Cycle: links between digital disadvantaged and digital exclusion, *Telecommunications Policy*, **31**, 374–88.

Warschauer, M. (2004) *Technology and Social Inclusion: rethinking the digital divide*, MIT Press.

Witten, I. and Bainbridge, D. (2003) *How to Build a Digital Library*, Morgan Kaufmann.

Witten, I., Loots, M., Trujilo, M. and Bainbridge, D. (2001) The Promise of Digital Libraries in Developing Countries, *Communications of the ACM*, **44**(5).

Worcman, K. (2002) Digital Division is Cultural Exclusion. But is digital inclusion cultural inclusion? *D-Lib Magazine*, **8** (3), www.dlib.org/dlib/march02/worcman/03worcman.html.

CHAPTER 8

Users' interactions with digital libraries

T. D. Wilson and Elena Macevičiūtė

Introduction

Over the past ten years, the spread and diversity of digital libraries has increased enormously. Not only are 'traditional' libraries extending the scope of their activities by creating digital libraries of one kind or another, but learned societies, interest groups and other organizations are creating digital libraries of specialized scope to serve the information needs of their intended user groups and of the public at large.

The purpose of this chapter is to provide an overview of current trends in research on the interaction between users and digital libraries, to reveal the main results of that research and to explore the applicability of existing models of information behaviour to the digital library sphere. Generally, we have not sought to limit our definition of the digital library to a particular form, but have accepted what is described in the retrieved literature as a digital library. However, from the perspective of the information user, it seems reasonable to question why the term 'library' is used in this context.

Methods and scope of this study

If we perceive a library as nothing more than a room with books, then, by analogy, a file of electronic documents can be described as a 'digital library'. The modern library, however, is much more than a room with books; it has associated services of various kinds, from reference services to interlibrary lending, and services directed to particular groups such as, in the public library sector, children's libraries and business libraries. Traditionally, special libraries in industry and beyond have offered translation and current-awareness services. Our proposition, therefore, is that the richer the array of services offered in the digital sphere, the more like a bricks-and-mortar library the digital library will be, and the richer the user experience of the library. The poorer the digital library is in these terms, the more like a repository or an archive it will be. One of the papers retrieved by the authors highlighted the difference between web archives and digital libraries, which provide more structured collections and enable the use of metadata, controlled vocabularies and authority files in the execution of searches. Thus, the quality of services and documents supplied by digital libraries played a distinctive role in their definition (Agosti, Crivellari and Di Nunzio, 2011, 15).

We began our analysis with a literature search, using Scopus because of its wider coverage of the journal literature in the field, searching for papers produced over the past five years, using the search formulation, 'digital library or libraries and user needs or information seeking or information behaviour'. After removing duplicates and irrelevant items, we were left with 166 papers, 55% of which were from journals and 45% from conference proceedings. The journal papers were from 58 journals, led by the *Journal of the American Society for Information Science and Technology*, with 13 papers, and *Electronic Library*, with 9. The leading conference was the ACM International Conference on Digital Libraries, with 18 papers (24%), followed by the ACM/IEEE Joint Conference on Digital Libraries, with 12 papers, and the International Conference on Asian Digital Libraries and the European Conference on Digital Libraries, with 10 papers each (the latter conference was renamed the International Conference on Theory and Practice of Digital Libraries with effect from the 2011 event).

Lines of research in user studies

Turning to the subjects covered by the papers, we detect four lines of research:

1   the activities of users in general, or specific groups of users, such as children and academics
2   specific activities of the user, such as searching and browsing
3   design aspects related to user behaviour, such as visualization, navigation and metadata
4   research and evaluation methods, such as eye-tracking, log analysis and social research methods such as card-sorting and focus groups.

As Chowdhury points out, user studies have 'become an integral part of digital library research over the past decade' (2010, 208). According to his calculations, usability and user studies cover over a third of the literature on digital libraries published between 1997 and 2007 and include such areas as interface interaction and design, human–computer interaction and accessibility. Liew confirmed the findings of Chowdhury in her review of digital library research over 11 years (1997–2007). Of her sample of 577 articles, 199 (34.5%) addressed use and usability of digital libraries (2009, 248). Often these issues are investigated within a certain user group or in relation to a particular resource (e.g. e-books, images or one of the digital libraries), especially for their evaluation. Thus, the evaluation of different elements of digital libraries is another goal closely connected to the usability studies. Zhang et al. (2008) investigated the features in the search and browsing designs of three digital libraries and established those that hindered user performance. The user interface design area also brought other tools to the design and development of digital libraries, such as the creation of personas. Personas represent user archetypes or the typical profiles of certain user groups. Koltay and Tancheva (2010) describe how Cornell University Library used personas for assessment of user needs and the information landscape of the library, as well as to identify gaps in service provision and decision making. Collecting the requirements of the main user groups for the design of digital libraries, and involvement of users in their development, can also be named as one of the reasons for user studies. Different approaches are used to achieve one or both of these goals. Abdullah and Zainab (2006) have used the Zachman Framework, a logical structure that provides a representation of an enterprise, in different dimensions, with each dimension capable of being perceived from different perspectives. The authors applied the Framework to collecting requirements from different user groups for the design of a collaborative digital library for an urban secondary school in Malaysia. Bastien et al. (2009) explored the needs of the European Navigator (a digital library on the history of European integration) user communities through discussions with their expert representatives. The groups of experts suggested a number of ideas on the digital library that were used for its redesign.

A number of articles explore the information seeking behaviour of academic researchers and staff. It is necessary to emphasize that these studies are broader and treat digital libraries among other resources available to this group. One of the largest studies was undertaken by Niu et al. in 2009 by conducting a survey of 2063 natural and applied sciences academic researchers from five universities in the USA. The survey proved that scientists mainly retrieved electronic papers from library-subscribed electronic journals and open access journals. Many of them preferred to start searching through the library home pages as a pathway to academic resources and, because of the frustration of searching in multiple content sources, indicated a preference for meta-search tools. The simplification of the search interfaces used by libraries was suggested as a possible reason for these findings. The survey also has shown that 'although the number of visits to the physical library is decreasing, the amount of utilization of library resources has generally been increased [sic], especially for electronically delivered content' (Niu et al., 2010, 877). Wang et al. (2007) presented a cross-cultural study of information seeking online by researchers in the USA, China and Greece. It was found that the role of internet searching and digital resources had increased and bricks-and-mortar libraries had become less visible. There was no special emphasis on digital libraries, although some of them (e.g. the Association for Computing Machinery (ACM) Digital Library) figure prominently in the lists of resources used.

It seems that other, direct digital library services, especially communication and consultation with librarians, increase the use of digital services. However, the provision of digital materials and technological support to researchers should not be taken for granted, as the research into the information behaviour in the humanities shows. Audenaert and Furuta (2010) looked into the use of source materials by humanities scholars and discovered that these 'materials are studied as an integral part of a complex ecosystem of inquiry' in order to understand the context of their creation, transmission and use (Audenaert and Furuta, 2010, 290). The authors created a model of sources, context, actors and derived forms that integrates digital libraries (mainly of cultural heritage materials) as tools providing wider access to source materials and editorial contributions and other support or means of dissemination.

Researchers and academic staff also become an object of research in relation to the use of specific tools, technologies or digital objects. Having in mind that digital libraries increase the complexity of the research environment, Alhoori and Furuta (2011) explored dynamic information needs and collaborative information use in relation to social reference management systems such as Connotea and CiteULike. Researchers at the University of Alberta participated in a user-evaluation study of Searchling, a visual interface with a bilingual thesaurus for query formulation and enhancement. This investigation provided a number of insights into multilingual search processes and the improvement of search support (Shiri et al., 2011). A visual interface as an aid in exploratory search was evaluated by Krestel, Demartini and Herder (2011), who discovered that 'different visualizations lead to fundamentally different kinds of exploratory behaviour' (Krestel, Demartini and Herder, 2011). This type of investigation usually concerns the evaluation of certain components or tools related to digital libraries.

A number of surveys conducted and reported by different actors (libraries, publishers or e-book aggregators) between 2005 and 2009 investigated the usage of e-books mainly accessed through academic libraries by academic staff and students. Their results are summed up by Mincic-Obradovic (2011, 120–34) and highlight users' awareness of e-books and their influence: e-book usage, sources, the purposes and frequency of reading e-books, preferred channels and formats, as well as the importance of e-books for users.

Researchers and students, more than any other groups, seem to attract attention of researchers. But there is a general lack of information on behaviour in relation to digital libraries among professionals and practitioners. Some research is addressing cultural heritage workers: cultural heritage experts (Amin et al., 2008) and museum practitioners (Chen, 2007). D'Alessandro, Kreiter and Peterson (2004) explored the use of digital libraries and resources, in comparison with other information sources, by general paediatricians. It was found that a short introduction to the use of a paediatrics digital library increases the number of questions pursued and answered using computer resources and decreases the time spent in getting an answer.

The existence of the International Children's Digital Library (ICDL) has become a focus of several research projects on children's use of digital libraries. Druin (2005) summarized her long-term work on development and participative design of the ICDL, involving children from seven to eleven years old working together with researchers. In line with other projects, the team found that children have positive views of technology and have particular needs and ways of interacting with it, including with digital libraries. As adult developers seem to be more interested in technological issues and think that they can remember their childhood, children's needs, especially those of the younger ones, who may be non-readers and rely on visual and auditory cues, are neglected. In the development of the ICDL adult and child researchers worked in brainstorming sessions, tested new ideas and implemented technologies. The research has revealed that children have special requirements for digital libraries in all their manifestations: 'different collections, different ways of cataloging materials, and different tools–technologies to access and use collections on the Web' (Druin, 2005, 34). The author has formulated seven design principles for digital libraries for children that emerged from her own and earlier work:

1   Children should be involved in the design of their libraries, as they make crucial input.
2   Digital collections should include books from different cultures, languages and periods.
3   Visual icons for searching are most important, but children need a variety of search tools, as they use multiple ways to find books.
4   Children-specific search criteria related to feelings, colours, shapes and sizes should be developed.
5   Interfaces for children's digital libraries should be customizable.
6   Digital library tools should be suitable for use at home collaboratively by many children or children and parents.
7   There is a need to balance innovation with broad access by users (Druin, 2005, 36).

These principles were also confirmed by other researchers. Abbas (2005) explored search terms that children used in the context of ARTEMIS Digital Library. She used an experimental technique to obtain search terms from middle school children and compared them with controlled vocabularies. Her findings show that the terms used to index digital library resources are not adequate and suitable for users in this age-group and that involvement of children in the development of representations not only improves the quality of the latter, but also increases understanding of how children interact with digital libraries (Abbas, 2005, 1520).

A team at the ICDL developed three digital library book readers (standard linear, comic strip and spiral) using contextual inquiry, participatory design and technology immersion techniques. A group of children and adults tested the readers (Hourcade et al., 2003). The findings showed that children have no clear preferences and use all three readers, although the standard one produced the best results for some tasks, the spiral one required more time for task completion and was rather confusing for younger children, while the comic strip reader was the favourite with adults. All three readers are in use in the ICDL.

The ICDL not only provides access to children's books but also supports the development of multicultural communities for children, formed around its book collection. One of the teams has assessed the ICDL Communities prototype, which provides tools for communication among children with different linguistic and cultural backgrounds, remotely and without machine translation (Komlodi et al., 2007). The team ran two preliminary evaluations with some children from the USA and Hungary and a group from the USA and Argentina using the ICDL prototype communication tools, followed by the main evaluation with children from the USA and Mexico. The complicated remote usability-testing method combined with ethnographic enquiry produced complex data relating to team building, identity, story creation, communication, emotions etc. It also showed that 'adult designers and developers have difficulty forecasting children's preferences, strengths, and weaknesses in … cross-cultural online communication'. The findings were surprising for designers and it turned out that the involvement of children in the development and evaluation of tools and processes is essential. Moreover, children from different countries and nations should be involved if the software is intended for international use, although it may be very challenging to arrange this (Komlodi et al., 2007, 509).

Bilal and Bachir have assessed the cross-cultural usability of the ICDL further by looking into the interaction of Arabic-speaking children with the library interface and collections. The assessment of the interface revealed that most of the features supported the children's searching activity, but the younger children had difficulties in recognizing the representations and icons on the interface (Bilal and Bachir, 2007a, 2007b). The overall interaction of the Arabic-speaking children with the ICDL for finding and reading books was a positive and pleasant experience: they appreciated the ease of use and the possibility of reading Arabic books online. All of them managed to complete most of the tasks. However, before interacting with the ICDL, children experienced anxiety, uncertainty and fear, although this was reduced by the presence of sympathetic adult researchers. Thus, an affective component was introduced into the (so far) cognitive and action input of children into the development of the ICDL. Children also indicated a number of problems, such as too small a collection of books in Arabic, consisting mainly of the books that they had read in Bibliotheca Alexandrina, and the lack of an Arabic interface and keywords (Bilal and Bachir, 2007a, 2007b). On the basis of this study, Bilal and Sarangthem built a model of the children's interaction with digital libraries associated with the tasks the children had performed. It consists of seven steps: Start – Recognize – Browse – Differentiate – Read – Explore – Finish. The model itself is similar to others modelling information seeking in digital environments. The authors used it to trace the levels of children's iterative interactions with the digital library related to their acquaintance with the collection, their age and internet experience, motivation and the nature of tasks (Bilal and Sarangthem, 2009).

Research methods for interaction studies

User interaction with digital libraries is explored using a number of methods, some usual for information-behaviour research and others drawn from information-systems or information-technology research. Some participative design and user-centred approaches have become a part of user research methods, but more traditional research methods, such as surveys, interviews and focus groups, are also used. Experimental and observational data are also used quite frequently. Kiran and Singh (2008) have used focus groups with postgraduate students to explore users' perceptions and experiences of libraries that offer digital services. The outcome showed that the most important issues of concern to the users are easy access, technical help and communication with service providers.

Log analysis seems to be as popular for exploring digital library users' activities as are surveys and interviews. An exhaustive review of the studies using log analysis (92 studies) over the last decade is provided in Agosti et al. (2011). Log analysis falls into two categories: analysis of web search engine logs and analysis of digital library system logs, which is of interest in this chapter.

'Log analysis is a primary source of knowledge about how digital library [DL] patrons actually use DL systems and how systems behave while trying to support user information seeking activities' (Agosti et al., 2011, 18). According to the authors, some areas benefit well from log analysis: one is users' interaction with current library systems, which is particularly useful as an evaluation method, providing input for management decisions, establishing the priorities and exposing the directions for system improvement (19). The review examines both the benefits and shortcomings of log data analysis as a method. The benefits are 'improving performance by recording effective evaluation data, helping in designing and testing of user interfaces and better allocation of resources' (18), supporting examination of very large numbers of search sessions and queries that the scale of qualitative studies cannot match (20). However, the method is criticized as being unable to provide in-depth information about user interaction with the digital library. In addition, log records have to be clean and of a well-defined structure, which requires careful preparation of the data for the analysis. And even when this is ensured, the data may remain incomplete, incompatible with log data from other systems, and ambiguous, due to poorly specified semantics. The 'generalization for all users is difficult as the data describes a particular system user searching specific collections' (20). The authors of the review describe attempts to overcome some of these shortcomings by designing specific log formats and structures; by combining various kinds of data, for example query logs and click streams, logs and observation data, online questionnaires, or interviews; and by conducting comparative log analysis of two or more digital libraries.

So far, log analysis has been applied for studying search behaviour in OPACs (e.g. Assadi et al., 2003; Koch, Ardö and Golub, 2004); video (Hopfgartner et al., 2008) and text (Christel, Maher and Li, 2009) retrieval; and book-centred reading behaviour using the logs from the ICDL (Chen, Rose and Bederson, 2009).

The wider application of log analysis so far has been inhibited by a lack of recent and long-term data sets that would enable the verifiability and repeatability of the experiments. The first steps in this direction were taken in 2009 under the Cross-Language Evaluation Forum (track LogCLEF). But the use of log analysis will grow not only in the areas that already apply it, but also in new applications, such as comparing behaviour recorded in logs from different devices (smartphones, laptops and tablet computers).

Eye-tracking analysis is one of the less-used methods. Sykes et al. (2010) used eye-tracking as part of user evaluation of Europeana. The eye-tracking data showed that users had not consciously considered what they looked at during search sessions and the data did not relate to many of their habitual actions. These data were valuable for designing more intuitive search functions. Another useful technique that helps researchers to track users' interaction with digital libraries is the think aloud method. Makri, Blandford and Cox (2010) have presented in detail a think aloud study of lawyers' interactive use of digital libraries according to the PRETAR framework developed by Blandford et al. (2008). The article provides methodological insights into the process of planning data collection, the actual data collection process, transcription, analysis and the reporting of findings.

It seems that user interaction with digital libraries can be explored using a wider variety of methods, expanded by constantly widening technological options.

Models of user information behaviour in digital libraries

If we consider information behaviour as the field of investigation that deals with people's interaction with information and information systems, then interaction with digital libraries is clearly a part of that field. However, models of information behaviour have generally treated information systems of any kind simply as one of the possible sources of information to which an individual may have access. Consequently, the investigation of the minutiae of interaction has generally been left to the information systems field, the human–computer interaction field or the investigation of information retrieval, especially interactive information retrieval.

In so far as we may be interested in the actions performed by a digital library user in searching digital library, models of interactive information retrieval, especially that of Saracevic (1997), may be considered sufficient. If, however, the digital library of interest to the user has more functionality than simple search for and retrieval of documents and/or images, then a wider range of interactions, which may be modelled separately from the retrieval process, are possible.

For example, a public digital library may offer the possibility of reserving a document for collection in the library, or mailing it to the user, rather than simply identifying its existence. Or an academic digital library may draw the user's attention to the alerting services of different publishers or journals. Or browsing and visualization capabilities may be presented by some digital libraries and not others. Some digital libraries offer special exhibitions for viewing, others do not. And so on and so on.

Thus, in modelling information behaviour in these contexts, we recognize that the behaviour is determined, to a significant extent, by the functionality of the system. Figure 8.1 shows a simple generic model of the user's relationship to the digital library:

Clearly, all interaction between the user and the system is mediated by the interface and, consequently, information behaviour is reduced to those actions and operations (in activity theory terms, see Wilson (2006)) performed by the user through the capabilities offered by the interface. In effect, the user has no scope

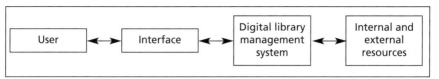

Figure 8.1 *Block diagram of a digital library system and user*

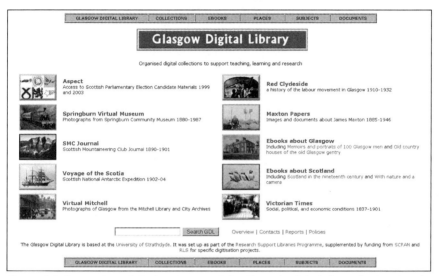

Figure 8.2 *Screen shot of the home page of the Glasgow Digital Library (University of Strathclyde; http://gdl.cdlr.strath.ac.uk/)*

for activity independent of what the system presents and, consequently, there is no scope for a general model of information behaviour. All the researcher can do is model the actual activities carried out by the user, within the constraints set by the system.

We can illustrate this by reference to any digital library: Figure 8.2 shows the opening page of the Glasgow Digital Library from the University of Strathclyde. We see immediately that the top and bottom menu bars are identical and guess that the first menu item designates the home page we have found. Ignoring the administrative links above the bottom menu bar, we find that the user who arrives at this page has the possibility of making a variety of choices for further action. There is some ambiguity on the page, since we do not know whether 'Collections' includes the 'Ebooks' collections, or whether 'Documents' includes the 'Maxton papers'. Disregarding these difficulties, there are about 20 different actions the user can take at this point: if he or she is interested in, say, 'shipbuilding', the obvious thing to do is to enter that term into the search box. On the other hand, if the user is simply browsing a newly found resource, he or she might click on 'Red Clydeside' simply to discover what is there; or, if the user's interest is in working class movements on Clydeside, then his or her first action may be to click on the 'Red Clydeside' link.

The point we make is that whatever action the user takes is not capable of being predicted by any general model of information behaviour. The action will depend upon the user's reason for exploring the site and making a choice to satisfy that need, from among the possibilities presented; further, if the motivation is simply curiosity to discover what is there, we have no way at all of predicting what actions a user will perform, or the sequence in which they will be performed.

The consequence of this is that 'user studies' in the context of digital libraries must relate to the design, testing, evaluation and re-design of the interface, and to this end a number of modelling languages can be employed. Perhaps the most widely known such language is UML (Unified Modelling Language), which is widely used in system-design work. UML employs the idea of 'use cases', that is, the set of steps taken by a user in interaction with a system in order to achieve a specific goal. Thus, we could create a use case for the user interested in trade union activity in the Clydeside shipyards during the 1926 General Strike. Recovery of a relevant document might result from more than one set of actions. For example, the user might enter 'Clydeside General Strike' into the search box on the home page and would then be presented with approximately 50 items relating to the search, the first one of which is: 'Red Clydeside: The General Strike on Clydeside 1926'. Alternatively, the user might choose to browse by clicking on 'Red Clydeside' on the home page, and then on the link 'Timeline of events', which brings up a page on which a link to the same document is found. A third approach would be for the user to click on the top menu item, 'Subjects'; this reveals a page of subject headings that includes 'General Strike, Great Britain, 1926'. Clicking on that heading brings up a list of documents that does *not* include the item found earlier, but does include two documents from the Maxton Papers collection. Thus, we have here two types of use case, which we can label 'searching' and 'browsing', and two alternative tracks through the system for the browsing mode.

Use cases are not generally used in this way; rather, they are means of specifying what the system *ought* to enable. However, we can see that, when modelling user behaviour in digital libraries, the idea has value and that, through log analysis, we could model the use cases of many digital library users to discover the modes of discovery they employ, the difficulties they encounter in the course of searching or otherwise using the resource, and the end results they appear to be aiming for.

We can also apply concept mapping to the analysis of user's interaction with a digital library system. Figure 8.3 shows a concept map for the two kinds of interaction described above – searching and browsing. Naturally, the map is very simplified when compared with actual behaviour. For example, there may be several iterations of a search before the user finds material of interest, and searching may be followed by browsing as an alternative strategy, and several iterations of browsing may take place, or the user may move between searching and browsing in a haphazard manner. The work by Bilal and Sarangthem (2009) on children's use of digital libraries, referred to earlier, is an interesting example of the modelling process at a level of complexity that expands upon Figure 8.3.

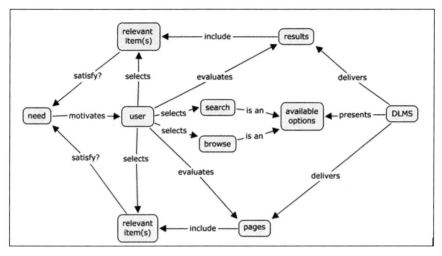

Figure 8.3 *A concept map of digital library interactions*

If a digital library offers other services, such as online reference chat, the user may take up this option also and pursue a chat session with a librarian, who may draw attention to specific items in the library or direct the user to particular pages on the system or to a completely different information source. If the digital library offers the possibility of a general web search, the user may actually leave the library at which they started and engage in interactions with other websites. All of these variants could be modelled in the same way; however, only those functions delivered by the digital library could be explored by the user and modelled by the researcher.

Summary

The study of digital library users is now a well established specialism within the field of information science, and one that is pursued by a wide range of other specialists, from sociologists to computer scientists. There is perhaps too much attention paid to the 'captive' audiences of academia, students and faculty members, and there is a need for much more work in the more specialized areas of the workplace. There are digital libraries designed for many specialized occupations, from engineering (e.g. the Institute of Engineering and Technology digital library[1]) through nursing (e.g. the Virginia Henderson International Nursing Library[2]) and various science specialisms (e.g. the Analytical Sciences Digital Library[3]), to economics (the Ludwig van Mieses Institute[4]), philosophy (the Marxists Internet Archive[5]) and many more. With few exceptions, the users and use of these libraries have gone unresearched and, if we are to learn more about the interaction activities of different interest groups and occupations, this is a gap that needs to be filled.

With regard to methods of investigation, it would seem that there are two possibilities: the first, and most popular at present, is to use 'non-obtrusive' methods such as log analysis. These have the advantage that the data is collected automatically and without users' personal intervention; the disadvantage is that, unless ways are found to augment the information with more demographic data about the users (see, e.g., Nicholas, Huntington and Jamali, 2008), we know little about the people behind the logs. Other methods demand more co-operation from users and, consequently, are likely to provoke some 'artificial' activity on their part. For example, when users know that eye-tracking is being used, they may subtly change their behaviour in ways that are difficult to recognize and account for. Similarly, an unusual degree of reflection on the part of the user may be prompted if they are asked to 'think aloud' when using a digital library. All other methods are also intrusive, whether they involve survey questionnaires or interviews after a session of digital library use, or employ experimental techniques involving predetermined search questions or topics for online reference chat. These difficulties and limitations of research methods apply, of course, to all other investigations of the information seeker and user and must be coped with through repeated studies of the same phenomena.

In one form or another, the digital library seems likely to be the dominant form of organized information, whether in specific institutions or generally available over the web. The more focused the collection and the more limited the audience, the more likely it is that specialized services will be developed, with use of such services being restricted to subscribing members or, for example, society members. There will be a continuing need, therefore, for user studies in this area for the foreseeable future.

Notes

1   http://digital-library.theiet.org/.
2   www.nursinglibrary.org/vhl/.
3   www.asdlib.org/.
4   http://mises.org/literature.aspx.
5   www.marxists.org.

References

Abbas, J. (2005) Out of the Mouths of Middle School Children: I. Developing user-defined controlled vocabularies for subject access in a digital library, *Journal of the American Society for Information Science and Technology*, **56** (14), 1512–24.

Abdullah, A. and Zainab, A. N. (2006) Ascertaining Factors Motivating Use of Digital Libraries and Formulating User Requirements Using Zachman Framework, *Malaysian Journal of Library and Information Science*, **11** (2), 21–40.

Agosti, M., Crivellari, F. and Di Nunzio, G. M. (2011) Web Log Analysis: a review of a decade of studies about information acquisition, inspection and interpretation of user interaction. In *Data Mining and Knowledge Discovery*, Springer, Netherlands, 1–34, doi: 10.1007/s10618-011-0228-8.

Alhoori, H. and Furuta, R. (2011) Understanding the Dynamic Scholarly Research Needs and Behavior as Applied to Social Reference Management. In Gradmann, S., Borri, F., Meghini, C. and Schuldt, H. (eds), *Proceedings in Research and Advanced Technology for Digital Libraries – International Conference on Theory and Practice of Digital Libraries, TPDL 2011, Berlin, Germany, September 26–28*, Springer Verlag, 169–78.

Amin, A., Van Ossenbruggen, J., Hardman, L. and Van Nispen, A. (2008) Understanding Cultural Heritage Experts' Information Seeking Needs. In Larsen, R., Paepcke, A., Borbinha, J. and Naaman, M. (eds), *Proceedings of the 8th ACM/IEEE-CS Joint Conference on Digital Libraries, Pittsburgh, PA, USA – June 16–20, 2008*, ACM Press, 39–47.

Assadi, H., Beauvisage, T., Lupovici, C. and Cloarec, T. (2003) Users and Uses of Online Digital Libraries in France. In Koch, T. and Solberg, I. (eds) (2003) *Proceedings of the 7th European Conference on Research and Advanced Technology for Digital Libraries (ECDL2003)*, Lecture Notes in Computer Science, vol. 2769, Springer Verlag, 1–12.

Audenaert, N. and Furuta, R. (2010) What Humanists Want: how scholars use source materials. In Hunter, J., Lagoze, C., Giles, L. and Li, Y-F. (eds), *Proceeding of the 10th Annual Joint Conference on Digital Libraries*, ACM Press, 283–92.

Bastien, J. M. C., Brangier, E., Dinet, J., Barcenilla, J., Michel, G. and Vivian, R. (2009) The Expert Community Staff: an innovative method for capturing end-user's needs. In Norros, L., Koskinen, H., Salo, L. and Savioja, P. (eds), *ECCE 2009 – European Conference on Cognitive Ergonomics: designing beyond the product – understanding activity and user experience in ebiquitous environment*, VTT-Technical Research Centre of Finland, 374–7.

Bilal, D. and Bachir, I. (2007a) Children's Interaction with Cross-cultural and Multilingual Digital Libraries: I. Understanding interface design representations, *Information Processing and Management*, **43** (1), 47–64.

Bilal, D. and Bachir, I. (2007b) Children's Interaction with Cross-cultural and Multilingual Digital Libraries: II. Information seeking, success and affective experience, *Information Processing and Management*, **43** (1), 65–80.

Bilal, D. and Sarangthem, S. (2009) Meditating Differences in Children's Interaction with Digital Libraries through Modeling their Tasks, *Proceedings of the American Society for Information Science and Technology*, **46** (1), 1–19.

Blandford, A., Adams, A., Attfield, S., Buchanan, G., Gow, G., Makri, S., Rimmer, J. and Warwick, C. (2008) The PRET A Rapporter Famework: evaluating digital libraries on the think-aloud technique, *Information Processing and Management*, **44** (1), 4–21.

Chen, R., Rose, A. and Bederson, B. B. (2009) How People Read Books Online: mining and visualizing web logs for use information. In Agosti, M., Borbinha, J. L., Kapidakis, S., Papatheodorou, C. and Tsakona, G. (eds), *Proceedings of the 13th European Conference on Research and Advanced Technology for Digital Libraries (ECDL2009)*, Lecture Notes in Computer Science, vol. 5714, Springer Verlag, 364–9.

Chen, Y.C. (2007). From Exhibits to Screen: a comparison of technology applications in physical and virtual museums - a case study of the Burke Museum. In Montgomerie, C. and Seale, J. (eds.), *Proceedings of the World Conference on Educational Multimedia, Hypermedia and Telecommunications 2007*, AACE, 424-9.

Chowdhury, G. G. (2010) From Digital Libraries to Digital Preservation Research: the importance of users and context, *Journal of Documentation*, **66** (2), 207–23.

Christel, M. G., Maher, B. and Li, H. (2009) Analysis of Transaction Logs for Insights into Use of Life Oral Histories. In Heath, F., Rice-Lively, M. L. and Furuta, R. (eds), *Proceedings of the 2009 Joint International Conference on Digital Libraries, JCDL 2009, Austin, TX, USA, June 15–19, 2009*, ACM Press, 371–2.

D'Alessandro, D. M., Kreiter, C. D. and Peterson, M. W. (2004) An Evaluation of Information Seeking Behaviors of General Pediatricians, *Pediatrics*, **113** (11), 64–9.

Druin, A. (2005) What Children Can Teach Us: developing digital libraries for children with children, *Library Quarterly*, **75** (1), 20–41.

Hopfgartner, F., Urruty, T., Villa, R., Gildea, N. and Jose, J. M. (2008) Exploiting Log Files in Video Retrieval. In Larsen, R. L., Paepcke, A., Borbinha, J. L. and Naaman, M. (eds), *Proceedings of the 8th ACM/IEEE-CS Joint Conference on Digital Libraries*, ACM Press.

Hourcade, J. P., Bederson, B. B., Druin, A., Rose, A., Farber, A. and Takayama, Y. (2003) The International Children's Digital Library: viewing digital books online, *Interacting with Computers*, **15** (2), 151–67.

Kiran, K. and Singh, D. (2008) Exploring User Experiences with Digital Library Services: a focus group approach. In Buchanan, G., Masoodian, M. and Cunningham, S. J. (eds), *ICADL – the 11th International Conference of Asian-Pacific Digital Libraries*, Springer Verlag, 285–93.

Koch, T., Ardö, A. and Golub, K. (2004) Browsing and Searching Behavior in the Renardus Web Service; a study based on log analysis. In Chen, H., Wactlar, H. D., Chen, C.-C., Lim, E. P. and Christel, M. G. (eds), *JCDL '04. Proceedings of the 4th ACM/IEEE-CS Joint Conference on Digital libraries*, ACM Press, 378.

Koltay, Z. and Tancheva, K. (2010) Personas and a User-centered Visioning Process, *Performance Measurement and Metrics*, **11** (2), 172–83.

Komlodi, A., How, W., Preece, J., Druin, A., Golub, E., Alburo, J., Liao, S., Elkiss, A. and Resnik, P. (2007) Evaluating a Cross-cultural Children's Online Book Community: lessons learned for sociability, usability, and cultural exchange, *Interacting with Computers*, **19** (4), 494–511.

Krestel, R., Demartini, G. and Herder, E. (2011) Visual Interfaces for Stimulating Exploratory Research. In Newton, G., Wright, M. and Cassel, L. (eds), *Proceedings of the 11th Annual International ACM/IEEE Joint Conference on Digital Libraries*, ACM Press, 393–94.

Liew, C. L. (2009) Digital Library Research 1997–2007: organisational and people issues. *Journal of Documentation,* **65** (2), 245–66.

Makri, S., Blandford, A. and Cox, A. L. (2010) This is What I'm Doing and Why: reflections on a think-aloud study of DL users' information behaviour. In Hunter, J., Lagoze, C., Giles, L. and Li, Y.-F. (eds,) *Proceeding of the 10th Annual Joint Conference on Digital Libraries*, ACM Press, 283–92.

Mincic-Obradovic, K. (2011) *E-books in Academic Libraries*, Chandos Publishing.

Nicholas, D., Huntington, P. and Jamali, H. R. (2008) User Diversity: as determined by deep log analysis, *Electronic Library*, **26** (1), 21–38.

Niu, X., Hemminger, B. M., Lown, C., Adams, S., Brown, C., Level, A., McLure, M., Powers, A., Tennant, M. R. and Cataldo, T. (2010) National Study of Information Seeking Behaviour of Academic Researchers in the United States, *Journal of the American Society of Information Science and Technology*, **61** (5), 869–90.

Saracevic, T. (1997) The Stratified Model of Information Retrieval Interaction: extension and application, *Proceedings of the 60th Annual Meeting of the American Society for Information Science,* **34**, 313–27.

Shiri, A., Ruecher, S., Bouchard, M., Stafford, A., Mehta, P., Anvik, K. and Rossello, X. (2011) User Evaluation of Searchling: a visual interface for bilingual digital libraries. *Electronic Library*, **29** (1), 71–89.

Sykes, J., Dobreva, M., Birrell, D., McCulloch, E., Ruthven, I., Unal, Y. and Feliciati, P. (2010) A New Focus on End-users: eye-tracking analysis for digital libraries. In Lalmas, M., Jose, J., Rauber, A., Sebastiani, R. and Frommholz, I. (eds), *Research and Advanced Technology for Digital Libraries, Proceedings of the 14th European Conference on Research and Advanced Technology for Digital Libraries (ECDL 2010)*, Lecture Notes in Computer Science, vol. 6273, Springer Verlag, 510–13.

Wang, P., Dervos, D. A., Zhang, Y. and Wu, L. (2007) Information Seeking Behaviors of Academic Researchers in the Internet Age: a user study in the United States, China and Greece. In *Proceedings of the Annual Meeting of the American Society for Information Sciences and Technology*, **44**, 1–29.

Wilson, T. D. (2006) A Re-examination of Information Seeking Behaviour in the Context of Activity Theory, *Information Research*, **11** (4), paper 260, http://informationr.net/ir/11–4/paper260.html.

Zhang, H., Li, Y., Liu, J. and Zhang, Y. (2008) Effects of Interaction Design in Digital Libraries on User Interactions, *Journal of Documentation*, **64** (3), 438–63.

CHAPTER 9

Digital libraries and scholarly information: technology, market, users and usage

Jeonghyun Kim, Angel Durr and Suliman Hawamdeh

Introduction

In today's technology-driven society, the means by which information is conveyed to information seekers is changing in ways never before possible. It is interesting to note that medical professionals were one of the first groups of users to see the potential in mobile devices for information acquisition and access (Murray, 2010). Therefore, medical libraries were among the earliest adopters of mobile technology and digital library services. Initially, many libraries were slow to adopt mobile-device technologies and integrate them into their services because they did not know whether the use of these devices was merely another technology trend, quick to rise and even quicker to pass (Murray, 2010).

However, as it appears, mobile-device technology is here to stay and is rapidly becoming more and more streamlined. Completing tasks that were once only possible with a variety of devices, such as a personal computer, GPS devices and an MP3 player, is now possible through the use of one petite and portable mobile device. Additionally, the task of viewing web pages and viewing web information on mobile devices has become much more user friendly and is almost identical to viewing this same information on a personal computer.

Today's information seekers are unlike any that the information profession has ever encountered before. These users will often describe themselves as 'dependent' on technology. Technological advances like the internet have made users believe that any information they require at any given time can be instantaneously retrieved by merely clicking a button. In other words, this distinctive user believes it is possible to access all the information of the vast and endless universe anytime and anywhere. As an information professional how does one meet the needs of this type of user, while at the same time providing the same quality of services that the information profession has been trained to provide for well over a hundred years?

Luckily, technology has made possible a variety of advances that can be utilized by both the information professional and the recreational information user. A few examples of rapidly dispersing global technologies are e-journals, e-books, e-readers and other mobile technologies. These technologies, and a variety of others, are finding their way into libraries around the world. Information professionals are finding unique and inventive ways to weave modern technologies into their already offered services. These innovations both enhance the overall user experience and ensure the presence of libraries for generations to come by proving just how necessary libraries truly are to the users who frequent them now and will do so in the future.

In order to better understand the changing needs of library users, this chapter will attempt to examine and discuss the changes that are currently taking place in the retrieval and demonstration display of scholarly information within digital libraries. This discussion includes electronic publishing and how its accessibility is changing the way in which individuals view and share academic information. By understanding the nature of contemporary information users and the currently available digital library technologies, librarians may be able to plan ahead to meet the needs of future users more effortlessly.

Electronic publishing

There are two prevalent definitions of electronic publishing. As a general term, electronic publishing refers to the use of electronic equipment to create and reproduce text and graphic images of all kinds and combinations. Electronic publishing also refers to the use of digital media, i.e. non-print, as the final communication format, including CD-ROMs, digital documents, web pages, online publications, presentation documents and more.

The history of electronic publishing is considerably short when compared with traditional forms of publishing, but its influence is just as significant. The first electronic publications were developed in the 1980s in the form of plain-text e-mails. They were either e-mailed to subscribers or made available through FTP in strict plain-text format. Later, the CD-ROM format was used for distribution, but it quickly became obsolete as electronic publishing emerged. The period from 1985 to 1995, referred to as the 'digital revolution', brought the shift from analogue to digital treatment of information, as presented in Figure 9.1.

E-journals

The very first electronic journal came from Syracuse University's Kellogg Project (Figure 9.1). The Kellogg Project had a mission to provide broader access to the university's adult education materials and to facilitate the exchange of information and learning using the very latest technologies where possible. In the autumn of 1987, the Kellogg project released its first official e-journal, titled *New Horizons in Adult Education* (Hugo and Newell, 1991). In 1990, *Postmodern Culture*, the oldest surviving e-journal, arrived as a ground-breaking experiment in scholarly publishing (Amiran and Unsworth, 1991). The following year, Elsevier experimented with a project called TULIP (The University Licensing Program), which distributed electronic text of journals to libraries

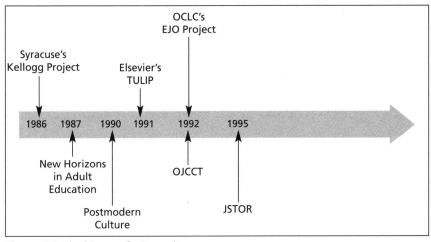

Figure 9.1 *The history of e-journals*

via computer tapes, which were mounted locally. At that time, TULIP was the leading experimental project to test the networked desktop delivery of e-journals (Elsevier, 2003). The *Online Journal of Current Clinical Trials (OJCCT)*, the first biomedical e-journal and the first pre-web electronic journal with a graphical user interface (GUI), arrived in 1992. In the same year, the Online Computer Library Center (OCLC) developed an online journal system that combined a centralized database server and full-text search engine with an intuitive client software product called Guidon. Guidon controlled communication with the server and offered near-print-quality display of selected articles, and it also served as a model for later web-based electronic-only journals (Hickey, 2001). In mid-1994, a pilot project was launched under the direction of the University of Michigan to develop a working prototype system in order to provide digital access to back issues of journals and to provide access to that database to the test sites. As a result of this University of Michigan project, JSTOR was founded as an independent, not-for-profit organization in 1995 (Guthrie, Kirchhoff and Tapp, 2003). In addition, the world wide web, which changed almost everything, came into being and created a powerful opportunity in electronic publishing that not only enabled more individuals and small organizations to participate, but also made small-market publishing economically viable.

E-journal growth

The number of e-journals available has grown steadily since the 1990s. A large portion of this increase has been in scholarly or academic electronic journals. The Association of Research Libraries' *Directory of Electronic Journals, Newsletters and Academic Discussion Lists*, published annually since 1991, displays this growth. The number of e-journals listed in the 1991 directory was 27; by the 2000 directory, the number had risen to 3500

(Association of Research Libraries, 2000). The global acceptance of the world wide web facilitated the growth of e-journal publishing in the mid-1990s, but much of the growth since 1996 can be attributed to the electronic debut of many commercial publishers. The growth in parallel publishing, which may be defined as the publication of an electronic version of a traditionally print journal, has greatly increased the number of scholarly journals available electronically and may possibly have affected the acceptance of journals in this format.

E-books

Another information format that arose from the expansion of electronic publication is the e-book. Project Gutenberg was started by Michael Hart, who is widely credited with creating the first official e-book in 1971, with the digitization of the US Declaration of Independence (Lebert, 2010) (Figure 9.2). In 1985, Grolier, one of the largest publishers of encyclopedias in the USA, published a text-only version of the *Academic American Encyclopedia*, which it renamed *The New Grolier Electronic Encyclopedia*. This work has the distinction of being the very first book published on a CD-ROM (Rickelman, Henk and Melnick, 1991). The Rocket e-book, the first official e-reader, was launched in 1998. It was in that same year that Kim Blagg received the first ISBN issued for an e-book and introduced e-books to the publishing world through her company Books OnScreen at the 1998 Book Expo America. In the academic world, e-books started with NetLibrary in 1999. Three years later, in 2002, OCLC took over NetLibrary. In 2004, two new aggregators started their businesses, one of which was Google, which started the Google Print Library Project. The Google library project was itself part of a larger initiative initially known as Google Print and later renamed Google Book Search. Google worked with the New York Public Library and the universities of Michigan, Harvard, Oxford and Stanford in order to make digital versions of their library books available online (Google Inc., 2004). However, the principal prompt for widespread e-book adoption came in 2006. Surprisingly, the boom in e-book technology did not occur as a result of the invention of e-ink, an electronic paper commonly used in electronic devices and e-readers, but because Springer, one of the chief scientific publishers, formally released its Springer eBooks offering. Although e-books have been available for less than 20 years, the technology only started receiving serious attention in the last 10 years and the e-book industry is still experiencing growing pains.

The e-book market has expanded significantly in the past ten years. According to the International Digital Publishing Forum and the Association of American Publishers (IDPF, 2011), wholesale numbers for e-book sales in 2011 are 77 times more than those in 2002, expanding from 1.5 million to 119.7 million. Overall, e-books make up 40% of the annual trade wholesale figures, compared with only 0.5% in 2002. While not all e-books are read with a specific reader, it is important to note that a Harris Interactive poll conducted in July 2011 found that almost one in six Americans (15%) uses an e-

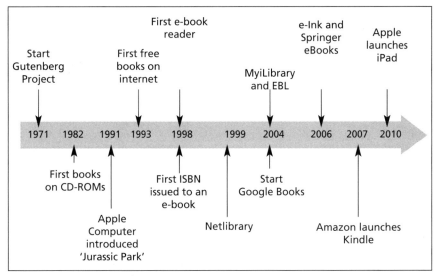

Figure 9.2 *The history of e-books*

reader device, up from less than one in ten (8%) a year previously. In addition, among those who did not have an e-reader, one in six (15%) said they were likely to get an e-reader device in the next six months (Harris Interactive, 2011).

E-books in libraries

E-book usage is flourishing in libraries too. According to a 2011 e-book survey conducted by the *Library Journal* and *School Library Journal* (Miller, 2011), 95% of academic libraries offer e-books, and total e-book collections increased by 93%. Additionally, those within the academic community have started to understand the importance of integrating e-books into their curriculum. The desire for e-books in public libraries has grown significantly; 66% of public libraries reported a steep increase in requests for e-books, and 82% now offer them to patrons. Recently, the 'eBook Feasibility Study for Public Libraries' was undertaken by the Chief Officers of State Library Agencies (COSLA). The study interviewed public library directors and managers to better understand how to improve the e-book experience for their patrons. Library directors and managers agreed that they needed ways to educate the staff and the public on issues relating to e-books; to make it easier to borrow the e-books; to become advocates to obtain better funding; to negotiate for better licensing models and reasonable copyright permissions; and to create a better learning community (COSLA, 2010).

E-books in the scholarly environment

The use of e-books in the scholarly environment was investigated by several projects. In the UK, the JISC national e-books observatory project was created to observe the impact and behaviours of end users using e-books and to find innovative methods to encourage e-book production. Its user survey revealed that more than 65% of teaching staff and students have used e-books to support their work or study, or for leisure purposes, and that more than half of those users used e-books from their university library. The project also found that students and faculty primarily use e-books to print out pages for handwritten note taking or citations, as well as to copy and paste into other documents. However, the project discovered that users prefer to use hard-copy text for prolonged reading, citing ease of note taking, reduced distractions and the ability to browse one or several works at once (Rowlands et al., 2009). In the USA, the University of California Libraries initiated the Springer e-Book Pilot Project with the goals of developing appropriate systemwide processes for acquiring and managing licensed e-books and of informing future licensing activities. The project survey reported that 58% of its survey respondents use e-books in their academic work, but 34% prefer e-books. The study also identified the ability to search within and across e-book content as the primary advantage of e-books, regardless of whether a respondent prefers print books or e-books (Li et al., 2011).

Not surprisingly, the growth in use of e-books has led to a slight decline in the check-out of print materials for most libraries. Yet, most still prefer print materials when it comes to academic materials. E-books have been very useful for academic libraries in terms of providing e-reference information to patrons, due to the ability to allow patrons to search within text to quickly find information regarding specific topics. Patrons can simply type in a term or subject and find all the instances of that particular term in an instant and be linked to any pages at the click of a mouse. This has completely revolutionized the way users access and use information. Previously, this type of instantaneous information seeking would have been possible only through the use of an index at the end of a text work. However, this also means that few patrons read more than a few pages of an e-book. If they want to read entire books or entire sections, most will still refer to print holdings. This is especially true for faculty, who are usually, on average, much slower than the student population to adopt e-book technology. 'According to Schonfeld and Housewright's 2010 survey of faculty habits and attitudes, only 50% of faculty believed in the importance of preserving e-books, and less than half of these faculty deemed e-books important to teaching or research. In rating the importance of a variety of electronic resources for teaching and research, e-books came in last place' (Shen, 2011, 185). Perhaps the reason why e-book technology is ranked so low among faculty users is because e-book usage in academia is not as widespread as it is among leisure readers. E-book producers should be working harder to attract academic publishers. There are far too few academic e-books available for use, therefore the technology is not being utilized by this type of user.

E-book readers

E-book usage is certainly on the rise; however, the same cannot necessarily be said of dedicated e-book readers. Since technology has made it possible to view e-books on a variety of platforms other than dedicated e-readers, whose only function is to allow readers to view and interact with e-books, use of e-reader technology has not expanded as rapidly as has the use of e-books. Since users can now access e-books from their personal computers and their smartphones for free, many do not believe it is necessary to purchase a dedicated e-reader whose sole function is to perform this task. Users want one technological device that can house information and serve a variety of functions. Therefore, libraries were correct in not jumping to purchase and adopt e-reader technology when it first arrived on the market. At this point, it is certainly unclear how e-readers will prove their place in the digital marketplace, unless it suddenly becomes no longer possible to view e-books on any other platform. Therefore, e-reader technology will have to evolve to meet the needs of a multi-tasking and singular-device-oriented user, or risk becoming another passing technological fad.

Access to digital material

Despite the shift of focus from print to electronic materials, libraries need to remember that their focus should still remain on the patrons and their physical needs. With less space allotted to print materials, libraries are now freeing up valuable space that is being used to draw more users into the physical library for activities that cannot be carried out in the electronic library realm. This is presenting libraries with unique opportunities to expand their patron base to a group that might otherwise never set foot in a traditional library. Libraries are providing the creative, quiet and collaborative spaces that patrons need in order to complete their educational endeavours. Many libraries are creating spaces known as 'information commons', into which users can enter in a variety of formats and use the tools provided by libraries to customize their learning and information-gaining experiences. Patrons want not only highly usable library spaces, but spaces that are aesthetically pleasing and provide students with the tranquillity and creative atmosphere they need in order to create high-quality work. By so doing, libraries are guaranteeing their place in the future of education, and proving to patrons that they are indeed flexible, and willing to evolve in response to the changing needs of their patron base (Gerke and Maness, 2010).

   Initially digital technology was expensive. Access to the internet and electronic databases cost libraries large sums of their already tight budgets. However, the widespread availability has substantially decreased the costs associated with digital technologies. The vast majority of US citizens now have access to the internet and a cellular phone. In fact, according to Informa Telecoms and Media's Global Mobile Forecasts (www.informatandm.com/section/home-page/), by the end of 2012 there will be over 5.3 billion mobile phone users globally. Interestingly this report states that 'it took over 20 years to reach 3 billion subscriptions . . . but another 1.9 billion net additions are forecasted [*sic*] in just six years, with global total nudging past the 5 billion milestone in 2011'. Informa Telecom and Media is one of the largest technological business research companies in the world. Based on this same 2009 report, McKiernan (2010) stated: 'North America and Western Europe will contribute only 8% of total additions, reflecting a high level of saturation . . . Globally, [mobile phone] subscription penetration will approach the 75 percent mark in 2013, while some countries will push past the 150 percent barrier' (48). These figures were not nearly as high just five years ago, in 2007. Mobile usage has seen tremendous expansion worldwide in the last several years, especially in developing countries. For those who are still unable to afford internet or mobile services there are even government agencies that provide these services for free, or at a greatly reduced cost to consumers. According to a 2009 study conducted by the Pew Internet & American Life Project, a staggering 56% of the American public currently access the web via a wireless device (McKiernan, 2010). With more individuals than ever before having access to the web and mobile devices, more users want the convenience that comes along with this access.

Digital information is now available via the internet from a wide variety of free sources, including several that claim to provide users with information that is scholarly in nature. One example of this sort of website is the widely used Google Scholar. Google Scholar uses the same search engine-type interface that users are accustomed to accessing, and provides instant access to information that is deemed scholarly in nature. Therefore, academic users no longer have to doubt whether the information they are obtaining via the internet is produced by a reputable and knowledgeable source. Additionally, Google Scholar provides full citation information for the resources it provides, so users can ensure the resources are indeed accurate. Google Scholar has done an excellent job working with libraries around the globe to link its search results to actual local library holdings. Therefore, when a user searches for a subject or type of article, on receiving their search results they will also be able to link instantly to their local library's own holdings to further enhance those search results. This feature has benefited libraries all over the world by providing them with an additional way to market their services and holdings to users, who might otherwise have only accessed information via the internet.

Additionally, Google Scholar links with local libraries in what is commonly referred to as a 'mashup'. A mashup is a combination of two unexpected items that link together to make something better or different than they would individually offer. Google Scholar and local libraries are both benefiting from this mashup, and combining the two services allows the user to get a far better experience than they would if they used the two services separately. Libraries can also use mashups with their own digital materials to combine tools in unexpected ways so as to provide a more engaging and interactive user experience. One example would be to create an application for smartphones that allowed users not only to access the library catalogue but also link them to mapping services that allowed them to see a map of the exact location within the library of the item they were seeking (Mason, 2010).

In addition to Google Scholar there is Microsoft Academic Search. Microsoft Academic was created with the same types of research functions that are provided by Google Scholar and, like Scholar, it is also a completely free resource. However, Microsoft Academic was officially released after Google Scholar. Currently, Microsoft Academic is primarily utilized for information in the field of computer science, as this subject area has the most completely indexed information. However, Microsoft Academic also offers additional information in a variety of other disciplines and subject areas. Microsoft Academic offers a variety of mapping tools that allow users to visually arrange and view data and information regarding authors and topics; however, the information provided is not always as complete or thorough as that of Google Scholar. It will be interesting to see if Microsoft Academic will truly become a contender in the information realm in the same way that Google Scholar has.

Emerging trends and new opportunities

The growth in digital technology and information has been applicable not only to large institutions, but also on the individual level. Individuals are increasingly looking to digital technologies to store vast amounts of personal information in a place that is both easily accessible, protected and enduring. Librarians are masters of information storage and have worked hard to ensure that digital information is safe and secure so as to be enjoyed by various users for generations to come. This same knowledge could easily be shared with and then utilized by individual users. Libraries have a unique opportunity to provide an excellent community service by teaching the general public to understand archival and preservation techniques in order to maintain data for future access and retrieval on a personal level. Most people do not understand data security and risk losing treasured personal information. Users often think that simply 'backing up' data will keep it safe; however, archiving is necessary to keep information accessible for future use. Even seemingly simple tasks, such as selecting appropriate file-storage types, can evade the common user. According to Copeland and Barreau, 'the library's primary role of collecting information has evolved to focus on providing access, but public libraries may once again focus on collecting if the need to preserve digital information is perceived as a public good. . . . As libraries have traditionally made materials available to those who can least afford them, they may also help individuals appreciate the value of personal artifacts and help them to preserve and share those treasures' (Copeland and Barreau, 2011, 645).

The New Media Consortium (NMC) in the USA is a non-profit member organization that aims to guide educators and learning organizations through the implementation and use of new technologies to improve and facilitate cohesive learning. The Consortium publishes a widely read and highly regarded annual report detailing up-and-coming technologies. Its report provides a timeline for horizon technologies and guidelines for by when they should be implemented. According to its most recent report, published in 2011 (Johnson et al., 2011), there are several technologies that should be implemented by all education organizations within the following year. These include cloud computing, collaborative environments, electronic books and mobiles. Libraries across the USA have already done an excellent job of implementing these technologies and integrating them effectively, far ahead of most academic professionals.

The report also provides a list of technologies that should be adopted within the next two to three years, as well as the next four to five. According to NMC, the technologies that need to be adopted in the next two to three years are augmented reality, game-based learning, open content and visual data analysis. By learning about these technologies far before their adoption, libraries can get a jump-start on technological trends and find creative ways to utilize them in their training.

Augmented reality

Augmented reality is a type of visually based learning application that can help students to visualize learning concepts in order to better understand them. One example of augmented reality already being utilized is by The Powerhouse Museum in Sydney, Australia. According to the 2011 Horizon Report Short List, it has 'developed an augmented reality application that allows visitors to use their mobile phones to see Sydney, Australia as it appeared one hundred years ago: www.powerhousemuseum. com/layer/' (New Media Consortium, 2011, 6). Users are thus able to use the application to explore and discover, based on their personal or academic interests, in a way that was previously unthought of. Augmented reality has the potential to create a very personal and malleable learning experience for users.

Game-based learning

Similarly to augmented reality, game-based learning allows students to use games for educational endeavours. Educational gaming offers educators a very accessible way to engage students in a variety of topics and help them to learn and build valuable problem-solving skills. Games are becoming an increasingly popular part of society, so educators should be looking for ways to incorporate these platforms into the realm of education.

Open content

The next technology, open content, is a term that many library professionals should already be familiar with. Open content technologies allow information to be inexpensively shared and customized, based on the needs of the individuals utilizing it. A very popular example of open content is wikis, which are being utilized by a variety of organizations.

Visual data analysis

The final technology listed for adoption in the next two to three years is visual data analysis. This allows users to view and easily interpret sets of data for a specific topic or trend. This allows them to then analyse the data visually and utilize it appropriately. One example of visual data analysis is a site called Crimespotting. According to the NMC 2011 Horizon Report, 'Crimespotting is an interactive map of crimes in San Francisco and Oakland that visualizes crime by location, type, date, and time, allowing users to quickly grasp patterns and trends: http://sanfrancisco.crimespotting.org' (New Media Consortium, 2011, 9).

Visual learning

These horizon technologies have one obvious thing in common: they all utilize visual learning, which is clearly a dominant theme in the up-and-coming horizon technologies. As a result of mobile technology, today's users are increasingly reliant on visual stimulation to better understand the world around them. Therefore, when planning and implementing services, library professionals should remain keenly aware of this fact and ensure that they are taking advantage of the wide variety of visual technologies that are increasingly becoming available. Another commonality these horizon technologies share is their relatively low implementation costs, since the only tool necessary to implement and produce them is a personal computer. There are also a variety of resources available that make applying these technologies simple and fast.

Conclusion

The rates at which mobile technologies are developing and the speed at which mobile devices are becoming integrated into daily life have had a substantial impact on information seeking practices and interpersonal communication. Technology expansion and digital information are changing consumers' behaviour, choices and lifestyle. In today's technology-focused and knowledge-based society, it is no longer enough for libraries to continue providing traditional services that may be comparatively inconvenient, inefficient and unsatisfactory for new generation of technology-savvy, digital native users who value convenience and efficiency. Librarians, in addition to keeping up with advances in technology, must research and seek a better understanding of the changing patterns in user behaviour, and take into consideration increasing user expectations. Today, the role of the library as an institution is shifting from collection-based services to information- and knowledge-based services where the awareness of service value, ease of use and access to information using mobile and communication technology impacts significantly on the users' overall perception of the library.

References

Amiran, E. and Unsworth, J. (1991) Postmodern Culture: publishing in the electronic medium, *The Public-Access Computer Systems Review*, **2** (1), 67–76.

Association of Research Libraries (2000) *Directory of Scholarly Electronic Journals and Academic Discussion Lists*, Washington, DC, Office of Scholarly Communication, Association of Research Libraries.

Copeland, A. and Barreau, D. (2011) Helping People to Manage and Share their Digital Information: a role for public libraries, *Library Trends*, **59** (4), 637–49.

COSLA (2010) *eBook Feasibility Study for Public Libraries: final report*, www.cosla.org/documents/COSLA2270_Report_Final1.pdf.

Elsevier (2003) *E-journals at Elsevier*, www.elsevier.com/wps/find/authored_newsitem.cws_home/companynews05_00021.

Gerke, J. and Maness, J. M. (2010) The Physical and the Virtual: the relationship between library as a place and electronic collections, *College & Research Libraries*, **71** (1), 20–31.

Google Inc. (2004) Google Checks Out Library Books, press release, www.google.com/press/pressrel/print_library.html.

Guthrie, K. M., Kirchhoff, A. and Tapp, W. N. (2003) The JSTOR Solution, Six Years Later. In P. Hodges, M. Sandler, and J. P. Wilkin (eds), *Digital Libraries: a vision for the 21st century: a festschrift in honor of Wendy Lougee on the occasion of her departure from the University of Michigan*, Scholarly Publishing Office, the University of Michigan University Library.

Harris Interactive (2011) One in Six Americans Now Use E-reader with One in Six Likely to Purchase in Next Six Months, press release, www.harrisinteractive.com/vault/HI-Harris-Poll-eReader-2011-09-19.pdf.

Hickey, T. B. (2001) Integrating Guidon with the World Wide Web, *Journal of Library Administration*, **34** (1/2), 67–71.

Hugo, J. and Newell, L. (1991) New Horizons in Adult Education: the first five years (1987–1991), *The Public-Access Computer Systems Review*, **2** (1), 77–90.

International Digital Publishing Forum (2011) *Industry Statistics*, http://idpf.org/about-us/industry-statistics.

Johnson, L., Smith, R., Willis, H., Levine, A. and Haywood, K. (2011) *The 2011 Horizon Report*, New Media Consortium.

Lebert, M. (2010) *History of Project Gutenberg*, www.gutenbergnews.org/about/history-of-project-gutenberg/.

Li, C., Poe, F., Potter, M., Quigley, B. and Wilson, J. (2011) *UC Libraries Academic E-book Usage Survey: Springer e-book pilot project*, www.cdlib.org/services/uxdesign/docs/2011/academic_ebook_usage_survey.pdf.

Mason, D. (2010) Library Mashups: exploring new ways to deliver library data. *The Electronic Library*, **28** (5), 757–8.

McKiernan, G. (2010) Worldwide Mobile Phone Adoption and Libraries, *Searcher*, **18** (3), 48–51.

Miller, R. (2011) *Dramatic Growth: LJ's second annual ebook survey*, www.thedigitalshift.com/2011/10/12/dramatic-growth-ljs-second-annual-ebook-survey/.

Murray, L. (2010) Libraries Like to 'Move it, Move it', *Reference Services Review*, **38** (2), 233–49.

New Media Consortium (2010) *NMC Horizon Project: 2011 short list*, www.nmc.org/pdf/2011-Horizon-Short-List.pdf.

Rickelman, R. J., Henk, W. A. and Melnick, S. A. (1991) Reading Technology: electronic encyclopedias on compact disk, *The Reading Teacher*, **44** (6), 432–4.

Rowlands, I., Nicholas, D., Huntington, P., Clark, D. and Nicholas, T. (2009) *JISC National E-books Observatory Project: key findings and recommendations*, www.jiscebooksproject.org/reports/finalreport 2009.

Shen, J. (2011) The E-book Lifestyle: an academic library perspective, *Reference Librarian*, **52** (1/2), 181–9.

CHAPTER 10

Digital libraries and open access

Gobinda Chowdhury and Schubert Foo

Introduction

Open access, defined simply as access to digital content free at the point of use, is a movement that began nearly two decades ago. It had its origins on the one hand in the exponential rise in the costs of scholarly information sources, especially journals, and on the other hand in the ease of publication and communication facilities that became available with the advent and proliferation of the internet and various new e-publishing models and standards. However, there is a bigger and altruistic reason behind the open access initiative. It has been driven by the need to provide better access to and sharing of information for research and scholarly activities. Open access facilitates research and scholarly activities in a number of ways, for example, by opening research and scholarly knowledge to all so that more researchers can access that knowledge build on it, thereby meeting another goal of less duplication of research efforts (JISC, 2011a). Open access benefits different stakeholders. Through open access:

- researchers can reach a greater audience and thus their research can be more widely read and cited
- institutions gain an enhanced reputation, and thus a better competitive edge, as their research becomes more visible
- funding agencies see a greater return on their investment because the research funded by them can reach more people
- publishers find that the impact of their journals increases as a result of greater access.

Thus, although the open access movement was initiated to find an alternative to the problems facing academic and scholarly communities due to the soaring price of journals, it does more social good by promoting better and easier access to knowledge for everyone, not necessarily the small group of people who are associated with relatively rich institutions. However,

Open Access is not self-publishing, nor a way to bypass peer-review and publication, nor is it a kind of second-class, cut-price publishing route. It is simply a means to make research results freely available online to the whole research community.

(JISC, 2011b)

This chapter discusses the issues of open access and institutional repositories in the context of open access digital libraries. It briefly introduces the concept of Open Archives Initiative (OAI) and institutional repositories. It then discusses how open access initiatives, coupled with recent developments in cloud computing technologies and some associated developments such as the Hargreaves Review and JISC initiatives in the UK, can help to build digital libraries that are free at the point of use, and thus facilitate better access to and dissemination of knowledge.

Open archives

The open access movement emerged in the early 1990s with the establishment of the open archive known as arXiv.org (formerly xxx.lanl.gov) in order to provide free access to literature on high-energy physics. Now arXiv provides access to research literature in physics, mathematics, computer science, nonlinear sciences, quantitative biology and statistics (arxiv.org). Subsequently, many open archives or open access digital libraries, like Cogprints, the Networked Computer Science Technical Reports Library (NCSTRL) and the Networked Digital Library of Theses and Dissertations (NDLTD) emerged. The objective of the open access initiative is to facilitate free and easy access to research and scholarly information. The Open Archives Initiative (OAI) was launched in the Santa Fe Convention in 1999, with a mission to develop and promote interoperable technologies and frameworks for the dissemination of e-prints in order to facilitate the efficient dissemination of content. Major standards and tools developed by the OAI include:

- Protocol for Metadata Harvesting (OAI-PMH), a set of standards designed to ensure the interoperability of open access repositories. According to this protocol, repositories use structured metadata via OAI-PMH and service providers make the OAI-PMH service requests to harvest that metadata. Further details of OAI-PMH, including an online tutorial, are available from the OAI website (Open Archives Initiative, n.d.a).
- Object Reuse and Exchange (OAI-ORE) specification, which defines standards for the description and exchange of aggregations of web resources, sometimes called compound digital objects, that may combine distributed resources with multiple media types, including text, images, data and video. These specifications and user guides are available on the OAI website (Open Archives Initiative, n.d.b).

The Open Access Initiative

The Budapest Open Access Initiative (BOAI) in 2001 ushered in a new era in scholarly communication, promising free access to scholarly information (Cullen and Chawner, 2011). Open access in this context means free access to research output, permitting any user to make lawful access to, and use of, research content and data, with appropriate acknowledgement. However, open access to content comes with some economic challenges. The BOAI realized that 'achieving open access will require new cost recovery models and financing mechanisms, but the significantly lower overall cost of dissemination is a reason to be confident that the goal is attainable and not merely preferable or utopian' (Budapest Open Access Initative).

In order to provide open access to scholarly journal literature, two complementary strategies were recommended in the BOAI:

1 Self-archiving, also known as the 'green route', where scholars deposit their referreed journal articles in open electronic archives. When these archives conform to standards created by the OAI, users will be able to access literature from all the repositories, without having to know in which specific repository the content is stored.
2 Open access journals, also known as the 'gold route', provide free access to literature. It is proposed that such open access journals will not charge users and these new journals will not charge subscription or access fees, and will adopt alternative business models for generating their revenues.

Both the gold and green routes provide access to information free at the point of use. The difference is that, for the green route, the authors are required to publish their scholarly output in commercial journals but at the same time to self-archive them in a repository that can be accessed for free, while for the gold route, journal publishers need to raise funds for their operations, for example by charging authors or their institutions, and so on, instead of charging the end-users. In either case, users can have free access to scholarly information, and thus the approaches promote better access to knowledge and new knowledge creation. Green open access repositories can be thematic, thereby creating subject repositories like arXiv, or they can be institution-based, thereby creating institutional repositories.

Institutional repositories

Institutional repositories may 'contain the intellectual works of faculty and students – both research and teaching materials – and also documentation of the activities of the institution itself in the form of records of events and performance and of the ongoing intellectual life of the institution. [They] will also house experimental and observational data captured by members of the institution that support their scholarly activities' (Lynch, 2003). The first institutional repository in the UK was set up in Southampton in 2001 (Cullen and Chawner, 2011). In the USA the first open access repository was set up in 2002 at the Massachusetts Institute of Technology 'as a new strategy that allows universities to apply serious, systematic leverage to accelerate changes taking place in scholarship and scholarly communication' (Lynch, 2003).

An institutional repository can, ideally, provide access to every intellectual output of the academics, researchers and students of an institution. It may contain research publications, research data, teaching materials as well as various other outcomes of the scholarly activities – for example, artistic works, exhibitions etc. – of an institution's member community. Over the past decade several new technologies, softwares and standards have emerged, facilitating the creation and management of institutional repositories. By building and combining the institutional repositories of all higher education and research institutions, it is possible to provide free access to all the scholarly and research output of a country and, by extension, to the academic and scholarly output of virtually the entire world. Thus, it is possible to build national and international digital libraries of research and scholarly information.

Challenges

Institutional repositories can vary significantly in size, from very small institutional services providing access to only a few thousand resources, to large federated services providing access to thousands or even millions of resources. Some popular and robust open source platforms such as DSpace, Fedora and Eprints and standards like OAI-PMH (discussed in Chapter 2 and also earlier in this chapter) are used to build institutional repositories. Both open access and commercial software platforms are used for open access journals, and many library management systems provide integrated access to open access resources. However, while there has been some progress and there are a number of common building blocks, the technological, technical, social and economic challenges of open access and institutional repositories are still quite significant.

In the UK, the Joint Information Systems Committee (JISC) has been playing a key role in promoting the development, management and use of institutional repositories (for details see Jacobs, Amber and McGregor, 2008; JISC, 2011c). Similar efforts are being made in other countries to build and promote institutional repositories. Cullen and Chawner (2011) note that:

- the OpenDOAR database at the University of Nottingham records a significant growth in the number of repositories over the past five years, from just over 300 in mid-2006 to over 1800 by January 2011
- nearly three-quarters of institutional repositories are available in North America (24%) and Europe (45%), while there are only 17% in Asia, 6% in South America, 4% in Australia, and 2% in Africa
- typically these repositories hold a mix of journal articles, theses and dissertations,

unpublished working papers, conference papers, books and book chapters as well as multimedia and other audiovisual materials.

Many recent studies (see, for example, Davis and Connolly, 2007; Connell, 2011; Cryer and Collins, 2011; Cullen and Chawner, 2011; MacDonald, 2011; St Jean et al., 2011) point out that the progress of institutional repositories has not been as great as was originally envisaged and cite a number of reasons for this:

- lack of understanding and commitment of faculty members regarding participation in the initiative
- various challenges associated with the understanding and management of copyright issues by faculty members and the repository management team
- the lack of a continuous funding stream to support the development, management and preservation of content and data at the institutional level, exacerbated by rapidly changing technologies and standards
- a lack of proper and acceptable evidences of better citation and academic rewards resulting from institutional repositories
- additional workload on faculty members that is associated with the process of self-archiving information, and so on.

While currently each individual institution takes on the stewardship of its own repository, the economic and environmental costs of managing such repository services can be significantly reduced by co-operating and sharing resources. For example, the new initiatives of JISC will promote better access to and use of institutional repositories in the UK:

> Open access research is now more accessible as JISC has developed a new search engine to help academics, students and the general public navigate papers held in the UK's open access repositories. . . . But now, using the COnnecting REpositories tool or CORE, people can search the full text of items held in 142 approved Open Access repositories.
>
> (JISC, 2011c)

Efforts similar to those of JISC have been made elsewhere, for example, at the global level through the Digital Repository Infrastructure Vision for European Research (DRIVER) project, whose objective is to establish an appropriate infrastructure for all European and worldwide digital repositories, thereby providing scientific information in an open access model (Peters and Lossau, 2011).

Cloud computing and open access

There are many definitions of cloud computing (see, for example, Vaquero, Rodero-Merino and Moran, 2011; Hayes, 2008), but, as mentioned in Chapter 4, cloud computing may be regarded as an internet utility service that can be used to create, manage and use information without requiring individual users or institutions to invest in a massive ICT infrastructure. In a way, it can be regarded in a similar way to the electricity that we get in our homes, offices, factories, etc. We can build several applications based on electricity to suit our personal and/or organizational needs without having to worry about the potential investment in electricity generation and the associated equipment and infrastructure that is used to carry electricity from its source to the point of use. All we do is pay for the amount of electricity that we use; and we have the flexibility of paying more or less in our electricity bills as our energy consumption goes up or down. Cloud computing can be regarded as a computing utility service for consumers. The Berkeley definition of cloud computing encapsulates these ideas:

> Cloud Computing refers to both the applications delivered as services over the Internet and the hardware and systems software in the datacenters that provide those services. The services themselves have long been referred to as Software as a Service (SaaS). The datacenter hardware and software is what we will call a Cloud. When a Cloud is made available in a pay-as-you-go manner to the general public, we call it a Public Cloud; the service being sold is Utility Computing.
>
> (Armbrust et al., 2009)

Economic benefits of cloud computing and open access

The cost of building the data centres for institutional repositories can be amortized and the overall cost of the digital library service can be reduced quite significantly. The Berkeley report (Armbrust et al., 2009) identifies three unique benefits of cloud computing:

1   the availability of infinite computing resources on demand, which means that the cloud users do not need to make plans for future provisions of computing equipment – software and hardware, etc. – at the beginning of a business or a project
2   the elimination of upfront commitment, which means that users do not have to make huge initial investments in computing resources, and which will promote more ventures and innovations
3   the provision for pay-as-you-go for computing resources, which is based on shared and optimum use of computing resources among a large number of users who are not known to each other, but who eventually share the overall cost, which is only a small fraction of the overall cost of computing and infrastructure.

Overall, there is a significant potential for cost savings because the operational responsibilities are shifted to the cloud-based digital library service provider, which is then responsible for the ongoing maintenance of the hardware as well as the network security, control and performance (Leavitt, 2009; Cervone, 2010). The service provider benefits from the economies of scale and statistical multiplexing, while consumers enjoy the convenience of having the services available from any location without realizing where the content is coming from (Armbrust et al., 2009; Baliga et al., 2011).

Environmental benefits

Information and communication technologies (ICTs) have been a major driving force behind the evolution of digital library services over the past few decades. Of late, internet, web and mobile technologies have been the major forces behind the creation of a new era of digital information systems and services that have significantly changed the ways in which we create, distribute, seek, access, use, share and re-create information. On the one hand there has been an unprecedented growth in the volume and variety of digital information; on the other hand there has been an exponential growth in the use of computer and communication technologies. However, the increasing use of ICTs in the creation, management and use of digital information has significant economic and environmental implications. Individuals, institutions, governments, businesses etc. are making increasing use of computing and communication technologies, so there is greater demand for economic resources to acquire, manage and upgrade technologies because of the relatively short lifespan of computer and communications equipment. This makes the task of planning, managing and implementing digital library projects that require substantial use of ICTs more and more difficult. Moreover, the increased use of ICTs in managing and providing digital library services results in more demand on energy consumption, which has adverse environmental impacts. It was estimated in 2009 that universities and colleges in the UK alone:

- used nearly 1,470,000 computers, 250,000 printers and 240,000 servers
- would have ICT-related electricity bills of around £116 million for the year 2009
- were indirectly emitting over 500,000 tonnes of carbon dioxide (CO_2) from this electricity use (James and Hopkinson, 2009).

Furthermore, it was estimated in 2008 that, globally, ICTs contributed to about 2% of current greenhouse gas emissions (The Climate Group, 2008), and this figure would increase rapidly over the coming years. However, it was also estimated that improved and appropriate use of ICTs can reduce 'annual man-made global emissions by 15 per cent by 2020 and deliver energy efficiency savings to global businesses of over EUR 500 billion' (The Climate Group, 2008). Research shows that energy consumption can be a significant percentage of the total cost of ICT services, and cloud computing can offer significant energy savings by sharing of computing resources through techniques such as the virtualization and consolidation of servers and by developing and using energy-efficient data centres and advanced cooling systems (Baliga et al., 2011). Increasingly, large cloud data centres are being set up in places where alternative sources of energy and natural cooling facilities are available (Andrew, 2010; Greenstarnetwork Technology, n.d.; Pawlish and Varde, 2010).

In the context of digital libraries, cloud computing technologies can facilitate shared use of computing and networking resources, thereby avoiding waste of computing resources and the corresponding energy consumption, while at the same time providing round-the-clock access to digital library services. For institutional repositories, cloud computing technologies can bring significant environmental and economic benefits. Such economic benefits arise from the shared use of computing and networking resources and, more importantly, will not require individual institutions to make large investments in the ICT infrastructure required for the setting up of repositories.

Intellectual property law and open access

It is widely recognized that the intellectual property (IP) laws that were devised in the pre-internet era are not appropriate for the digital era, and therefore some major changes are required to make them suitable for today's environment. Consequently, recommendations for changes in the copyright laws and development of suitable business models have been made at different levels, for example, in the recent Hargreaves Review that was submitted to and accepted by the UK government (HM Government, 2011), and in earlier recommendations and even models proposed by others (see, for example, Chowdhury, 2009a, 2009b).

The Hargreaves Review, commissioned by the British Prime Minister, was published in May 2011. The Review acknowledged that the two key enablers of growth are currently ICT and IP law, which control access to and the use of information. It also pointed out the inadequacy of the current IP laws to promote the British digital economy and the measures that need to be taken by IP law to facilitate easy access and use of digital information. The Hargreaves Review made ten specific recommendations, some with many subsections. One of the major recommendations of the Review was to set up a cross-sectoral digital copyright exchange 'to boost UK firms' access to transparent, contestable and global digital markets' (Hargreaves, 2011, 8).

The future of open access digital libraries

Open access resources and institutional repositories based on the cloud computing architecture will eventually provide access to the lion's share of the academic and scholarly output and data of an entire country or region, thereby creating a digital library of research and scholarly information of a country, and eventually of the entire world. Furthermore, such a cloud-based service of open access repositories, once linked with other individual cloud research and content services, for example, in the UK, those of the National Health Service for health research, various government departments and research institutions, nongovernmental organizations, etc., will eventually provide access to almost all the research and scholarly output of Britain. The economic and management responsibilities of individual institutions can be reduced by joining cloud initiatives, such as those proposed by JISC (mentioned earlier in this paper and detailed in JISC, 2011a, 2011b and 2011c), and a more sustainable repository of national academic and scholarly output and data can be developed and made available to everyone – not only in the academic and research communities, but to those in government, business and industry and others.

Sustainability issues

Open access and institutional repositories significantly depend on economic as well as technological resources. It is always a challenge to balance the distribution of available resources efficiently, and this is exacerbated by the rapidly changing technological environment and the changing nature of users and academic and research environments. Technology infrastructure and tools and end-user requirements are dynamic and tend to change very quickly, requiring continuous updating and modernization (Stathopoulos, Houssos and Stavrou, 2011). Thus the economic sustainability of open access digital libraries is closely related to technological and social sustainability. Furthermore, significant dependence on ICTs has an impact on the environmental sustainability of digital libraries that are based on open access resources and institutional repositories. The sustainability issues of digital libraries are discussed further in Chapter 15.

Cloud computing technologies, especially virtualization and cloud-based software or platform services (SaaS/PaaS), can significantly improve the economic and environmental sustainability of open access resources and institutional repositories (Stathopoulos, Houssos and Stavrou, 2011). However, cloud-based services come with some inherent challenges such as portability, interoperability, long-term management and preservation, abuse and misuse of the service, legal and access management issues, and so on.

Conclusion

OAI protocols, cloud computing technologies and new IP laws and frameworks, such as those proposed in the Hargreaves Review, will play a major role by creating a simple and easy-to-use platform for making the intellectual output of research and scholarly activities (irrespective of who owns the copyright – the author or researcher, the institution, the publisher, etc.) lawfully accessible to academia, businesses and industries, especially those that are heavily engaged intellectual and innovative activities. They will also encourage and facilitate new knowledge creation by not only making existing knowledge – research output and research data – available to interested institutions and individuals, but also making it possible for them to make use of content lawfully for further/new innovative and creative activities. The proposed digital copyright exchange will facilitate access to information and data by clearly indicating the terms of access, and by facilitating lawful access by automatic payment or clearance that are required for any content access/transaction activity. Furthermore, commercial publishers and data service providers, especially in niche areas, may also join such a service, in which case the digital copyright exchange can play a key role by providing an effective platform for information access, information research and new product development.

References

Andrew, A. M. (2010) Going Green, *Kybernetes*, **39** (8), 1392–5.

Armbrust, M., Fox, A., Friffith, R., Joseph, A. D., Katz, R. H., Konwinski, A., Lee, G., Patterson, D. A., Rabkin, A., Stoica, I. and Zaharia, M. (2009) *Above the Clouds: a Berkeley view of cloud computing*, Electrical Engineering and Computer Sciences, University of California Berkeley, Technical Report No. UCB/EECS-2009-28, www.eecs.berkeley.edu/Pubs/TechRpts/2009/EECS-2009-28.html.

arXiv.org, http://arxiv.org/.

Baliga, J., Ayre, R. W. A., Hinton, K. and Tucker, R. S. (2011) Green Cloud Computing: balancing energy in processing, storage, and transport, *Proceedings of the IEEE*, **99** (1), http://ieeexplore.ieee.org/stamp/stamp.jsp?arnumber=05559320.

Budapest Open Access Initiative, www.soros.org/openaccess/read.

Cervone, H. F. (2010) An Overview of Virtual and Cloud Computing, *OCLC Systems and Services*, **26** (3), 162–5.

Chowdhury, G. G. (2009a) Towards the Conceptual Model of a Content Service Network. In *Globalizing Academic Libraries Vision 2020, Proceedings of the International Conference on Academic Libraries, Delhi, October 5–8, 2009, Delhi*, Mittal Publications, 215–20.

Chowdhury, G. G. (2009b) Towards a New Service Model for the Content Supply Chain, plenary speech, *The Seventh Book Conference, University of Edinburgh, 16–18 December 2009*, http://booksandpublishing.com/2009/04/book-studies-conference-plenary-speakers-added/.

The Climate Group (2008) *SMART2020: enabling the low carbon economy in the information age*, www.theclimategroup.org/publications/2008/6/19/smart2020-enabling-the-low-carbon-economy-in-the-information-age/.

Cogprints, http://cogprints.org/.

Connell, T. H. (2011) The Use of Institutional Repositories: the Ohio State University experience, *College & Research Libraries*, **72** (3), 253–74.

Cryer, E. and Collins, M. (2011) Incorporating Open Access into Libraries, *Serials Review*, **37** (2), 103–7.

Cullen, R. and Chawner, B. (2011) Institutional Repositories, Open Access and Scholarly

Communication: a study of conflicting paradigms, *Journal of Academic Librarianship*, **37** (6), 460–70.

Davis, P. M. and Connolly, M. J. L. (2007) Institutional repositories: evaluating the reasons for non-use of Cornell University's installation of DSpace, *D-Lib Magazine*, **13** (3/4), www.dlib.org/dlib/march07/davis/03davis.html.

Greenstarnetwork Technology (n.d.), www.greenstarnetwork.com/node/6.

Hargreaves, I. (2011) *Digital Opportunity: a review of intellectual property and growth. An independent report*, www.ipo.gov.uk/ipreview-finalreport.pdf.

Hayes, B. (2008) Cloud Computing, *Communications of the ACM*, **51** (7), 9–11.

HM Government (2011) *The Government Response to the Hargreaves Review of Intellectual Property and Growth*, www.ipo.gov.uk/ipresponse-full.pdf.

Jacobs, N., Amber, T. and McGregor, A. (2008) Institutional Repositories in the UK: the JISC approach, *Library Trends*, **57** (2), 124–41.

James, P. and Hopkinson, L. (2009) *Green ICT: managing sustainable ICT in education and research*, www.jisc.ac.uk/publications/programmerelated/2009/sustainableictfinalreport.aspx.

JISC (2011a) *Open Access*, www.jisc.ac.uk/openaccess.

JISC (2011b) *Open Access for UK Research: JISC's contributions – summary of achievements*, www.jisc.ac.uk/publications/programmerelated/2009/openaccesscontributions.aspx.

JISC (2011c) *UK's Open Access Full-text Search Engine to Aid Research*, 3 October, www.jisc.ac.uk/news/stories/2011/09/openaccess.aspx.

Leavitt, N. (2009) Is Cloud Computing Really Ready for Prime Time? *Computer*, **42** (1), 15–20.

Lynch, C. (2003) *Institutional Repositories: essential infrastructure for scholarship in the digital age*, ARL Bimonthly report no. 226, Association of Research Libraries, www.arl.org/resources/pubs/br/br226/br226ir.shtml.

MacDonald, R. (2011) Starting, Strengthening, and Managing Institutional Repositories, *Electronic Library*, **29** (4), 553–4.

NCSTRL, Networked Computer Science Technical Reference Library, www.ncstrl.org.

NDLTD, Networked Digital Library of Theses and Dissertations, www.ndltd.org.

Open Archives Initiative, www.openarchives.org/.

Open Archives Initiative (n.d.a), *Protocol for Metadata Harvesting*, www.openarchives.org/pmh/.

Open Archives Initiative (n.d.b), *Object Reuse and Exchange*, www.openarchives.org/ore/.

Pawlish, M. and Varde, A. S. (2010) Free Cooling: a paradigm shift in data centers, *5th International Conference on Information and Automation for Sustainability, ICIAfS 2010; Colombo; 17–19 December 2010*, 1–28, doi: 10.1109/ICIAFS.2010.5715732.

Peters, D. and Lossau, N. (2011) DRIVER: building a sustainable infrastructure for global repositories, *Electronic Library*, **29** (2), 249–60.

St Jean, B., Rieh, S. Y., Yakel, E. and Markey, K. (2011) Unheard Voices: institutional repository end-users, *College & Research Libraries*, **72** (1), 21–42.

Stathopoulos, P., Houssos, N. and Stavrou, G. (2011) Technology Trends, Requirements and Models for Providing Sustainable Technological Support for Libraries in an Evolving Environment. In Katsirikou, A. (ed.), *Open Access to STM Information: trends, models and strategies for libraries*, IFLA Publication 153, IFLA, 167–76.

Vaquero, L. M., Rodero-Merino, L. and Moran, D. (2011) Locking the Sky: a survey on IaaS cloud security, *Computing*, **91** (1), 93–118.

CHAPTER 11

iSTEM: integrating subject categories from multiple repositories

Christopher C. Yang and Jung-ran Park

Introduction

Subject categories with a hierarchical structure (e.g. classification, subject directories, taxonomy) are frequently used in organizing resources in many libraries and institutions. There are enormous challenges for information professionals in integrating the distinct subject directories into a unified subject directory while retaining the knowledge captured in each collection. The core of the challenges stems from the fact that each of these subject directories evinces a complex semantic and syntactic structure that is embedded in local collections. Subject directories from different repositories use different organizational structures (e.g. hierarchical/non-hierarchical) and different hierarchical relationships between topic and subtopic, resulting in many-to-one mappings or vice versa.

In addition, the disparity in the levels of granularity assigned to particular subject areas brings forth hindrances in unifying the two subject directories. In natural language, mappings between word forms and meanings can be many-to-many. In other words, the same meaning can be expressed by several different forms (e.g. synonyms) and at the same time the same forms may designate different concepts (e.g. homonyms). In addition, the same concept can be expressed by different morpho-syntactic forms (e.g. noun, adjective, compound noun, phrase, clause etc.). The complex nature of mappings between forms and meanings adds intricacy and richness. On the other hand, these same phenomena engender significant hindrances in accurate and consistent semantic mapping between two or among different vocabulary schemes, such as subject directory and thesauri (Park, 2006).

Figure 11.1 shows some of the conceptual mismatches that can be expected to be encountered in any library setting in the process of semantic mapping between two or more vocabulary schemes (Park, 2002; Yang and Lin, 2007; Yang, Lin and Wei, 2010).

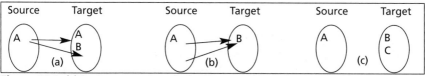

Figure 11.1 *(a) Source concept equivalent to several target concepts; (b) two or more source concepts equivalent to one target concept; (c) no conceptual equivalent between the source concept and the target concept*

In this chapter, we will present our onoing project, called iSTEM, on integrating and expanding taxonomy and subject categories derived from multiple repositories in science, technology, engineering and mathematics. The goals of this study lie in determining relationships between subject categories from different repositories through several text-classification models and developing operations and processes for integration based on the identified subject-category relationships from different repositories.

Background: ontology integration

In this section, we will briefly present an overview of the current state of ontology integration and its limitation. The literature review is not meant to be exhaustive.

Substantial effort has been made on ontology integration over the last decade. Ontology is a model that represents a set of concepts within a domain and the relationships between concepts. Noy and Musen (2000, 2001) developed the PROMPT system to align ontology by measuring the linguistic similarity between concepts. Ryutaro, Hideaki and Shinichi (2001) developed the HICAL system that utilized machine-learning techniques to select the most similar concepts for integration, but disregarded the hierarchical structure of ontology. Doan et al. (2003) developed the GLUE system, which employed multi-strategy learning techniques to compute concept similarity.

However, the above-mentioned ontology integration systems can only partially support subject directory integration. Although concepts are similar to the labels of categories in subject directories, categories consist of documents and the labels are merely representing the hidden themes of categories which depend on the assigned documents in categories. The integration of subject directories must consider the documents in categories, but not the labels alone.

In addition to ontology integration there was recent work on category-tree integration, which generally used the categorization information in the source category tree to improve the underlying text-classification models. Agrawal and Srikant (2001) flattened the hierarchical structures of the target category tree and extended the naïve Bayes approach to build an enhanced classification model that exploits the categorization information embedded in the source category tree. Zhang and Lee (2004a, 2004b) proposed to adopt the support vector machine algorithm and the co-bootstrapping technique as analysis to tackle the same problem. Wu et al. (2008) suggested a hierarchical shrinkage algorithm to organize child documents according to their parent categories, in order to improve category tree integration. Cheng and Wei (2008) divided each source category into multiple subcategories and merged them into the most similar master categories. These techniques attempted to use the categorization information of the source category tree to improve the text-classification models and perform integration at the document level.

However, the hierarchical structure of the source category trees was discarded in favour of the master subject directory (Figure 11.2), and therefore the knowledge embedded in the original category tree structures was not retained. The integration was

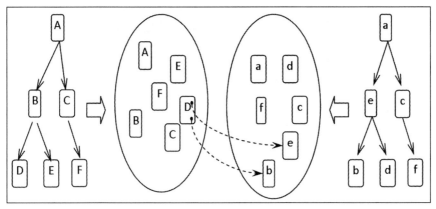

Figure 11.2 *Illustration of discarding category structure during integration*

also likely to result in structural incoherency and conflicting relationships between documents and subject headings in the final subject directory.

The iSTEM project: objectives and repositories

The objective of the iSTEM project is to integrate subject categories from one subject directory into another. Specifically, the two sources, a *source* subject directory and a *master* subject directory, must be defined. The source subject directory is defined as a hierarchical tree from which subject categories are drawn. In contrast, the master subject directory is defined as a hierarchical tree into which the source categories will be integrated. Based on this definition, the goal of the proposed solution is to integrate the subject categories from source subject directory into an appropriate location in the master subject directory, taking into account the structures of both master and source subject directories. With this integration approach, we overcome the shortcomings of the existing solution, in the sense that the structure of the integrated subject directory will reflect and retain the knowledge of information professionals who model the source and the master taxonomies. Figure 11.3 illustrates the integration of the two subject-category trees (i.e. subject directories).

In the iSTEM project, we develop techniques for facilitating an effective integration task and developing open source tools which enable information professionals to successfully integrate and expand taxonomy and subject categories derived from different repositories. This integration process is aimed at retaining the structures of both original subject directories and building a unified and expanded subject directory. As a result, the knowledge captured in each subject directory can be preserved. The integration provides a uniform interface for users to reduce the tedious and time-consuming process of browsing through two separate subject categories. In contrast, through the utility of the proposed tool and after integration users may be able to experience seamless information access by navigating through one unified and expanded subject directory.

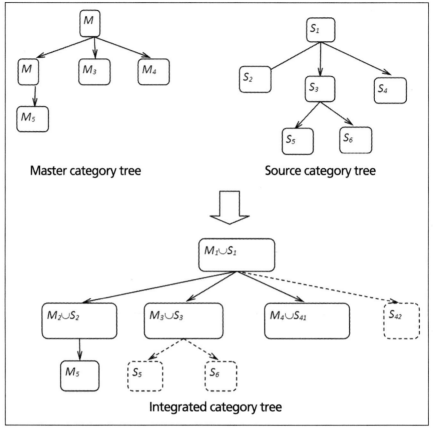

Figure 11.3 *Illustration of the integration of two category trees into a unified category tree*

The selected repositories in iSTEM (as presented in Table 11.1) cover STEM resources from diverse information providers/sources including repositories drawn from the results of high quality National Science Foundation (NSF) research projects (e.g. NSDL Science Refreshers, AMSER, Engineering Pathway, Math Common Core, BEN), academic institutions (e.g. IPL2, Center for Research Libraries, arXiv.org) and commercial and open platforms (e.g. Yahoo Directory and Open Directory). In particular, the Center for Research Libraries covers materials of emerging regions such as Africa, Middle East and Southeast Asia from an international consortium of institutions and libraries.

Table 11.1 *Ten STEM repositories*

Repository	Description	URL
NSDL Science Refreshers	High-quality science content from trusted providers organized by subject areas for K-6 (primary education).	http://nsdl.org/refreshers/science
Applied Math and Science Education Repository (AMSER)	A portal of educational resources built for community and technical colleges and funded by the National Science Foundation (NSF).	http://amser.org/
Engineering Pathway	A collection of teaching and learning resources in applied science and maths, engineering, computer science/information technology, and engineering technology for K-12 primary/secondary school and university.	www.engineeringpathway.com/
Math Common Core	A National Science Digital Library (NSDL) collection to associate digital learning objects with educational standards.	http://nsdl.org/browse/commcore/math/
BiosciEdNet (BEN)	Over 15,000 reviewed resources covering 77 biological sciences topics, managed by the American Association for the Advancement of Sciences (AAAS).	www.biosciednet.org/
Internet Public Library (IPL2)	The second generation of IPL, merging the collection of resources from IPL and Librarians' Internet Index (LII), and hosted at the Drexel University.	www.ipl.org/
Center for Research Libraries (CRL)	An international consortium of university, college and independent research libraries. Most of the materials in CRL repositories are collected from emerging regions of the world such as Africa, Middle East, South-East Asia, etc.	www.crl.edu/
arXiv.org	A directory of over 630,000 electronic resources in physics, mathematics, computer science, quantitative biology, quantitative finance and statistics provided by Cornell University Library.	http://arxiv.org/
Yahoo Directory*	A high-quality web directory.	http://dir.yahoo.com/
Open Directory*	A human-edited directory of web resources. Similar to Wikipedia, it is constructed and maintained by a vast and global community of volunteer editors. There are over 100 search engines and portals, such as Google, World of Education and Education America Net, using the Open Directory.	www.dmoz.org/

*Note: We focus only on STEM categories in Yahoo Directory and Open Directory. iSTEM focuses on the integration of ten valuable and high-quality repositories in science, technology, engineering and mathematics (STEM). These STEM repositories provide important resources for K-12 primary/secondary school and college education. These resources are essential for equipping future generations with the skills necessary for continual success in our knowledge-based economy. Educators and students tend to find it tedious and time consuming to browse through multiple STEM repositories to identify materials for teaching and learning. A unified subject directory will greatly enhance their teaching and learning experience and increase productivity. Table 11.1 lists the ten STEM repositories that we are currently integrating. These repositories cover resources from diverse information providers/sources, including repositories drawn from the results of high-quality National Science Foundation research projects and academic institutions, as well as commercial and open platforms.

The iSTEM project: learning category relationships and developing integration operations and processes

Category relationships

Determining relationships between subject categories is a critical step in establishing the appropriate location in the master subject directory into which the source category will be integrated. The integration operations define the manner of integrating a subject category from the source subject directory with the corresponding category in the master subject directory. Subject categories can be considered as a set of documents. Given two subject categories, we apply set theory to define five relationships between them. Figure 11.4 illustrates the category relationship using Venn diagrams:

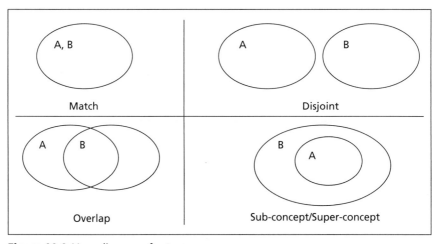

Figure 11.4 *Venn diagram of category*

Match: If all documents in category A can be assigned to category B and vice versa, A and B are said to have a match relationship.

Disjunction: If none of the documents in category A can be assigned to category B and vice versa, A and B are said to have a disjoint relationship.

Sub-concept: If all documents in category A can be assigned to category B, but only some documents in category B can be assigned to category A, A is said to be a sub-concept of B.

Super-concept: If some documents in category A can be assigned to category B, but all documents in category B can be assigned to category A, then A is said to be a super-concept of B.

Overlap: If some documents in category A can be assigned to category B and vice versa, A and B are said to have an overlap relationship.

To determine category relationships, conditional probability $P(A|B)$ is utilized where $P(A|B)$ is defined as the number of documents that are labelled B that are predicted to be labelled A, then *divided by* the number of documents labelled B.

A trained text classifier is then employed to derive the number of documents predicted to be labelled into a certain category. By applying conditional probability to the initial definition of category relationships, we can rewrite the relationship in a formal manner. For example, category A is considered to have a *Match* relationship with category B if and only if $P(A|B) = 1$ and $P(B|A) = 1$. In this ongoing project, we investigate several text-classification models and examine their effectiveness in determining the category relationships. These text-classification models include Rocchio classification, naïve Bayes classification, k nearest neighbourhood classification and support vector machines. The performance of these classification models varies depending on the distribution of documents in categories, the term vectors representing documents and the domain of documents.

Integration operations and processes

Map, *insert* and *split* are the three operations that can be performed to integrate a subject category from the source subject directory with a subject category in the master subject directory (Figures 11.5 and 11.6). These operations are utilized depending on the category relationships and the parent–child relationships of the integrating categories.

Map: A source category S is mapped to an existing category M in the master subject directory. After the integration, all documents in the source category will be labelled M.

Insert: A source category S is inserted as a new category M_{new} in the master subject directory. After the integration, all documents in the source category will be labeled M_{new}.

Split: A source category S is split into n sub-categories, $S_1, S_2, ..., S_n$. After splitting, each sub-category will be either mapped to an existing category or inserted as a new category into the master subject directory.

One of the three integration operations will be performed whenever a category is integrated from the source subject directory into the master subject directory. There are three major criteria to determine the selection of an integration operation to be activated. These criteria are 1) the category relationship between the given category in the source subject directory and the categories in the master category, 2) the hierarchical structure of the source subject directory, and 3) the hierarchical structure of the master subject directory.

In the iSTEM project, we adopt two approaches: a rule-based approach and a path-similarity approach. In the rule-based approach we will develop decision rules to activate an integration operation given a set of conditions. The conditions are the parent–child

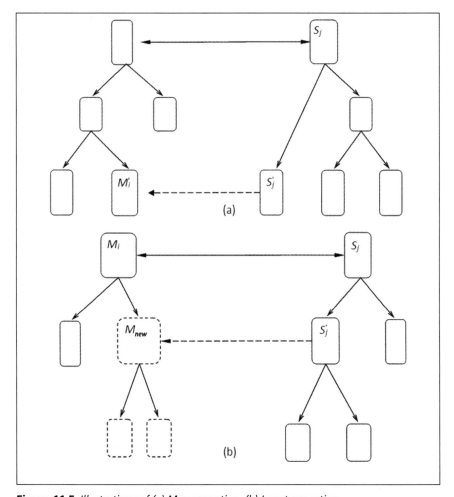

Figure 11.5 *Illustrations of (a) Map operation, (b) Insert operation*

relationships and category relationships of the potential integrating categories. Through utilization of these rules, the integration must not violate the parent–child relationships in the source and master taxonomies in order to retain the knowledge of collection organization. A top-down approach is adopted so that the root category can be considered first, and the breadth-first approach may be utilized to integrate the categories from the highest level until the leaf categories are reached. We take integration samples generated by cataloguing and information professionals as a set of training cases and utilize case-based reasoning algorithms to deduce integration rules. The integration rules learned in this approach should emulate the ways that cataloguing and information professionals integrate subject categories.

In the path similarity approach, we aim at measuring the similarity between the paths in source- and master-category directories. A path is defined as a sequence of categories

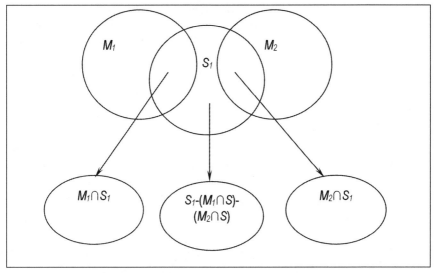

Figure 11.6 *Illustration of splitting S₁ into three subcategories. S₁ is overlapping with M₁ and M₂*

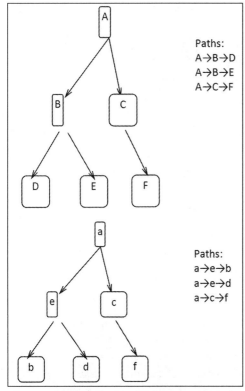

Paths:
A→B→D
A→B→E
A→C→F

Paths:
a→e→b
a→e→d
a→c→f

Figure 11.7 *Paths extracting from master and source category trees*

from a root category to a leaf category. A leaf category is a category that does not have any subcategory. Figure 11.7 illustrates the paths extracting from category trees. We develop a path similarity measurement to identify the best matching between a path in the master-category subject directory and a path in the source-category subject directory by utilizing the category relationship. By identifying optimum matching, we integrate the categories from the path in the source-category subject directory to the path in the master-category subject directory with a minimum cost. We also develop an algorithm to resolve conflicts that occur in path integration.

We have conducted an experiment to integrate the Yahoo! directory and Open Directory as a pilot test. The result shows that the proposed techniques achieve higher than 80% of integration accuracy. The iSTEM project is an ongoing project. We are continuing our efforts to integrate the other eight directories one by one as well as communicating with the resource providers to evaluate the usefulness of the integrated directory.

Conclusion

Owing to the information explosion, many libraries face the necessity of building unified collections derived from different sources of repositories and resource types from different institutional repositories. In this situation, it is desirable to integrate the distinct subject directories into a unified subject directory while retaining the knowledge captured in each collection. This will facilitate federated searching of information resources and will, in turn, enhance the user experience of seamless information access. Furthermore, the importance of information and resource sharing through collaboration across libraries, museums and other institutions has been increasingly recognized. There is thus a critical need to integrate subject categories and taxonomy.

Currently, there is no existing tool to support the integration task. It demands as much time and effort to rebuild a subject directory for the combined resources as to integrate them manually. Reconstructing the subject directory implies abandoning the original subject directories, in the process sacrificing accumulated knowledge. In order to overcome such obstacles, it is necessary to devise a semi-automatic tool to support information professionals in apprehending relationships from the subject categories of different repositories and in recommending plausible changes and fine-tuning of the integration process.

The iSTEM solution takes into account the knowledge of information professionals encoded in the structure of both master and source taxonomies to generate the expanded taxonomy. This approach attempts to address the shortcomings of existing taxonomy-integration approaches where the structure of source taxonomy is often discarded before integration. Creating high-quality taxonomy is an arduous effort, as it requires the knowledge of domain experts to logically classify the content of the collection into a hierarchical structure of subject headings. As such, we believe that a high-quality integrated taxonomy can be constructed by retaining the knowledge of information professionals from all available sources during the integration process.

The generated taxonomy through the iSTEM project may serve as an intermediary that assists information professionals in the task of building a refined integrated taxonomy. Using the iSTEM tool to automatically generate a preliminary integrated subject directory, information professionals can in turn use the generated taxonomy as a starting-point and employ their own domain knowledge to augment the final modelling of the expanded taxonomy. The semi-automatic approach is aimed at considerably reducing the amount of laborious work required to create an integrated taxonomy from scratch. Information professionals may not have to manually collate a large number of collection records located in hundreds of subject categories so as to model the structure of the integrated taxonomy. Instead, they can focus efforts on improving the quality of the expanded subject directory by relocating documents and subject headings manually or adjusting the merging parameters of the integration tool.

From the information seeker's perspective, the integrated subject directory can help to reduce the effort required to find specific information. Without the expanded taxonomy, users must browse through multiple directory trees. Often, this results in redundant information being found, owing to variations of subject classification and granularity. By providing a unified and logical view of collection items and their subject headings aggregated from multiple sources, we expect that users may spend considerably less time browsing through the subject directory tree. There has been a growing number of STEM resources in the last decade; however, the distributed resources indeed make it more difficult for users to identify desirable resources seamlessly. The integration of STEM repositories has a potential to provide a promising mechanism for federated browsing and searching. It may enhance the teaching and learning experience of K-12 primary/secondary and college educators and students.

References

Agrawal, R. and Srikant, R. (2001) On Integrating Catalogs, *Proceedings of WWW10 Conference, Hong Kong, May 1–5*, 603–12.

Cheng, T. H. and Wei, C. (2008) A Clustering-Based Approach for Integrating Document-Category Hierarchies. *IEEE Transactions on Systems, Man, and Cybernetics Part A: Systems and Humans*, **38** (2), 410–24.

Doan, A., Madhavan, J., Dhamankar, R., Domingos, P. and Halevy, A. (2003) Learning to Match Ontologies on the Semantic Web, *The VLDB Journal*, **12**, 303–19.

Noy, N. F. and Musen, M. A. (2000) PROMPT: Algorithm and Tool for Automated Ontology Merging and Alignment, *Proceedings of the 17th National Conference on Artificial Intelligence*, AAAI Press/ MIT Press, 450–5.

Noy, N. F. and Musen, M. A. (2001) Anchor-PROMPT: using non-local context for semantic matching, *Proceedings of the Workshop on Ontologies and Information Sharing at the International Joint Conference on Artificial Intelligence*, 63–70.

Park, J. R. (2002) Hindrances in Semantic Mapping Involving Thesauri and Metadata: a linguistic perspective, *Journal of Internet Cataloging* [renamed *Journal of Library Metadata*], **5** (3), 59–79.

Park, J. R. (2006) Semantic Interoperability and Metadata Quality: an analysis of metadata item records of digital image collections, *Knowledge Organization*, **33** (1), 20–34.

Ryutaro, I., Hideaki, T. and Shinichi, H. (2001) Rule Induction for Concept Hierarchy Alignment, *Proceedings of the Workshop on Ontologies and Information Sharing at the 17th International Joint Conference on Artificial Intelligence*, Morgan Kaufman, 26–9.

Wu. C-W., Tsai, R. T.-H. Lee, C-W and Hsu, W.-L. (2008) Web Taxonomy Integrations with Hierarchical Shrinkage Algorithm and Fine-grained Relations. In *Expert Systems with Applications*, **35**, 2123–31.

Yang, C. C. and Lin, J. (2007) Integrating Web Directories by Learning their Structures. In *Proceedings of the International World Wide Web Conference (WWW'07), Banff, Alberta, Canada, 8–12 May.*, http://www2007.org/proceedings.html.

Yang, C. C., Lin, J. and Wei, C. (2010) Retaining Knowledge for Document Management: category-tree integration by exploiting category relationships and hierarchical structures, *Journal of the American Society for Information Science and Technology*, **61** (7), 1313–31.

Zhang, D. and Lee, W. S. (2004a). Web Taxonomy Integration through Co-Bootstrapping, *Proceedings of the 27th Annual International ACM SIGIR Conference on Research and Development in Information Retrieval (SIGIR'04)*, ACM Press, 410–17.

Zhang, D. and Lee, W. S. (2004b) Web Taxonomy Integration Using Support Vector Machines, *Proceedings of WWW 2004, New York, USA, May 17–22*, http://dl.acm.org/citation.cfm?id=988672&picked=prox&CFID=102377760&CFTOKEN=87004591.

CHAPTER 12

The usability of digital libraries

Sudatta Chowdhury

Introduction

Simply stated, the term 'usability' means how easily a product or a service can be used. In the context of digital libraries, usability studies involve both user studies and evaluation of digital library products and services. A number of models of usability have been proposed in the literature. However, usability studies originated in, and have been largely conducted in the context of, the field of human–computer interactions (HCI). Hearst (2009) comments that usability is an important quality of a user interface. Nielsen (2003, 2006) comments that usability depends on five qualities of the interface of an information service: learnability, efficiency, memorability, errors and satisfaction. These parameters focus on measuring the features of user interfaces and are built on the design guidelines of user interfaces proposed by Shneiderman and Plaisant (2010).

However, the usability of a digital library is not limited to its interface features; rather, it should focus on the overall digital library service. Kuniavsky (2003) suggests that there are four major steps in a usability study of information systems:

1 Define the users and their goals.
2 Create tasks that address these goals.
3 Select a group of study participants for the usability study.
4 Watch them try to perform the specified tasks using the service or product whose usability is being measured.

While these guidelines may be used for conducting usability studies of digital libraries, a number of challenges are involved here. This chapter addresses these issues and, drawing examples from several usability studies, it discusses different approaches and techniques for conducting usability studies of digital libraries. Some socio-economic issues affecting the usability of digital libraries, such as the digital divide and emerging business models, are also mentioned.

Usability

ISO 9241 Part 11 (1998) defines usability as the extent to which a product can be used by specified users to achieve specified goals with effectiveness, efficiency and satisfaction in a specified context of use. This definition reminds us that the users should be able to use an information product or service with effectiveness, efficiency and satisfaction in a specified context of use.

ISO 9241 Part 210 (2010) prescribes guidelines for user-centred design and usability metrics. According to these guidelines, in order to measure the usability of a digital library, we need to:

- conduct usability studies involving digital library users, and therefore identify a subset of the target users of the digital library and involve them in the study
- study the selected users' context and the goals for which they are going to use the concerned digital library
- assess how the chosen users use the digital library to accomplish their tasks
- find out how efficiently the study participants can use the various features and functions of the digital library concerned
- find out what their overall perception and level of satisfaction with the digital library service is.

A variety of data-collection methods and tools are used for conducting usability tests (for details, see Chowdhury and Chowdhury, 2011). Selection of the appropriate methods and tools depends on the type of usability test being conducted, such as formative or summative evaluation. Formative evaluation takes place throughout the design process; it is an iterative process conducted by the design team or experts, sometimes with a small number of users. Summative evaluation is conducted when the prototype has been designed and before implementation; it is conducted in a real-life situation involving end-users. Other factors to be considered while conducting a usability study include a clear understanding of the study objectives, the characteristics of study participants, and availability of budget, staff and time.

Usability tests can be conducted in a controlled laboratory environment, or at user sites when real-life data collection is desired. For the latter, the researcher needs to decide whether the tests have to be conducted in one or multiple locations so that they will be conducted in specific user contexts. A variety of usability guidelines, including some international standards, are available (e.g. the ISO 9241 series of standards), and a researcher can choose and use a variety of usability metrics to measure several parameters from system performance data to assess the level of user satisfaction. However, in order to develop a usable information product or service, and to keep it up to date with the changing market conditions and user demands and expectations, usability studies should be a continuous process throughout the lifecycle of a product or service. In the early stages of product or service design, usability studies can be conducted with minimum user involvement or through heuristic (expert) evaluation, and as the product matures or once it is in the market such studies can be conducted by involving a number of participants or user groups in one or more study locations. Such usability tests can be conducted in a controlled environment where only a selected number of parameters are measured while other factors are either disregarded or carefully avoided, or in uncontrolled, real-life settings. Similarly a variety of data-collection methods can be employed, some of which may generate qualitative data while others may produce quantitative data and measurable statistics, and, depending on the study objectives and approaches, the data collected may be combined and compared to generate various usability figures and metrics. The success of a usability study depends significantly on proper and careful planning as well as on the selection of study participants and appropriate study methods and data-collection tools and techniques.

Usability studies of digital libraries

Usability studies of digital libraries primarily aim to find out how easily users can interact with the interface, how quickly and easily they can find useful information, how easily they can use the retrieved information to accomplish their specific tasks and what the general impressions of the users are about the various features and functionalities of the digital library (Chowdhury and Chowdhury, 2011). Thus, a well designed digital library should have good usability features (Chowdhury, Landoni and Gibb, 2006). However, Chowdhury and Chowdhury (2011) suggest that usability is a relative concept and must be judged on the basis of a digital library's intended goals.

A number of usability and evaluation studies, using a variety of usability study techniques and methods, have taken place in the field of digital libraries over the past two decades. Several models for usability and evaluation of digital libraries have also been proposed by researchers. Research on the usability of digital libraries has broadly used two main approaches (Chowdhury and Chowdhury, 2011):

- empirical techniques which involve testing systems with users
- analytical techniques which involve experts assessing systems, i.e. heuristic evaluation, using established theories and methods.

Blandford and Buchanan (2003) list the following criteria for assessing the usability of digital libraries:

- Achieving goals – how effectively and efficiently can the user achieve their goals with a digital library system?
- Learnability – how easily can the user learn to use the digital library?
- Help and error recovery – how well does the digital library help the user to avoid making errors, or recover from errors?

- User experience – how much does the user enjoy working with the digital library?
- Context – how well does the system fit within the context in which it is used?

These usability criteria are similar to those proposed by Nielsen (2003) and they focus largely on the user interfaces of digital libraries. Blandford et al. (2004) emphasize that user needs should be the driving factor for studying the usability of digital libraries. Research also shows that 'it is now vital to obtain an in-depth knowledge of the users, their information requirements in given situations, the circumstances and contexts in which their information needs arise, the action users take to resolve matters, and the use they make of the information once found' (Pinto and Sales, 2007, 534). A more comprehensive set of usability criteria has been proposed by Chowdhury (2004a):

1   Interface features:
   - types of interface (e.g. simple vs. expert search interface)
   - language(s) of the interface
   - navigation options, shortcuts and system information
   - screen features, i.e. use of colours, typography, layout and graphics
   - personalization of the interface, e.g. choice of interface language and/or retrieval level, number of records on one page, sort options etc.
2   Search process. Database/resource selection:
   - options for selection
   - cross-database search facilities.
3   Query formulation facilities:
   - formulation and modification of queries
   - building search sets
   - saving searches.
4   Search options:
   - specific search options for text, multimedia, specific collection etc.
   - multiple access points: search fields.
5   Search operation:
   - use of search operators
   - natural language queries.
6   Results manipulation:
   - format(s) for display of records
   - number of records that can be displayed
   - navigation in the list of records
   - marking of records
   - sort options
   - printing, exporting and e-mailing of records.
7   Help features:
   - appropriateness and usefulness
   - context-sensitive help

- consistency of terminology, design and layout
- linguistic correctness.

These usability criteria focus mainly on the system features of digital libraries. However, user-centric issues are equally important usability criteria for a digital library. Liew (2005) discusses the usability and user interface features of a digital library of Máori cultural heritage that focus on the interface as well as search and retrieval features of a digital library. Many researchers have conducted usability studies to find out how digital libraries are used by target users to accomplish their tasks or to meet their information needs. Probably one of the earliest and most widely known impact studies was conducted by Borgman and her colleagues (Borgman, 2002, 2004; Borgman et al., 2000, 2004, 2005; Borgman and Rasmussen, 2005) in the context of a digital library of spatial data and content.

Some digital library usability and evaluation studies

Given that digital libraries are designed for specific users and to provide support for specific activities, they should be evaluated in the context of their target users and their specific contexts. A variety of research methods and techniques have been used in the course of various usability and evaluation studies of digital libraries conducted within the Digital Library Federation (Covey, 2012). These include think aloud, transaction log and systems analysis, heuristic evaluation, card sorting and survey research. A recently conducted usability study of Europeana used a combination of focus-group studies and eye-tracking technologies. It focused on a number of areas, including (Dobreva and Chowdhury, 2010):

- ease of use and intuitiveness of Europeana, especially in the case of users who visit the website for the first time
- identification of 'future' user needs as the younger generation grows up
- styles of use of the prototype for knowledge discovery amongst young users
- expectations, including how users see trustworthiness
- similarities and differences between the groups from different countries.

As Europeana was designed to meet the information needs of users in European countries, especially in the area of cultural heritage information, multiple sites were used to conduct this usability study. Data was gathered from selected participant groups in four countries – Bulgaria, Italy, the Netherlands and the UK. Similarly, in order to collect rich data sets, a combination of data-collection techniques were used, such as questionnaires, recordings of discussion sessions, queries saved in My Europeana by each participant and eye tracking data (Dobreva and Chowdhury, 2010). Furthermore, data wsa visualized as heat maps and gaze plots, in order to study the participants' eye movements as they interacted with the Europeana interface (Skykes et al., 2010). The researchers noted that eye-tracking data used in conjunction with other data gathered by other usability methods can provide reliable data on and insights into the user's information behaviour, as well as on actual usage patterns, preferences, etc.

As discussed in Chapter 4, information-access features and facilities in digital libraries often vary depending on the objectives and the underlying business models of the libraries. While some digital libraries are part of the publishing business model of a parent organization, such as the ACM Digital Library, which can be accessed through membership and subscription, most digital libraries are funded by either an institution, a consortium or grants and charities/voluntary contributions. Examples of such digital libraries include Europeana, PubMed, NDLTD (Networked Digital Library of Theses and Dissertations), NSDL (National Science Digital Library) and various institutional repositories, such as Strathprints (2012) and Enlighten (2012). However, very few researchers have conducted usability studies from the perspectives of the funding models and economic sustainability of digital libraries.

Chowdhury, McMenemy and Poulter (2008) proposed a generic model, called MEDLIS, for usability and evaluation of digital libraries that, among other things, looks at the business models and economic sustainability of digital libraries. They recommend that the usability study of a digital library should begin with some broad questions, and it is important to find out who should best provide the answers to these questions. For example, information related to the origin and objectives of the digital library service, the management and business model etc. can be obtained from the management and the service website. Although some of this information can also be obtained by studying various documents – minutes of meeting, memos, design documents etc. – access to some information is usually restricted and can be obtained only through agreement with the management in question. Similarly, some information, such as the reasons for using the service, ease of use of the service, user satisfaction etc., can be obtained only from the users. Furthermore, in order to assess the economic sustainability vis-à-vis the underlying business model etc. it is also necessary to conduct a market scan and find comparable digital library services and their strengths and weaknesses compared with the digital library model being studied. Therefore a variety of data-collection methods and analysis techniques needs to be employed in order to study the economic models and sustainability of digital libraries. More sustainability issues of digital libraries are discussed in Chapter 15.

Social factors of usability

The usability of information products and services are influenced by a number of social factors, such as the digital divide and the information skills of users and web accessibility (Chowdhury and Chowdhury, 2011). Broadly speaking, the digital divide is a disparity between the information and technology 'haves' and the 'have nots'; but it can be of different types (Norris, 2001; Chowdhury, 2004b):

• the social divide: the difference in access among diverse social groups

- the global divide: the difference in access to ICTs in general and the internet in particular
- the democratic divide: the different applications and uses of online information to engage and participate in social life.

Access to digital libraries can be affected by poor access to ICTs. Thus, poor access to and use of digital libraries can be attributed to the problem of digital divide. Similarly, access to digital libraries can be affected by the poor information skills of users. The other important factor that can affect access to digital libraries is related to web accessibility, especially for people with different degrees of physical and learning disabilities, poor language skills and so on (Chowdhury and Chowdhury, 2011). The digital divide and usability are thus inherently linked in a vicious circle: without access, users are not able to develop the required skills, and without skills they are unable to access and use digital information properly (Mossberger et al., 2003).

Fortunately, due to a variety of national and international initiatives, overall, a growing numbers of people across generations are becoming increasingly engaged with ICT, internet and mobile technologies. Some form of divide can also be noticed in ICT skills, ICT use and expectations among the younger generation, the so-called Google generation or digital natives, versus the older generation, who were not born in the digital age and had to learn to use and adopt modern digital technologies. Selwyn (2009) reminds us that we should remain especially mindful of the wider political and ideological agendas underlying the persistence of the 'digital native' discourse in society. However, some researchers believe that the gap between the Google generation and the rest of today's society in their use of the internet and ICTs is not as great as it is often perceived to be (see for example, Gunter, Rowlands and Nicholas, 2009; Rowlands et al., 2008; Selwyn, 2009). Rowlands et al. (2008) point out that, contrary to popular belief, the ubiquitous presence of the internet and ICTs in the life of the younger generation does not result in improved information retrieval, information seeking or evaluation skills. So, according to these researchers, the usability of digital libraries should not be influenced by the division of younger and older generations of users. There are alternative views and research findings as well. For example, in the context of the usability of Europeana, Dobreva and Chowdhury (2010) noted a significant difference among younger and older generations of users and they recommend that some simple search-engine-like features are preferable for younger users.

Summary

Since users are at the core of any usability study and user studies have remained a major area of research within the information science community, many methods and techniques that were developed for user studies have been adopted and used in usability research (Chowdhury and Chowdhury, 2011). While significant amounts of progress have been made in usability research in digital libraries and information services, many new challenges have also appeared over the past few years. Some of these challenges are due to the changing nature of the web and the emerging technologies, standards etc., while others are caused by the very nature of the web and ICTs, which are affected by many factors, including the digital divide, digital and information literacy and the fast-changing nature of society caused by the culture of web and mobile technologies, social-networking technologies and so on. These emerging technologies and culture bring tremendous opportunities as well as challenges for usability researchers within the information science community (from Chapter 10). Several technology-related factors especially the growing ICT and internet infrastructure, regulations and facilities vis-à-vis the digital divide have a significant impact on the usability of digital libraries.

Usability studies provide valuable information for designers and providers of digital library services. However, digital libraries are also significantly influenced by various external factors, such as the changing business patterns and the emerging players and services in the information marketplace, some prominent examples being Google Books, Google Scholar and Microsoft Academic ReSearch. The question remains, however, of what the nature of the new and emerging digital libraries will be and whether digital library managers should focus more on building and managing content, while leaving access and retrieval to the big search-engine services like Google, Microsoft etc.; or whether large digital libraries and institutional repositories should work alongside the search-engine services in order to provide better information access and retrieval facilities for end-users. It will be interesting to see how ICTs, the information marketplace and intellectual property law shape up to meet the emerging needs and challenges of digital libraries. These new developments will no doubt force digital library researchers and service providers to conduct several new usability studies and develop benchmarks for the assessment of the qualities and success of digital libraries. The basic user-related questions as discussed in this chapter, and also by Chowdhury (2012) and Dobreva, O'Dwyer and Feliciati (2012) in the context of the usability of digital libraries, should be studied alongside the emerging technological, economic and legal frameworks, in order to ensure the sustainability of digital libraries.

References

Blandford, A. and Buchanan, G. (2003) Usability of Digital Libraries: a source of creative tensions with technical developments, *TCDL Bulletin*,
www.ieee-tcdl.org/Bulletin/current/blandford/blandford.html

Blandford, A., Keith, S., Connell, I. and Edwards, H. (2004) Analytical Usability Evaluation for Digital Libraries: a case study. In Chen, H., Wactlar, H. and Chen, C. (eds), *Proceedings of the 4th ACM/IEEE-CS Joint Conference on Digital Libraries, ACM/IEEE, 7–11 June 2004*, 27–36.

Borgman, C. L. (2002) Evaluation of Digital Libraries: testbeds, measurements, and metrics, *Fourth DELOS Workshop. Computer and Automation Research Institute (MTA SZTAKI)*,

Hungarian Academy of Sciences, Budapest, Hungary, 6–7 June 2002, Final report to the National Science Foundation,
www.sztaki.hu/conferences/deval/presentations/FINAL%20REPORT%20TO%20NSF%20CISE_10_2.doc.

Borgman, C. L. (2004) Evaluating the Uses of Digital Libraries. In *DELOS Workshop on Evaluation of Digital Libraries, Padova, Italy,*
www.delos.info/eventlist/wp7_ws_2004/Borgman.pdf.

Borgman, C. and Rasmussen, E. (2005) Usability of Digital Libraries in a Multicultural Environment. In Theng, Y.-L, and Foo, S. (eds), *Design and Usability of Digital Libraries: case studies in the Asia-Pacific,* Information Science Publishing, 270–84.

Borgman, C. L., Gilliland-Swetland, A. J., Leazer, G. L., Mayer, R., Gwynn, D., Gazan, R. and Mautone, P. (2000) Evaluating Digital Libraries for Teaching and Learning in Undergraduate Education: a case study of the Alexandria Digital Earth Prototype (ADEPT), **49** (2), 228–50.

Borgman, C. L., Leazer, G. H., Gilliland-Swetland, A., Millwood, K., Champeny, L., Finley, J. and Smart, L. J. (2004) How Geography Professors Select Materials for Classroom Lectures: implications for the design of digital libraries. In *Proceedings of the 4th ACM/IEEE-CS Joint Conference on Digital Libraries, Tucson, Arizona,* 179–85.

Borgman, C. L., Smart, L. J., Millwood, K. A., Finley, J. R., Champeny, L., Gilliland, A. J. and Leazer, G. H. (2005) Comparing Faculty Information Seeking in Teaching and Research: implications for the design of digital libraries, *Journal of the American Society for Information Science,* **56** (6), 636–57.

Chowdhury, G. G. (2004a) Access and Usability Issues of Scholarly Electronic Publications. In Gorman, G. E. and Rowland, F. (eds), *Scholarly Publishing in an Electronic Era: International Yearbook of Library and Information Management, 2004/2005.* Facet Publishing, 77–98.

Chowdhury, G. G. (2004b) Access to Information in Digital Libraries: users and digital divide, paper presented at the *International Conference on Digital Libraries, New Delhi, 24–27 February,* New Delhi, TERI.

Chowdhury, G. G. and Chowdhury, S. (2011) *Information Users and Usability in the Digital Age,* Facet Publishing.

Chowdhury, G., McMenemy, D. and Poulter, A. (2008) MEDLIS: Model for Evaluation of Digital Libraries and Information Services, *World Digital Libraries,* **1** (1), 35–46.

Chowdhury, S. (2012) User-centric Studies. In Dobreva, M., O'Dwyer, A. and Feliciati, P. (eds), *User Studies for Digital Library Development,* Facet Publishing, 44–52.

Chowdhury, S., Landoni, M. and Gibb, F. (2006) Usability and Impact of Digital Libraries: a review, *Online Information Review,* **30** (6), 656–80.

Covey, D. T. (2012) *Usage and Usability Assessment: library practices and concerns,* Council on Library and Information Resources, Pub105, www.clir.org/pubs/reports/pub105.

Dobreva, M. and Chowdhury, S. (2010) A User-centric Evaluation of the Europeana Digital Library. In Chowdhury, G., Khoo, C. and Hunter, J. (eds), *The Role of Digital Libraries in a Time of Global Change, 12th International Conference on Asia-Pacific Digital Libraries, ICADL 2010, Gold Coast, Australia, June 21–25, 2010,* 148–57.

Dobreva, M., O'Dwyer, A. and Feliciati, P. (2012) *User Studies for Digital Library Development*, Facet Publishing.

Enlighten (2012) Research Publications by Members of the University of Glasgow, http://eprints.gla.ac.uk/.

Europeana, www.europeana.eu/portal/.

Gunter, B., Rowlands, I. and Nicholas, D. (2009) *The Google Generation: are ICT innovations changing information-seeking behaviour?*, Chandos Publishing

Hearst, M. (2009) *Search User Interfaces*, Cambridge University Press.

ISO (1998) ISO 9241-11:1998. *Ergonomic Requirements for Office Work with Visual Display Terminals (VDTs) – Part 11: Guidance on usability*, International Organization for Standardization.

ISO (2010) 9241-210:2010, *Ergonomics of Human–System Interaction – Part 210: Human-centred design for interactive systems*, International Organization for Standardization.

Kuniavsky, M. (2003) *Observing the User Experience: a practitioner's guide to user research*, Morgan Kaufmann.

Liew, C. L. (2005) Cross-cultural Design and Usability of a Digital Library Supporting Access to Máori Cultural Heritage Resources. In Theng, Y.-L. and Foo, S. (eds), *Design and Usability of Digital libraries: case studies in the Asia-Pacific*, Information Science Publishing, 284–97.

Mossberger, K., Tolbert, C. J. and Stansbury, M. (2003) *Virtual Inequality: beyond the digital divide*, Georgetown University Press.

NCSTRL, www.ncstrl.org/.

NDLTD, www.ndltd.org/.

Nielsen, J. (2003) *Usability 101: introduction to usability*, www.useit.com/alertbox/20030825.html.

Nielsen, J. (2006) Digital Divide: the three stages, *Jakob Nielsen's Alertbox*, www.useit.com/alertbox/digital-divide.html.

Norris, P. (2001) *Digital Divide: civic engagement, information poverty, and the internet worldwide*, Cambridge University Press.

Pinto, M. and Sales, D. (2007) A Research Case Study for User-centred Information Literacy Instruction: information behaviour of translation trainees, *Journal of Information Science*, **33** (5), 531–50.

PubMed.gov, www.ncbi.nlm.nih.gov/pubmed/.

Rowlands, I., Nicholas, D., Williams, P., Huntington, P. and Fieldhouse, M. (2008) The Google Generation: the information behaviour of the researcher of the future, *Aslib Proceedings: New Information Perspectives*, **60** (4), 209–310.

Selwyn, N. (2009) The Digital Native: myth and reality, *Aslib Proceedings: New Information Perspectives*, **61** (4), 364–79.

Shneiderman, B. and Plaisant, C. (2010) *Designing the User Interface: strategies for effective human–computer interaction*, 5th edn, Addison-Wesley.

Skykes, J., Dobreva, M., Birrell, D., McCulloch, E., Ruthven, I., Ünal, Y. and Feliciati, P. (2010) Focus on End Users: eye-tracking analysis for digital libraries. In Lalmas, M., Jose, J. M., Rauber, A., Sebastiani, F. and Frommholz, I. (eds), *Research and Advanced Technology for*

Digital Libraries: 14th European Digital Library Conference, Glasgow, September 14–16, Lecture Notes in Computer Science, 6273, 510–13.

Strathprints (2012) The University of Strathclyde Institutional Repository, http://strathprints.strath.ac.uk/.

CHAPTER 13

Intellectual property and digital libraries

Michael Fraser

Introduction

In recent years, there has been an increased use of the internet to search, gather and retrieve data and creative content. The shift to digital libraries has greatly impacted on the way people use physical libraries and the way libraries must collect, store and make information and content available to clients. After 20 years of journal subscription-price increases, the traditional commercial publishing model for academic research output is no longer financially sustainable on the same scale and new forms of scholarly communication and open access are becoming integral elements of library collection development activities (Rasmussen, 2009). Underlying these developments in digital libraries is the need to develop an economically sustainable library business model – as library budgets continue to be strained, particularly in the wake of the global financial crisis – while respecting and implementing the copyright entitlements of authors and publishers. This chapter proposes such a model.

The Big Deals

The introduction of publishers' so-called 'Big Deals' (discussed in more detail later in this chapter) in the 1990s, where libraries throughout the world started forming multiple coalitions to negotiate purchases collectively with big publishers, was an initial attempt to adapt to the new world of online publishing (PCG – Publishers Communication Group, 2011). Under the Big Deal system, many university and research libraries combined in groups to buy a single 'all-you-can eat' subscription for a set fee and for a set period, most commonly three years (Poynder, 2011). The fees were, and still are, usually based on the cost of the member institutions' historical print subscriptions. Under this system, universities started purchasing their subscriptions from large publishers in the form of bundled site licences, which allow electronic access to most of a publisher's subscription list at a price that depends on historical expenditure on print journals from that publisher. A publisher might supply a whole list for the price of the sum of the original print subscriptions of a library consortium, with an electronic premium added – generally in the range of between 5% and 15% – with a built-in percentage increase of around 6% per annum (Poynder, 2011). But while bundling electronic journals with print subscriptions provides researchers with extra access to journals, many librarians now find the long-term contract lock-ins inflexible. Elsevier, for one, provides a five-year package. Librarians have struggled with the sustained price increases of print subscriptions (Pool, 2010) and this has led to the gradual demise of the Big Deal.

One of the questions which publishers' site licences have raised is whether the terms and conditions of the licence entered into by a library negate the exceptions in copyright law or whether the statutory exceptions override the terms and conditions of the site licences. For example, in Australia, sections 49, 50 and 51A of the Copyright Act provide statutory exceptions for certain library copying and communication of books and journal articles. Section 49 provides exceptions for the reproduction and communication of works by libraries and archives for users. Section 50 provides exceptions for the reproduction and communication of works by libraries or archives for other libraries or archives. Section 51A provides exceptions for the reproduction and communication of works for preservation and other purposes. There is a debate over whether the conditions of publishers' contracts under site licences displace the free exceptions under the statute, or whether the statutory exceptions override any contract between the publishers and the libraries. The answer to this question will affect the extent to which the libraries are able to exploit the use of the materials purchased under the licences and will affect the value of the licence contracts to both libraries and publishers.

Open access

In light of the controversy over the Big Deals, the open access system was introduced by some libraries and institutions as a means of alleviating financial pressure on libraries. As also discussed in Chapter 10, open access offered a new model for dissemination of 'royalty free' information, defined as information produced by scholars without expectation of payment for the copyright use of their works (Epstein, 2008). Ultimately, the Open Access Initiative aims to make all journal articles freely available over the public internet without financial, legal or technical barriers. A reader is permitted to read, download, copy, distribute, print, search or link to the full texts of these articles, crawl them for indexing, pass them as data to software or use them for any other lawful purpose (Open Society Foundations, 2002),

But, in spite of the intentions of the open access system, budgetary constraints and funding continue to be a concern. Even though content under the open access system may be free to readers, libraries still have to cover the cost of maintaining the system. As also discussed in Chapter 10, the dependence of the open access system on author contributions and institutional funding has brought its long-term sustainability into question. Because the open access pricing model depends significantly on the funds made available through grants and university 'memberships', if granting bodies do not widely allocate enough money to cover system and publication costs, prices for publication will have to rise or other sources of revenue will have to be found (Chesler, 2004).

To ensure that the financial burden of the Open Access Archive does not fall once again on libraries, in the absence of government and university subsidies, other possible sources of revenue for libraries as open access publishers have been debated in the literature for many years. Increased submission fees for authors, university membership fees, pay-per-view charges, sponsorships and advertising have all been considered as alternatives for funding the Open Access Archive (Chesler, 2004). But there is another alternative to the open access publishing model which would be financially sustainable while maintaining a quality standard of content. A self-funding copyright registry of works with a market-based model of operation would provide direct access to works and the rights to reuse and repurpose them. The registry would enable a real metric of actual usages of the works, both the initial access and the downstream uses, which would provide both the author and the author's educational institution with the option of receiving remuneration, at a low transaction cost. The real metric of actual usages of the works would also allow the most-used material to rise to notice. Beginning with a discussion of the copyright framework and how, in some cases, it restricts easy access to and use of information in this digital age, this chapter describes the features of a digital copyright registry system and discusses how it could facilitate easy and lawful access to digital information.

Copyright framework

In this chapter the Australian Copyright Act has been chosen as a case study to discuss some of the inherent weaknesses of the copyright laws in meeting the demands of today's digital world. The Australian Copyright Act 1968 takes a public policy-based approach to copyright and a purposive approach to library exceptions. The Berne Convention stipulates that national parliaments are permitted to legislate for exceptions to copyright, provided that exceptions are limited to certain special cases that do not conflict with the normal exploitation of a work and do not unreasonably prejudice the legitimate interests of the rights holder (the 'three step test').

As noted above, the Australian Copyright Act contains exceptions to copyright in sections 49, 50 and 51A specifically for libraries. Under section 49 a library may copy text for clients who have requested it in writing and signed a declaration that they require it for research or study. Under section 50 a library can make a replacement copy of an item in its collection that has been lost, stolen or damaged, if a replacement copy is not available to buy. Under section 51A a library can copy a published, written, artistic or musical work in its collection for the preservation of that work. Section 51A of the Act allows digitizing of some material for preservation purposes and allows its use internally for library staff in limited circumstances, but this provision is rarely relied upon by libraries for digitization activities because of its complexity and narrow scope (Smith, 2002).

The 'flexible dealing' exception in section 200AB of the Australian Copyright Act applies to libraries, archives and educational institutions as well as to people and institutions assisting people with a disability. It can be used where the proposed use of the material falls outside the other specific exceptions for libraries or exceptions such as fair dealing for the purposes of research. The requirements for using the flexible dealing provision are that the use is a special case, no other exceptions apply, the use is non-commercial, the use will not prejudice the copyright holder and the use will not compete with or take profit from the copyright holder (Australian Digital Alliance, 2008).

Those in favour of the library exceptions under the Australian Copyright Act argue that libraries are simply doing what they've always done but have adapted to a digital context by making books and other works available for use by the public and promoting freedom of information by using digital technology. While there is a consensus that libraries should enjoy the benefit of exceptions for preservation purposes under section 51A, those opposed to the other library copyright exceptions believe that these provisions deny copyright owners their financial due for the copying and communication of their works. They argue that the copyright owner should be remunerated by libraries because libraries using these sections are, in effect, information brokers competing directly with copyright owners and other commercial content services. Some opponents of the library exceptions argue that if the exceptions are to be maintained so that libraries can copy for clients without permission of the copyright owners, then those exceptions should not permit free copying and communication; rather, the library exceptions should be remunerable, allowing libraries the benefit of the exception in that they may copy, but requiring them to pay equitable remuneration to the rights owners for the copying and communication they do under the exception.

Many authors and publishers believe that the current copyright laws do not effectively protect their intellectual property rights, and publishers have turned to licensing in order to protect their interests (Bosch, 2005). Libraries, on the other hand, support the system because they see it as analogous to the role libraries have always played in providing access to information in the library, but now making use of digital technologies. But although it was hoped that the licensing process would resolve the copyright issues faced by libraries and copyright owners, the shift to licences has heralded significant difficulties.

Licensing and the Big Deal

A significant problem for libraries under the publishers' licence system has been the way in which electronic journal access rights are managed under the business models of large journal publishers. Each publisher sells access to its electronic journals under licences and each licence may have different terms and conditions for use. Ensuring compliance with differing and complex licence terms has proved to be a formidable compliance challenge for libraries. In many cases libraries cannot employ in-house lawyers to provide advice to staff in order to construe the varying terms and conditions of publishers' licences (De Matteo, 2008). In the latter part of the 1990s, efforts were made to bring some standards and structures to the licensing process, which led to the introduction of more standard licence agreements (Bosch, 2005).

Adding to the burden of complex licensing arrangements has been the considerable expense of digital resources. Libraries felt that the expense of building digital repositories threatened their financial viability (Taylor-Roe, 2009). The 1993 Follett Report suggested that the inability of library budgets to keep pace with the escalation in journal prices posed a serious threat to future academic research (Taylor-Roe, 2009), and libraries claim that there were signs of market failure arising from the exercise of market power by a small group of journal-publishing giants. Three firms that dominated the sector – Reed Elsevier, Springer-Kluwer and Wily-Blackwell (McGuigan and Russell, 2008) – increased their prices for electronic journal subscriptions at a rate above the rate of inflation. The publishers' proposition was that libraries acquire both print and online versions and bundled subscriptions. Libraries complained that they were obliged to acquire less popular journals in order to gain access to flagship titles (De Matteo, 2008). Bundling deals in Australia are often based on multi-year contracts which do not allow for cancellation of any titles, and non-disclosure agreements prevent libraries from discussing the terms of the deals (Burrows, 2006).

These concerns have led to considerable tension between libraries and publishers. In an effort to increase their bargaining power and resolve the 'serials crisis', in the late 1990s libraries worldwide began dealing collectively with publishers under a purchasing model known as the Big Deal. Major research libraries in both Australia and the UK adopted the Big Deal approach in the early 2000s (Jump, 2011). The underlying rationale of the Big Deal is that, by paying a little more, libraries can get a lot more. Under the Big Deal, a group of libraries are able to bargain and contract collectively with a publisher to receive all, or a substantial portion of, a publisher's titles in electronic format. By bargaining collectively and agreeing to purchase large bundles of titles, libraries have been able to buy more digital works for less money (Kohl and Sanville, 2006).

The Big Deal has quickly become the overwhelmingly preferred mode of journal purchase for libraries worldwide (Kohl and Sanville, 2006) and this initiative has had a major impact on the size of journal collections in academic libraries, with many journal collections effectively doubling in size shortly after the late 1990s (Taylor-Roe, 2009). But, over time, doubts have emerged about the long-term sustainability of the Big Deal concept (Taylor-Roe, 2009). Publishers have continued to substantially increase the Big Deal fees over the years, at a rate regarded unreasonable by many libraries. A 2009 online survey of academic librarians in the UK higher education and research libraries community, conducted by Newcastle University, found that 41.9% of library respondents indicated that Big Deals consumed 26–50% of their library serials budget, and 38.7% of libraries said that Big Deals consumed more than half of their serials budget. This same study also indicated that 50% of respondents were less happy with these deals and 37% had either cancelled deals altogether or downgraded to smaller subsets of content (Powell, 2011).

In 2011, Research Libraries UK informed the publishers Elsevier and Wiley-Blackwell that they would not renew these deals unless there were significant real-terms price reductions (Jump, 2011). Because Big Deal agreements with publishers also usually extend over a number of years, librarians' ability to adapt their journal collections to match the changing information needs of their customer base is inhibited. Similarly, what some librarians regard as the forced indiscriminate bulk purchases of whole portions of publishers' collections that underpin the Big Deal leave little room for strategic or quality-controlled journal acquisition (Taylor-Roe, 2009).

Generally, libraries prefer to choose journal titles the old-fashioned way – year by year, title by title, based on the value of the content rather than the size of the package (Mitchell and Lorbeer, 2009). There has been a push for more flexible purchasing options, with the ability to exclude content and reduce costs and a pricing model for electronic content that does not rely on historical spending patterns (Taylor-Roe, 2009). But funding and budgetary constraints have remained a concern. The internet-based open access approach to disseminating scholarly works was introduced as a possible solution to this problem.

A new alternative: the Open Access Archive

As discussed in Chapter 10, interest in open access publishing gained support in the 1990s as the potential for the rapidly expanding internet to deliver information instantaneously to anyone with a computer and a network connection was realized. Open access journals are digital, online and free of any direct charge to readers. There are no price barriers to access, such as fees for subscriptions, licences or pay-per-view. While authors must be properly acknowledged and cited, most copyright and licensing restrictions are waived, permitting users to read, download, copy, distribute, print, search or link to the full texts of articles (Epstein, 2008). In other words, the rights holder's licence sets the value of the licence for access to the work at nought.

The Open Access Archive, defined as 'peer-reviewed journals whose content is made freely available on the internet upon publication for use by anyone anywhere for any purpose as long as the authors are properly acknowledged' (McGuigan and Russell, 2008), has aimed to make all journals freely available on the public internet without financial, legal or technical barriers (Open Society Foundations, 2002). Authors can achieve open access either by self-archiving their articles on the web or by publishing in an open access journal. Open access journals may themselves adopt a model of delayed open access, partial (or hybrid) open access or full and immediate open access (Morris, 2004).The archive is intended to be a cost-free alternative to academic journals supplied by publishers (Open Society Foundations, 2002). The reader is permitted to read, download, copy, distribute, print, search or link to the full texts of these articles, crawl them for indexing, pass them as data to software, or use them for any other lawful purpose (Open Society Foundations, 2002). Because price is perceived as a barrier to access, the Open Access Archive does not charge subscription or access fees, and costs are instead covered in other ways, ranging from 'author pays' models to subsidies from government grants or sponsoring institutions (McGuigan and Russell, 2008).

Open access has been readily adopted by tertiary education libraries and has quickly evolved into an international movement with active individuals, organizations and institutions (Franklin, 2003). Supporters of the scheme point to greater access to scholarly literature, faster dissemination of new knowledge, greater research impact and increased citation rates. A new movement has developed to network the archives managed by individual institutions, which are usually universities. However, despite widespread support, the Open Access Initiative remains unproven. Institutional repositories of open access material are comparatively new (Creaser et al., 2010) and author charges as a way of paying for scholarly communications have yet to be proven as a business model that truly reduces cost. The literature contains stories where costs in the author-pays model exceed current expenditures, and if the open access model does not reduce overall costs it does not fix the problem (Roberts, 2003). Moreover, open access does not reward writers and other creators of creative content or remunerate them for their creations via royalties (especially, those who aren't salaried) and this removes market incentives for authors and limits the range of authorship.

It was hoped by its proponents that the introduction of the open access system would solve the library funding crisis and that free journals would alleviate the pressure on library budgets. But there is an increasing gap between the amount of research information being published and libraries' ability to buy materials (Morris, 2004). In fact, 2011 data shows that the size of the gap between library funding and budgets and the cost of acquiring scholarly information for libraries has increased since the economic crisis beginning in 2008 (Powell, 2011). Although profit has been removed from the open access model significant costs are still required for the distribution of scholarly works (Bosch, 2005). Critics argue that the economics underpinning the model are flawed. For example, in cases where the author is charged a fee to place his or her work in the Open Access Archive, critics agree that it is fairer for an author to be remunerated for providing his work to the public. Some question also remains about the sustainability of the model's reliance on government funding, university project funding, grants, research funds and membership fees or, for that matter, author fees (De Matteo, 2008).

A further criticism is that because the system depends on ongoing funding, either from university funds or by sponsors, the government or the authors themselves, this compromises libraries' ability to make impartial, quality-controlled decisions in the selection of material for inclusion in the archive. It has been argued that the Open Access Archive may never be able to equal the stringent quality controls of most published academic journals. Each academic discipline generally attracts an established hierarchy of journals. A researcher on a given topic will often prejudge the importance of an article by the quality of the journal in which it is published. The absence of this informal hierarchy from open access may leave a researcher adrift in a sea of content without any real signpost to each article's quality or significance (Franklin, 2003).

Even where administrators of the Open Access Archive attempt to replicate the quality-selection role performed by publishers, the impartiality of the editor who selects and culls materials for a well regarded journal is lost under the influence of the author-pays or sponsorship models on which libraries are often reliant for financial support. The open access initiative has made the relationship between academic, open access publisher and library co-dependent, which may compromise the process of truly impartial selection and rigorous exclusion of materials by open archive librarians. The content available on the Open Access Archive is not driven by consumer demand and does not respond to market signals from readers.

Copyright registry: a viable solution

There are two primary problems with the current open access system. First, libraries continue to struggle financially under the open access scheme, and a more economically sustainable model for library access to digital works is required, especially as we move into the digital era. Second, critics often argue that quality control is not central to open access, and this is likely to become a bigger problem over time. Administrators may come to accept an increasing number of articles into the Open Access Archive in order to secure enough revenue to sustain the open access business model, diluting the overall quality of the material published and diminishing the value of the peer-review process (Chesler, 2004).

Chowdhury and Fraser have proposed a new business model for access to journal materials in libraries – the introduction of a national copyright registry (Chowdhury, 2009; Chowdhury and Fraser, 2011). A copyright registry would go a long way towards solving these difficulties, as well as having other benefits. The registry would hold content metadata linked to content held anywhere online and would enable access to content and the rights to reuse it. The long-term sustainability problem of the Open Access Archive would be resolved through the registry's built-in payment system, which would recover transaction costs, making the registry self-sustaining. The issues of quality control arising from the open access business model would be addressed through the registry's market-based model for operation, allowing the most sought-after and most reused quality material to be clearly identified. The registry would provide a proportional financial return to the author and to the author's institution or publisher where they applied a fee. Authors, institutions and publishers who chose to set a fee for use could receive remuneration for the use of their works according to usage, rather than having to pay simply to have their work included in an Open Access Archive.

To facilitate the smooth access to works via the proposed registry, content identifier and rights transaction metadata would be registered, and prices and conditions for buying the content and for the rights would be embedded in the metadata. Those who chose to set the price for their works at nought could of course do so. The matching linked metadata would also be embedded in the content itself, so that the content, which is stored anywhere, could be accessed online directly through the registry. The metadata in the registry would be active, enabling access to the online content and also enabling transactions for downloading and reusing the content, including transactions for free content. The registry would give consumers direct access to heterogeneous online content for downloading with the rights that consumers need to reuse, repurpose and super-distribute the content. It would allow consumers to search and download content and granular segments of content online, and to acquire the rights to copy and transmit the content, in a single online transaction.

Recent library studies have shown that content-enriched metadata contributes overall to higher circulation rates for serials and so, through the use of metadata, the registry would be facilitating the increased use of journals (Tosaka and Weng, 2011). The registry would therefore benefit all parties: publishers, by facilitating the use of and access to their content and a payment to the publisher for the use of its works; authors, through proportionate financial remuneration for the use of their works and by direct financial remuneration for use where they chose to self-publish through the capital registry; libraries, by generating cost-recovery revenue and creating a quality-controlled archive that included metrics of actual use; and consumers, by establishing a self-sustaining resource of content and making the most sought-after content readily available in response to consumer demand.

There would be several secondary advantages of the introduction of a copyright registry. Presently, academics are dependent on the citation of their articles as evidence of their research. However, library studies show that only a proportion of all the journal articles that are published are accessed. It is estimated that 5% of journals account for 40% of journal subscription use and that only 10% of papers are now available on open access (Poynder, 2011). The registry would measure actual access and downstream reuse transacted through the registry, giving a far better indicator of the usage of an article and the impact of an author's work. This would improve the way academic works are assessed and measured by academic institutions and academics.

There would also be a financial benefit to libraries associated with the introduction of the registry. First, from a budgetary perspective, purchasing journals under the Big Deal reduces the budgets of libraries and institutions to a handful of large, fixed-block expenditures, undermining budget flexibility. A large institution can expect to pay several million dollars for a Big Deal licence, and so Big Deals can quickly consume most of the serials budget of a library or other institution. Big Deals consume a large percentage of the total library materials budget, and often the purchase of books and monographs suffers because moneys have to be prioritized for journals. As library budgets have fallen relatively, and journal prices have risen, the problem has become increasingly serious. In early 2011 *The Economist* reported that 65% of the money spent on content in academic libraries now goes on journals, 'up from a little more than half ten years ago' (Poynder, 2011). The Registry can help library managers spend their budget smore appropriately, based on actual use of information.

Second, the actual cost of just keeping physical journals on shelves and maintaining physical library premises is significant. Libraries spend billions every year building, curating and maintaining their collections. A 1999 analysis based on Association of Research Libraries statistics found that a library's non-subscription operational costs are on average double its subscription costs, and this is without taking into account the considerable costs associated with constructing and maintaining library buildings – a factor which would lead to a higher estimate of non-subscription costs (Montgomery, 2000). Maintaining physical libraries requires a significant outlay in operating expenses and administrative overheads such as telecommunications charges, staff salaries, council rates, furniture and office equipment, insurance, rent, energy and cleaning. Library space costs alone account for 80% of the expense of providing bound journals collections (Montgomery, 2000). For example, the US library system costs $12 billion a year, and only $3–4 billion of that is spent directly on publishers' products (Open Content Alliance, 2011).

Electronic journals minimize the need for physical infrastructure and provide a cost-effective, immediate means of providing access to library users. A 2003 study by the University of California Berkeley established that if electronic access to journals is the primary method of access provided by a library, there is a potential cost saving to the university system as a whole (Cooper, 2003). An earlier, 2002, study found that the operational cost of housing bound journals in a university library was $205,000 a year – $245,000 if unbound journals were included – compared with just $5000 for electronic journals. A more recent JISC-funded study noted that the cost of book publishing in print is £15,750 per title, for e-only format the publishing cost is around £11,320 per title and for open access around £7380 per title. In other words, the cost of books in the open access digital library model would be less than half that of their printed counterparts. This study (Houghton et al., 2009) also shows that in a UK HEI (higher education institution) library, annual book handling costs are £90 per title for print and £28 per title for e-books and that, at this rate, book handling costs in UK HEIs during 2006–7 would have been around £360 million, had they all been print acquisitions, and £112 million had they all been e-books. The physical handling costs for bound journals, such as binding, labelling and reshelving, were $22,000 for bound journals, while electronic journals incurred none of these expenses. While electronic journals attracted other operational costs, the final analysis showed that the annual operational costs for bound journal collections totalled $258,000, as compared with just $138,000 for electronic journal collections (Montgomery, 2000).

The proposed copyright registry, by providing an interoperable infrastructure across all works to make the works and rights transactions available online, would significantly reduce distribution and transaction costs for content and rights.

Summary

As Stephen A. Roberts has observed, library funding has protected libraries from market rigour and shielded them from the stimulus of the market, even though sometimes it has also kept them short of revenue. If it had been otherwise, society might not have enjoyed the obvious benefits delivered by great library resources. But, he asks, can the trend be continued when the future seems to promise so much change? Libraries need to consider the variety and complexity of the new global information marketplace, where users potentially have access to not only global information content but also competing alternatives and services (Roberts, 2003).

The reality facing libraries in 2011 is much harsher than it has ever been in the last 15 years. The current global economic crisis may have originated in the USA, but the economic near-collapse of many countries has resulted and will continue to result in dramatic cuts in public spending. In the foreseeable future, many governments' education budgets, and library budgets more specifically, will either be reduced or certainly not increased. In Europe the cuts in higher education have hit a number of countries particularly badly (e.g. Ireland, the UK, Greece, Spain, Portugal), but the crisis is international. The Publisher's Communication Group estimates that budgets are unlikely ever to rise to their pre-2008 levels. The Big Deals negotiated by publishers and library consortia have become increasingly expensive over the years and decreasing library budgets will make it more difficult for institutions to afford these big purchases. Publishers need to develop a sustainable strategy in order to control their loss of revenue from libraries and this will require questioning the existing system. (PCG, 2011).

Even if the traditional open access system is still theoretically affordable, we need to consider whether the money of those who fund the increasingly expensive open access system – universities, research funders, governments and, ultimately, tax-payers – could in fact be better spent (Poynder, 2011). The introduction of a registry would reduce costs and keep library resources focused on payment for the actual use of content in a sustainable model which supported writing, publishing and affordable access in a digital network communications environment. The registry model offers a better outcome for authors, publishers, cash-strapped libraries and the tax-payer because it is self-sustaining. Under the current model tax-payers foot the bill for the authors' research and writing, the peer-reviewers and the library acquisition budget from which commercial academic publishers profit. The registry, in contrast, is a self-sustaining social infrastructure which supports libraries, rewards authors and publishers for the use of their work, and provides better access for readers.

References

Australian Digital Alliance (2008) *A User's Guide to the Flexible Dealing Provision for Libraries, Educational Institutions and Cultural Institutions*, 4–5.

Bosch, S. (2005) Licensing in Libraries: practical and ethical aspects, *Journal of Library Administration*, **42** (3/4), 65–6.

Burrows, T. (2006) Brave New World of Plus ça Change? Electronic journals and the academic library, *Australian Academic & Research Libraries*, **37** (3), 170–6.

Chesler, A. (2004) Open Access: a review of an emerging phenomenon, *Serials Review*, **30** (4), 292–7.

Chowdhury, G. G. (2009) Towards the Conceptual Model of a Content Service Network. In *Globalizing Academic Libraries Vision 2020, Proceedings of the International Conference on Academic Libraries, Delhi, Oct. 5–8, 2009*, Delhi Mittal Publications, 215–20.

Chowdhury, G. and Fraser, M. (2011) Carbon Footprint of the Knowledge Industry and Ways to Reduce It, *World Digital Libraries*, **4** (1), 9–18.

Cooper, M. D. (2003) *The Cost of Providing Electronic Journal Access and Printed Copies of Journals to University Users*, School of Information Management and Systems, University of California Berkeley.

Creaser, C., Fry, J., Greenwood, H., Oppenheim, C., Probets, S., Spezi, V. and White, S. (2010) Authors' Awareness and Attitudes toward Open Access Repositories, *New Review of Academic Librarianship*, **16** (S1), 145, 147.

De Matteo, S. (2008) Copyright, Open Access, Creative Commons: impacts on library services and budgets, *Open and Libraries Class Journal*, **1** (1), www.infosherpas.com/ojs/index.php/openandlibraries/article/view/16/27.

Epstein, B. A. (2008) Open Access: implications for evidence-based practice, *Journal of Emergency Nursing*, **34**, (6), 561.

The Follett Report (1993) *Joint Funding Council's Libraries Review Group: report*, www.ukoln.ac.uk/services/papers/follett/report/.

Franklin, J. (2003) Open Access to Scientific and Technical Information: the state of the art, *Information Service & Use*, **23** (23), 67–68.

Houghton, J., Rasmussen, B., Sheehan, P., Oppenheim, C., Morris, A., Creaser, C., Greenwood, H., Summers, M. and Gourlay, A. (2009) *Economic Implications of Alternative Scholarly Publishing Models: exploring the costs and benefits*, a JISC EI-ASPM Project report, http://eprints.vu.edu.au/15222/1/EI-ASPM_Report.pdf.

Jump, P. (2011) Libraries Reject 'Raw Deal' on E-journals, *Times Higher Education*, 18 August.

Kohl, D. and Sanville, T. (2006) More Bang for the Buck: increasing the effectiveness of library expenditures through cooperation, *Library Trends*, **54** (3), 394–410.

McGuigan, G. S. and Russell, R. D. (2008) The Business of Academic Publishing: a strategic analysis of the academic journal publishing industry and its impact on the future of scholarly publishing, *Electronic Journal of Academic and Special Librarianship*, **9** (3), http://southernlibrarianship.icaap.org/content/v09n03/mcguigan_g01.html.

Mitchell, N. and Lorbeer, E. (2009) Building Relevant and Sustainable Collections, *The Serials Librarian*, **57** (4), 4327–9.

Montgomery, C. H. (2000) Measuring the Impact of an Electronic Journal Collection on Library Costs: a framework and preliminary observations, *D-Lib Magazine*, **6** (10), www.dlib.org/dlib/october00/montgomery/10montgomery.html.

Morris, S. (2004) Open Access: how are publishers reacting?, *Serials Review*, **30** (4), 304.

Open Content Alliance (2011) *Economics of Book Digitization*, www.opencontentalliance.org/2009/03/22/economics-of-book-digitization/.

Open Society Foundations (2002) *Budapest Open Access Initiative*, www.soros.org/openaccess/read.shtml.

PCG (2011) *Library Consortia and the Big Deal: where to now?*, Publishers Communication Group, www.pcgplus.com/pdfs/15Library%20Consortia%20and%20the%20Big%20Deal.pdf.

Pool, R. (2010) Big Deal Packages Squeeze Recession-Hit Libraries, *Research Information*, www.researchinformation.info/features/feature.php?feature_id=269.

Powell, A. (2011) Times of Crisis Accelerate Inevitable Change, *Journal of Library Administration*, **51** (1), 112–13.

Poynder, R. (2011) The Big Deal: not price but cost, *Information Today*, **28** (8), 14.

Rasmussen, A. M. (2009) Library Collections in Transition: the future of books in libraries, *ICAS 6 Newsletter*, July, 11.

Roberts, S. A. (2003) Financial Management of Libraries: past trends and future prospects, *Library Trends*, Winter, 473.

Smith, N. (2002) Digital Agenda Report Card: how are libraries and the digital copyright amendments getting on year after commencement?, *Australian Academic and Research Libraries*, **33** (4), www.alia.org.au/publishing/aarl/33.4/full.text/smith.html.

Taylor-Roe, J. (2009) To Everything There is a Season: reflections on the sustainability of the 'Big Deal' in the current economic climate, *Serials*, **22**, (2), 113.

Tosaka, Y. and Weng, C. (2011) Re-examining Content-Enriched Access: its effect on usage and discovery, *College & Research Libraries*, September, 424.

CHAPTER 14

Digital preservation: interoperability *ad modum*

Milena Dobreva and Raivo Ruusalepp

Introduction

Digital preservation (DP) is defined as the set of activities which assure 'interoperability with the future' (Rusbridge at al., 2005, 1). It is a key aspect of digital libraries because, without it, future users will not be able to access the wide range of digital resources created and collected today. Not only does DP address the future, it is also a prerequisite for us today to access digital resources created in the past. From this point of view it would be more correct to define it as 'interoperability over time'.

But then one could ask, what makes digital preservation different from technical interoperability? Why should this be a separate domain in its own right? What is so special about the time dimension of interoperability that addressing it needs to be tackled as a separate research and development domain?

Being defined as 'the capability to communicate, execute programs, or transfer data among various functional units in a manner that requires the user to have little or no knowledge of the unique characteristics of those units' (ISO/IEC 1993), interoperability is a major concern within the digital library domain in a technological environment where multiple hardware and software systems and standards co-exist, and where the number of metadata schemas available is measured not in dozens, but in hundreds. Gradmann (2008) suggests that it is a multidimensional concept that can be expressed through six vectors (functionality, people, technologies, interoperational entities, information objects and multilinguality) and four abstraction levels (technical, syntactic, semantic and functional), thus forming an interoperability matrix. Where does DP fit into this matrix, or does it extend the matrix? This chapter is about digital preservation research and argues that what makes it a domain in its own right is that its primary focus is on applying interoperability *ad modum*, or in other words, advancing towards solutions that guarantee that digital objects will be rendered and used at any future point in time in ways that do not differ from their original intended uses. We believe that in the future digital preservation information systems will be a natural part of the 'fabric' of digital objects' entire lifecycle and not necessarily a separate activity, usually undertaken towards the end of that lifecycle.

The chapter starts with a review of work undertaken to date in this domain. It tracks past efforts to define research priorities for this domain. It then discusses the main driving forces that impact on digital preservation today and finally highlights new trends and future developments.

Digital preservation and its role

A very fundamental question to ask is why we need digital preservation. Let us consider some typical use cases:

Use case 1: Media failure. The curator of a small collection of digitized audio recordings based in the media studies department of a higher education institution has only one master copy of each recording. The digital files are stored on CD-ROMs dating back to 1994. When she gets a request to provide a particular file to a teacher from the department, she discovers that the CD-ROM on which this file is located cannot be read.

Use case 2: Format obsolescence. A national library has an extensive digitization programme that was implemented in the last decade. Initially files were stored in TIFF format as master copies and a PDF version was made for access, but recently a decision was taken to start using PDF/A. The digital collection manager needs to transform all images in the collection into PDF/A files so as to provide uniform access to the digital library.

These use cases are not exhaustive, but they illustrate typical situations where preservation action needs to be taken.

Let us imagine a DP system as a black box. What would such a black box do? There are different possible roles for it and places to find it. One possibility is that this box is used only when a user needs to use an older digital object and discovers that he or she cannot open it or render it properly. Ideally, the user would not need any sophisticated technical knowledge but would send the object to a 'preservation toolbox' or 'preservation doctor' and get back a fixed, usable version.

Another option is that the box is part of digital archives and repository and regularly takes care of any changes in digital objects so as to guarantee they can be used anytime by anyone.

Yet another scenario is to have DP as a part of an infrastructure service, like disk storage that computers use all the time, which automatically checks every day for potential preservation risks such as format obsolescence, loss of data or context, and recommends appropriate action when risk levels are above a fixed threshold.

These are three different scenarios. In the first case digital preservation is reactive (it is applied when a need to use an object arises), in the second it is preparatory proactive (all objects are maintained in a usable state) and in the third it is ubiquitous.

A more holistic point of view is to view DP not as a specialized system, but as an integral part of the overall digital-object lifecycle. As Julia Martin and David Coleman argued a decade ago,

> Data grows, lives, and dies, as do delivery systems. As never before, the task of keeping data alive requires frequent adaptations to and perpetual evolution of the archival system. To keep pace with technological flux, an ongoing process of selection – of media platforms, of preservation structures, of migratory patterns – is necessary to avoid data extinction. In these various ways, there is an ecological force at work.
>
> (Martin and Coleman, 2002)

Hence, there are several conceptual and technical alternatives available, some already implemented in practice, some still in the planning stages, but ultimately DP is about delivering accessible, usable and meaningful digital objects to those who want to use them. As such, DP could (and should) remain hidden from the end-users of digital objects and be a seamless service that runs 'in the background', as most interoperability tools do.

However, DP is not only about delivering objects to users and fulfilling the legal obligations of memory institutions, but now has a real economic dimension, because digital information has permeated all societal processes. Ensuring continuing accessibility of information is economically prudent across all domains where we find digital objects. The strategic role of digital preservation in the knowledge economy and e-infrastructures is explicitly stated in high-level policy documents of the European Commission (EC). In 2009, a study was commissioned by the EC in order to 'analyse the drivers for DP development, the potential socioeconomic impact of the preservation of born-digital content, and the technological, organizational, and economic conditions required for further progress of DP-related disciplines' (DPimpact, 2009). The DPimpact report emphasized:

> From a strategic point of view, the most relevant strength of DP is its potential multiplier effect on a key resource (born-digital content) for the knowledge economy.
>
> (DPimpact, 2009, 106)

This is further elaborated to 'integration of organizational policies in technological implementations', as well as 'interesting technological developments, such as more automated and scalable DP tools, increased capacity of support infrastructures, tools and procedures for addressing high volume, dynamic, volatile and short-lived content, as well as for re-using preserved content' (DPimpact, 2009: 106).

Is digital preservation domain specific?

DP is often considered in the context of particular subject areas in order to address their specific needs. The DPimpact study looked into three domains – memory institutions; scientific and research institutions; and business, companies and enterprises. It found that the memory institutions had 'very limited funding for preservation', compared with 'limited funding' in the scientific and research institutions and 'funding on project basis charged to overheads' in businesses, companies and enterprises (DPimpact, 2009: 34).) Thirteen out of 18 projects funded by the EC during 2001–11 were in the domain of memory institutions, while 12 projects were targeted for scientific institutions, 6 projects were targeted at enterprises and 6 for government organizations. However, even in the domain of memory institutions there are no ultimate solutions and the work continues (Strodl, Petrov and Rauber, 2011).

The importance of long-term preservation is also highlighted as a complementary effort to digitization; the report of the Comité des Sages (Reflection Group on bringing Europe's cultural heritage online) clearly stated the DP mandate of memory institutions (The New Renaissance, 2011, 6):

- Preservation is a key aspect in digitisation efforts. Digital preservation is also a core problem for any born digital content. The organisational, legal, technical, and financial dimensions of long term preservation of digitised and born digital material should be given due attention.
- The preservation of digitised and born digital cultural material should be the responsibility of cultural institutions – as it is now for non-digital material.
- To avoid duplication of effort by companies operating across borders and by the cultural institutions, a system could be envisaged by which any material that now needs to be deposited in several countries would only be deposited once. This system would include a workflow for passing on the copy to any institution that has a right to it under national deposit legislation.

Therefore, DP is no longer a challenging research problem for memory institutions to tackle as an additional burden, but a perceived need of modern society.

Major trends in DP research and development
What is being preserved: objects

The key challenge in preserving usability of digital content over time is overcoming technology obsolescence, but a set of other issues related to the management of collections of digital objects is also involved. Preservation is a complex activity because the complexity of digital objects is increasing and the context of use needs to be recreated. The gradual expansion of preservation to include a wider range of types of objects is presented in Figure 14.1.

Currently, complex objects and dynamic objects are the focus of research. For example, in 2011–12, JISC funded the POCOS (Preservation Of Complex Objects Symposia) project, which looked at the preservation of visualizations and simulations (see the edited collection that presents this domain, Delve et al., 2012), software art,

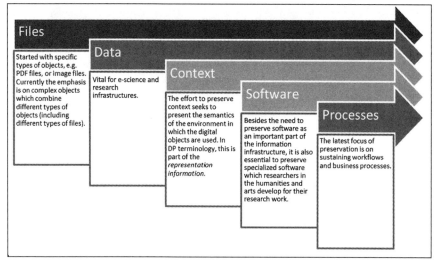

Figure 14.1 *Evolution of digital objects addressed by preservation*

and computer games and virtual worlds (collections presenting the challenges and current solutions for these domains are forthcoming at the time of this book's writing).

How to preserve: strategies

Currently, there are several strategies for sustaining the use of digital objects in the future (Figure 14.2).

The *techno-centric* strategy (see Chue Hong, 2012) aims to preserve original hardware and software in a usable state in the future. It involves regular *media renewal* in order to make sure that the physical digital objects are not corrupted.

Incremental change relies on constant migration of digital objects into new formats, so as to avoid format obsolescence. For software products this is done through emulation – which involves recreation of older software environments for newer equipment.

Analytical strategies are currently based on techniques used in computer forensics. The underlying logic for this strategy is to apply specialized methods for the recovery of objects which are in demand in the future, rather than 'mass preservation', which does not seem

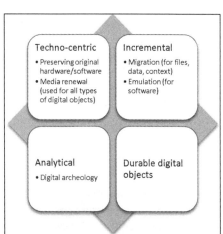

Figure 14.2
Major strategies for digital preservation

realistic, bearing in mind the volume of digital information. The pioneering work in this domain was called *digital archaeology* (see Ross and Gow, 1999) and is now continued as digital records forensics (see Digital Records Forensics Project).

Yet another strategy seeks for ways of changing the formats of the digital objects in a way that allows the objects themselves to invoke preservation actions. Such objects are called *durable digital objects* (see Gladney, 2008).

The first three strategies require rigorous organization of processes within organizations; the fourth is still under development.

It is also essential to emphasize that preservation can be divided into passive digital preservation (bit-level, taking care only of sustaining the physical object) and active digital preservation, which also takes care of preserving components of the context of use.

All the above strategies outline the principle that is applied in preservation; in practice, they are implemented through specialized lifecycles that integrate various tools and/or services.

Preservation decomposed

The diversity of digital objects and types of institutions that are responsible for their preservation means that a variety of tools are used in practice, but the underlying process could be described as universal. The pivotal standard in the domain, ISO 14721:2003 *Space Data and Information Transfer Systems – Open Archival Information System – Reference Model*, widely known as the OAIS reference model (ISO, 2003), is a functional framework that presents the main components and the basic data flows within a digital archive system. It defines six functional entities that synthesize the most essential activities within a digital archive: ingest, preservation planning, archival storage, data management, administration and access. Recently, these six stages have been combined into a smaller number of use-cases that preservation systems address. For example, a report of four major national libraries in Europe looks at three core functions – ingest, retention and access (BL, KB, DNB, NB, 2010).

The OAIS model looks at data stored in the digital archive as a fluid object that can (co-)exist as three types of information package (IP) – submission (SIP) is used to transfer data from the producer to the archive, archival (AIP) is used for archival storage and preservation, and dissemination (DIP) is used within the access function when consumers request archived materials. Table 14.1 presents a brief description of each OAIS functional entity.

As a reference model, the OAIS standard does not imply a specific design or formal method of implementation (Lavoie, 2004). Instead, it is for the repository to develop its own implementation by analysing existing business processes and matching them to OAIS functions. One of the confusing aspects for practical implementation has been the lack of active digital preservation (e.g. migration, emulation) as a separate functional entity.

Table 14.1 *Description of the OAIS functional entities*

Functional entity	Description	Functions implemented within this entity
Ingest	This entity provides the services and functions to accept SIPs from producers (or from internal elements under administration control) and prepare the contents for storage and management within the archive.	Ingest functions include receiving SIPs, performing quality assurance on SIPs, generating an AIP which complies with the archive's data formatting and documentation standards, extracting descriptive information from the SIPs for inclusion in the archive database, and co-ordinating updates to Archival Storage and Data Management.
Archival Storage	This entity provides the services and functions for the storage, maintenance and retrieval of AIPs.	Archival Storage functions include receiving AIPs from Ingest and adding them to permanent storage, managing the storage hierarchy, refreshing the media on which archive holdings are stored, performing routine and special error checking, providing disaster-recovery capabilities and providing AIPs to Access, to fulfil orders.
Data Management	This entity provides the services and functions for populating, maintaining and accessing both descriptive information, which identifies and documents archive holdings, and administrative data, used to manage the archive.	Data Management functions include administering the archive database functions (maintaining schema and view definitions, and referential integrity), performing database updates (loading new descriptive information or archive administrative data), performing queries on the Data Management data to generate result sets, and producing reports from these result sets.
Administration	This entity provides the services and functions for the overall operation of the archive system.	Administration functions include soliciting and negotiating submission agreements with producers, auditing submissions to ensure that they meet archive standards, and maintaining configuration management of system hardware and software. Administration also provides system engineering functions to monitor and improve archive operations and to inventory, report on and migrate/update the contents of the archive. It is also responsible for establishing and maintaining archive standards and policies, providing customer support and activating stored requests.

Continued on next page

Table 14.1 *Continued*

Functional entity	Description	Functions implemented within this entity
Preservation Planning	This entity provides the services and functions for monitoring the environment of the OAIS and providing recommendations to ensure that the information stored in the OAIS remains even if the original computing environment becomes obsolete.	Preservation Planning functions include evaluating the contents of the archive and periodically recommending archival information updates to migrate current archive holdings, developing recommendations for archive standards and policies, and monitoring changes in the technology environment and in the designated community's service requirements and knowledge base. Preservation Planning also designs IP templates and provides design assistance and review to specialize these templates into SIPs and AIPs for specific submissions. Preservation Planning also develops detailed migration plans, software prototypes and test plans to enable implementation of administration migration goals.
Access	This entity provides the services and functions that support consumers in determining the existence, description, location and availability of information stored in the OAIS, and allow consumers to request and receive information products.	Access functions include communicating with consumers to receive requests, applying controls to limit access to specially protected information, co-ordinating the execution of requests to successful completion, generating responses (DIPs, result sets, reports) and delivering the responses to consumers.

A number of models have been proposed that describe the lifecycle of digital preservation tasks. The pivotal standard in the domain, the OAIS reference model, presents a functional framework with main components and basic data flows within a digital archive system. It defines six functional entities which synthesize the most essential activities within a digital archive: *ingest, preservation planning, archival storage, data management, administration* and *access*. The recent DCC Digital Curation Life-Cycle Model[1] presents these core digital preservation activities in a wider context that also includes appraisal and disposal. Another variation on the composition of functional entities can be seen in the recent description of high-level preservation functions in report of four major national libraries in Europe (BL, KB, DNB, NB, 2010). The report uses three core functions – *ingest, retention* (in this context used in the sense of digital storage and associated management functions) and *access*.

The OAIS model also defines the principal structures used for the circulation of data flows within the archive. It introduces the concept of IP and makes the methodological assumption that the way data is stored in the digital archive (Archival

Information Package, AIP) is different from the way data is supplied to the archive (Submission Information Package, SIP) and accessed (Dissemination Information Package, DIP).

The nitty-gritty: digital preservation tools and services

Over the past decade, the automation of preservation functions has mainly been seen within the context of holistic software solutions that provide digital collection management as well as digital preservation tools. Digital repository software or digital archive software solutions have dominated the preservation software market while not always providing support for active digital preservation.

Since digital repository software such as EPrints, Fedora and DSpace have been available as open source, it has become very popular, especially for research libraries as 'institutional repositories'. Commercial software developers, such as IBM, Tessella, ExLibris and others, have developed dedicated software systems for digital archive management. Nowadays Fedora and DSpace collaborate to develop active DP functionality in their systems (see www.duraspace.org).

The Preserv2 project commented that 'the market for preservation services for repositories is undeveloped, and is unlikely to be developed until repositories establish clearer requirements, policy frameworks and budgets' (Hitchcock, 2009, 18). Thus the first recommendation of the project was: 'Promote a joint approach to repository preservation by repositories and preservation organisations and specialists' (Hitchcock, 2009, 19).

In the repository context, the software tools are for managing the whole digital archive and workflows within it. Most often, they do not include tools for active digital preservation (although they successfully manage passive digital preservation) and they expect these activities (e.g. file format migration, or emulation) to happen outside their system environment. This has prompted the development of software tools and services that explicitly address active digital preservation and its surrounding archive functions.

The existing systems, tools and their services were mapped to six entities of the OAIS functional model in 2007 in a European research project called CASPAR, in order to analyse how well the OAIS concepts were implemented in practice. Table 14.2 shows the number of systems, projects and tools studied by the CASPAR project (CASPAR, 2007), which analysed 34 preservation systems, repositories, project efforts and studies. Eleven of these systems had a specific focus on preservation, 14 provided preservation functionality as part of their solution, and 9 included tools/standards which could be implemented in the preservation domain but were not created especially to be used in it and that have components matching OAIS functional entities (note that the administration functional entity was excluded from analysis). The low number of preservation-specific solutions that implement OAIS functional entities is evident.

Table 14.2 Coverage of OAIS functional entities in digital archive systems

OAIS functional entity	Specific focus on preservation	Preservation by implication	Other
Ingest	3	3	0
Archival Storage	2	7	0
Data Management	0	4	0
Preservation Planning	5	6	0
Access	0	3	4
Totals	11	14	9

Note: The table presents the absolute number of systems (out of 34 systems analysed in total) which provide support for the various functional entities. The numbers do not add up to 34 because the options/features are not mutually exclusive.

Preservation planning was the most popular functional entity in the designated preservation applications; archival storage and preservation planning are the most popular OAIS functional entities within the systems that include preservation by implication.

A range of independent software tools has been developed in recent years to support individual preservation tasks. Digital preservation is implemented through complex procedures; breaking these lifecycle processes down into smaller, manageable tasks is one of the rationales for providing services that address a clear issue and solve it in an efficient way. This approach has become particularly relevant in distributed environments (like e-infrastructures) and also for smaller institutions or projects that do not have the capacity to develop bespoke solutions covering all preservation functions. Specialized services can also be integrated into in-house preservation systems where they can help to resolve a granular issue without compromising any of the primary functions of the preservation system.

Preservation services

Lately, we have witnessed a growing interest in the development of preservation services.

'Services' is a term with different contexts of use and has lately become very popular through the service-oriented architecture (SOA) concept. It is also used to refer to larger sets of consultancy-led activities. For example, in 2005 the Digital Preservation Coalition in the UK published the second edition of its directory of digital preservation repositories and services in the UK (Simpson, 2005), which features 6 archives, 11 data services, 6 deposit libraries, 4 libraries, 1 research centre, 5 research councils, 3 private sector data services and 4 companies active in consultancy and development. Gartner Research has offered a definition of an IT service that is widely used:

IT services refer to the application of business and technical expertise to enable organizations in the creation, management, optimization or access to information and business processes.

(Gartner Glossary)

It is difficult to find DP services that fully comply with this definition; one possible explanation is that acknowledgement of the business case for digital preservation is still in its infancy.

An approach that emerged a few years ago and represents a step away from integrated digital archive systems is to use *microservices*. These allow the flexible combination of specialized solutions for preservation, depending on the requirements of the institution. They are defined as follows by the UC Curation Center/California Digital Library (2010):

> Micro-services are an approach to digital curation based on devolving curation function into a set of independent, but interoperable, services that embody curation values and strategies. Since each of the services is small and self-contained, they are collectively easier to develop, deploy, maintain, and enhance. Equally as important, they are more easily replaced when they have outlived their usefulness. Although the individual services are narrowly scoped, the complex function needed for effective curation emerges from the strategic combination of individual services.

Microservices for digital preservation are currently under development at the California Digital Library (Merritt repository) (see Abrams, Kunze and Loy, 2010), for the Electronic Records Archives at the US National Archives, using iRODS (see Rajasekar et al., 2010, 60), and are also used in the open archival information system Archivematica (see web references).

The debate on the applicability of this approach is ongoing, for example (Challis, 2010):

> I'm not convinced the specs for these are well defined enough for general purpose use yet, but I can see the technique in general being very useful. If the same microservices can be called through multiple interfaces (command line, REST, etc.), then it should in theory make them language agnostic.

Work continues on the thorough breakdown and analysis of what constitutes a microservice and how various microservices can be orchestrated so that the major requirements for authenticity and integrity of preserved digital objects are not compromised. Further work is needed on elucidating the granularity and the requirements for various microservices, but the trend that is emerging from this is that workflow-based and microservices-based approaches could offer more flexible digital preservation solutions.

Preservation tools

In the overall landscape of digital preservation solutions, we could argue that services are currently an experimental area. In a rapid desk research and analysis of current offering, 190 software tools and services were identified. These are typically used in different preservation environments, but it is clear that they are used for an atomic task or a set of tasks. However, it was not always possible to determine whether they meet the criteria for being a service. Atomic tools can easily be developed into services, and for this reason the study also looked at tools that solve a clearly identified problem. The conceptual overlap between tools and services is also clearly demonstrated in recent overviews of digital preservation services. Managers of several projects or initiatives started to compile lists of useful digital preservation tools:

- A survey of the CAIRO project, which aimed 'to bring together existing tools in a documented, automated, integrated workflow, to produce repository-independent metadata packages, in the form of METS files, that could provide the basis for long term life cycle management' (Thomas et al., 2007), identified 54 tools under 15 categories, featuring identifier creator, metadata extractor, digital signature creator, format identifier, as well as very generic tools such as antivirus software.
- The National Digital Infrastructure Preservation Program (NDIPP) in the USA lists a collection of 38 tools and services that were used and/or developed by their partner institutions (NDIPP).
- The US Library of Congress lists ten tools for preservation metadata implementation supporting PREMIS (PREservation Metadata: Implementation Strategies).
- A mashup experiment organized by the AQuA (Automating Quality Assurance) project compared 44 tools and services to automatically detect quality issues in digitized collections both for ingest and checking the status of stored objects (see AQuA project).
- The blogs of the OpenPlanetsFoundation (OPF) are a valuable source of information on tools and services that are currently being developed and tested. Eight tools discovered on the OPF web pages were included in this study.
- The DigiBIC project offers a platform for presenting tools developed by EC-funded research and development projects in the field of digital libraries and content which could be exploited by research centres and small and medium-sized creative businesses. Thus far, the portal lists some 30 tools, five of which are preservation-related and appear under the 'Archives/Metadata/Search' heading (see DigiBIC).
- SourceForge offers a platform for publishing, searching and downloading open source software. A search for the terms 'preservation', 'ingest' and 'web archiving' returned 81 tools in all, which were downloaded 2450 times during one week (11–18 November 2011). This demonstrates a significant interest in open

software tools; downloads were made from virtually everywhere in the world excluding African countries. SourceForge was also the source that provided the highest number of tools for this analysis (see SourceForge).

The total number of tools covered by these sources is 249, but with some tools repeated across the sources, the number of different individual tools is 190. The most popular tools are DROID (Digital Record Object IDentification) and JHOVE (JSTOR/Harvard Object Validation Environment) – both mentioned in four sources.

The overall picture shows an abundance of tools and services, but there is a significant difference in the decomposition of digital preservation processes into services. For example, the service can be for digital preservation, but also specific to a particular institutional repository (e.g. the TIAMAT ingest service for the Tufts Digital Repository (Kumar, Kaplan and Rubinger, 2008)); or the service can be a global monitoring tool, like the PEPRS (Piloting an E-journals Preservation Registry Service), which maintains a registry of electronic articles and tracks if there is a preservation system where the electronic publications are deposited (Burnhill and Guy, 2010).

The distribution of identified tools and services shows that most of them deal with very practical tasks. The most popular type of tool is related to metadata, since tools for metadata extraction are used during pre-ingest and ingest, but are not per se preservation tools. Digital object analysis is part of ingest and preservation planning. Web archiving is a popular digital preservation domain at the moment.

What does this abundance of tools mean in practical terms? The fact that so many have been developed highlights that institutions that have development capacity tend to produce their own tools, fine-tuned to specific requirements and conditions. What need to be developed further are objective metrics that allow the comparison of tools in a transparent and easy-to-understand manner – this will help all those institutions that are looking for suitable solutions to make informed decisions about which tool from a particular category would be the most useful.

How digital preservation integrates with e-infrastructures

In recent years, significant attention has been paid to the development of technological and research e-infrastructures (or cyberinfrastructures, as they are called in the USA). Such infrastructures provide facilities, resources and related services in a particular domain. The fact that they provide access to resources means that they need to address the preservation aspect – in addition, the services they provide also need to be preserved because, without this, future users would not be able to understand or re-create the uses of those infrastructures.

Digital preservation has also been assessed lately from the point of view of research infrastructures. A quick survey of e-infrastructures in the arts and humanities shows that there is a clearly expressed interest in the preservation and curation of research data (see websites listed at end of chapter). For example, long-term preservation is recognized as an essential aspect of DARIAH (Digital Research Infrastructure for the Arts and Humanities; Willemse, 2007), which so far has published policies on institutional repositories and on collection ingest, management and preservation. The focus of the latter policy is expressed as follows: 'DARIAH's mission is to foster and support high quality digital research in arts and humanities. Part of this remit involves promotion of the importance of sustaining and preserving data for future use, so that scholars can benefit from and build upon earlier work in their field' (DARIAH, 2010).

TextGrid, a German research infrastructure aiming 'to support access to and exchange of data in the arts and humanities by means of modern information technology (the grid)' (see TextGrid) is part of DARIAH. The project released TextGrid v. 1.0 in September 2011 after five years of development. The architecture of TextGird is a three-layer service implemented on grid storage. Another major e-infrastructure for the humanities, CLARIN (Common Language Resources and Technology Infrastructure), issued a short guide on long-term preservation (see CLARIN).

Not all networks and consortia in the humanities and arts digital domain address preservation issues. For example, the recently started ESF (European Science Foundation)-funded project Network for Digital Methods in the Arts and Humanities (NEDIMAH) is focusing on new research methods but does not address preservation (see NEDIMAH). Another recent example of an e-infrastructure project is the Collaborative EuropeaN Digital Archive Infrastructure (CENDARI), which 'will provide and facilitate access to existing archives and resources in Europe for the study of medieval and modern European history through the development of an "enquiry environment"' (see CENDARI). This project has the aim of improving access to historical resources, but how it will approach preservation is still not clear.

There are also projects which explore how to create efficient e-infrastructure in the digital cultural heritage domain. The DC-NET (Digital Cultural heritage NETwork) project explored what are the most urgently needed services for cultural heritage institutions (see DC-NET). The Indicate project is exploring how grid technologies could be connected to memory institutions and is piloting it in practice (see INDICATE).

One area where preservation awareness is well established is that of *science infrastructures*. For example Aschenbrenner et al. (2011) argued: 'Overall, the diversity between (and even within) the [science] communities makes it impossible to aim for a single strategy or system of curation for technical, organisational and social (e.g. trust) reasons.' Two types of interaction between repository-based systems and grid technologies are considered: data to service and service to data. 'Both patterns, "data to service" and "service to data" require vertical functionalities that bridge repositories and services. This includes e.g. authentication and rights management' (Aschenbrenner et al., 2011).

Compared to the infrastructures dealing with science data, digital cultural heritage is a domain where special attention needs to be paid not only to born-digital data but also to digitized objects. As Eric Meyer et al. highlighted:

> While digitization projects and programmes are somewhat simpler than many advanced
> Grid infrastructure projects, taken together they are arguably contributing to a growing
> research infrastructure that supports e-Research in the humanities, whether or not it is
> formally called e-Research or e-Infrastructure.

(Meyer, Eccles and Madsen, 2009, 9)

Some examples are emerging of consortia created for digital preservation, e.g. Goportis in Germany (see Goportis), which brings together three libraries – the German National Library of Science and Technology, the German National Library of Medicine and the German National Library of Economics – but such co-operatives are still an exception rather than the rule. It could be argued that the current state of standalone preservation solutions is a result of the uniqueness of the digital holdings of every institution, which require tailor-made approaches. A recent comparison of digital preservation provision across major European national libraries and the German Computer Game Museum showed significant differences in the types of holdings that need to be preserved, collection policies, preservation systems and standards used. The National Library of France is developing its own in-house preservation system SPAR, OAIS-compliant and based on the use of METS and PREMIS-compliant metadata; the Royal Library of the Netherlands uses the e-Depot system, which is based on the IBM DIAS and uses extended Dublin Core bibliographic metadata. The German National Library has deployed a combination of tools, including kopal-DIAS and koLibRI, and has developed its own preservation metadata format, LMER (KEEP, 2009, 54–9). The continuing investment in in-house preservation systems is contributing to lack of interoperability and the fragmentation of resources into 'digital silos'. This standalone service architecture cannot be sustained over the longer term, as further fragmentation does not offer economies of scale. Instead, shared solutions for the creation, storage and use of digital resources, including e-infrastructures, will become the major component of the future knowledge economy.

Digital preservation research agendas: an overview

So far, we have outlined what DP is and what it involves, and have summarized what research in DP has looked at (the object and process levels), how to preserve it (lifecycles, repositories, DP tools), as well as what the current state of DP is (e-infrastructures and collaborative collection management). During the years when all these developments were happening, the preservation community also started to look at research trends – areas that need targeted effort in the near future either to answer emerging needs in the preservation domain or to develop new solutions for DP.

An overview of the various facets of digital preservation supports a view of interoperability (see Gradmann, 2008) that includes six vectors (functionality, people, technologies, interoperational entities, information objects and multilinguality) and four abstraction levels (technical, syntactic, semantic and functional) has still not been made in a systematic way.

In the last 20 years there have also been several attempts to define research agendas for the domain. This has not been done on a regular basis by the same professional community, as for example the regular Claremont Report on Database Research.[2] Although research priorities in DP are not analysed regularly, several efforts have been made towards achieving this goal.

In 2007, the DigitalPreservationEurope (DPE) project released a research agenda which identified ten fields of research (DigitalPreservationEurope consortium, 2006). A research seminar organized within the Dagstuhl series in 2010 analysed current demands and came up with seven suggested topics (Chanod et al., 2010). In the same year, the PARSE.Insight project produced a deliverable which looked at areas that need to be addressed within preservation infrastructures for scientific data (PARSE.Insight, 2010). Further, in May 2011 an expert seminar organized by the EC (Billenness, 2011) brainstormed on ten topics for future research. Table 14.3 draws together the topics that were discussed in these three different settings.

Table 14.3 Topics suggested within three recent research agendas

Topic	DPE (2007)	Dagstuhl seminar (2010)	PARSE. insight (2010)	EC work-shop (2011)
Objects				
Knowledge preservation				✓
Complex objects				✓
Self-preserving objects				✓
Specific activities				
Restoration	✓			
Conservation	✓			
Automation	✓			✓
Storage	✓	✓		
Policy and rule management		✓		
Extraction of preservation information				✓
Properties of objects and the preservation process				
Risk	✓			
Ethics, privacy, security and trust		✓		
Significant properties of digital objects (PARSE.Insight addresses authenticity)	✓		✓	
Context and beyond metadata	✓	✓		
Ease of use (e.g. implicit preservation) and private data				✓
Evaluation and benchmarking		✓		
Quality assessment (and certification of repositories in the case of PARSE.insight)			✓	✓

Table 14.3 *Topics suggested within three recent research agendas (continued)*				
Topic	DPE (2007)	Dagstuhl seminar (2010)	PARSE. insight (2010)	EC work-shop (2011)
Preservation strategies and systems				
Integrated access: time – systems – community				✓
Integrated emulation systems				✓
Preservation-ready systems		✓		
Virtualization of policies, resource and processes			✓	
Integration of digital preservation into digital asset management				✓
Economic aspects				
Market-driven and cost-benefit				✓
Financial infrastructure			✓	
Others				
Reformulate digital preservation as a computer-science question				✓
Experimentation	✓			
Application domains		✓		
Interoperability	✓			
Shared knowledge about representation information			✓	
Shared knowledge about hardware and software			✓	
Digital rights			✓	
Standards				✓

One point worth mentioning is that all these definitions of research priorities look at a mixture of issues pertaining to various domains, as described above. Some look into particular types of object, others at new strategies or at particular activities within digital preservation. There has been no holistic analysis across these different dimensions, so far.

Drivers for new models in automating digital preservation

There are three major drivers for looking for alternative models to the current repository-centric preservation models and software that support digital archiving:

Internal factors: These come from the preservation community, which in the past has sought to integrate preservation better into the overall digital object lifecycle. Examples of this are recent discussions on preservation-ready systems (Borbinha, 2010) and ways of integrating digital preservation components into other existing information systems; and work on new formats of digital objects that will help these objects to be self-preserving. The latter is a further development of the idea of durable digital objects; in the last EC consultation on areas for future research on digital preservation, self-preserving objects were suggested as one of the areas for future research (Billenness, 2011).

IT trends that are already being explored within the preservation community. The second major driver for rethinking digital preservation models is the rapid development of technological solutions for access, such as e-infrastructures, cloud computing and micro-services. For example, of the Quest Software (2011) *Ten Predictions for Technology Trends and Practices in 2012*, six are related to developments in cloud services and virtualization: 'SaaS growth will help drive wider adoption of cloud services.' These technologies will continue to advance and are being increasingly deployed by the digital preservation community. For example Askhoj, Nagamori and Sugimoto (2011) discuss a service model for shared archiving services via the cloud.

General awareness of the DP issues, clearly defining the mandate of DP in legal and other regulations (digital legal deposit, electronic record-keeping, open data, data protection, business need etc.).

The 'digital tsunami'. Another driver is the technologies developed to tackle 'big data', open data, massive production of voluminous data, e.g. from technologies that were not previously affordable but are today, e.g. 3D scanning. For example, the Gartner technology Hype Cycle for 2011 includes the 'Big Data' domain (Gartner Hype Cycle, 2011), which relates directly to the scalability of digital preservation solutions and their ability to handle rapidly growing volumes of digital assets. Systematic analysis of these predicted changes and their consequences for digital preservation are currently too low on the research agenda.

This chapter has shown that the preservation community is actively adopting new methods and technologies and is refining existing ones. Preservation models and systems are one area where increased granularity and definition of smaller composite units has been achieved. In 2004 Brain Lavoie and Lorcan Dempsey pointed out (Lavoie and Dempsey, 2004):

> Determining the extent to which digital preservation can benefit from a division of labor, in the sense of finding 1) a sensible deconstruction of the digital preservation process into a set of more granular services, and 2) the optimal degree of specialization across preserving institutions, is a key issue in the design of digital repository architectures.

Today, examples exist that map the OAIS functional entities to a layered service model, where APIs (application programming interfaces) are the services between PaaS (Platform as a Service) and SaaS (Software as a Service) layers and, indeed, other layers (e.g. Package layer, Archival layer and Record Management layer, as defined in Askhoj, Nagamori and Sugimoto, 2011). The SaaS models can now be hosted either locally or in the cloud.

The micro-services approach that emerged a few years ago also steps away from the encapsulated holistic digital archive systems and instead allows for combining flexible specialized solutions. The growing use of micro-services and increasing reliance on SaaS platforms and cloud technologies have changed these models, paving the way for e-infrastructures to become part of the digital preservation landscape.

Future trends

There are a large number of drivers and technology pushes that have an impact on how digital preservation develops. Picking out only a few of these as significant may seem unfair. However, we expect that five future trends to follow are:

- transparent enterprise-driven models for digital preservation that will help to identify specific and generic components of the preservation function
- launch of self-preserving objects – initially likely to be simple objects (text, images) that will still make a difference for the cultural heritage sector as the primary caretaker of these data types
- increased flexibility in digital preservation architectures – based on granular or layered structures (e.g. SaaS, PaaS, IaaS) (IaaS stands for Infrastructure as a Service, a typical cloud service) that are easy to adapt to a variety of preservation scenarios
- clearly defined sets of metrics or benchmarks for comparing preservation tools and services and their performance
- terminology and standards no longer likely to converge along professional community borderlines – besides interoperability across time, digital preservation will generate pressure for interoperability in real time, advancing the need to agree on terminology.

Conclusion

Preservation is inevitably intricate. Inbuilt hazards relate to scale (e.g. the quantity and variety of digital objects requiring preservation), speed (preservation research occurs within a rapidly shifting and multi-faceted technological environment) and incoherence (for example, a lack of consensus on best practices and preferred methods).

To some extent, the significant contextual or symbolic aspects of items and their probable use have always been important to knowledge organizations. Yet in a *digital* library these aspects themselves become targets for preservation (Chowdhury, 2010). All of this is to say that evaluating DP work with users is fraught with complication.

This chapter has looked at research in DP that demonstrates that there is already substantial know-how around, as well as numerous preservation tools and repository management systems. Research is still vibrant around DP topics – in fact we expect that further progress will be made in coming years and that in just a few years a chapter on this topic will deal with substantially different material and require a complete rewriting.

Acknowledgements

This chapter uses some of the results of the DC-NET – Digital Cultural heritage NETwork is an ERA-NET (European Research Area Network) project, financed by the European Commission under FP7's Capacities Programme, in particular those reported in Ruusalepp and Dobreva (2012).

Notes

1   www.dcc.ac.uk/resources/curation-lifecycle-model.
2   http://db.cs.berkeley.edu/claremont/claremontreport08.pdf.

References

Abrams, S., Kunze, J. and Loy, D. (2010) An Emergent Micro-Services Approach to Digital Curation Infrastructure. *International Journal of Digital Curation*, **5** (1), 172–86.

Aschenbrenner, A., Enke, H., Fischer, T. and Ludwig, J. (2011) Diversity and Interoperability of Repositories in a Grid Curation Environment, *Journal of Digital Information*, **12** (2), http://journals.tdl.org/jodi/article/view/1896.

Askhoj, J., Nagamori, M. and Sugimoto, S. (2011) Archiving as a Service: a model for the provision of shared archiving services using cloud computing. In *Proceedings of the iConference 2011*, 151–8, http://dl.acm.org/citation.cfm?doid=1940761.1940782.

Billenness, C. (2011) *The Future of the Past – Shaping New Visions for EU-research in Digital Preservation: report on the Proceedings of the Workshop Organised by the unit Cultural Heritage and Technology Enhanced Learning, European Commission, Information Society and Media Directorate-General, Luxembourg, 4–5 May 2011*, http://cordis.europa.eu/fp7/ict/telearn-digicult/future-of-the-past_en.pdf.

BL, KB, DNB, BN (2010) *Long-Term Preservation Services: a description of long-term preservation services in a digital library environment*, British Library, Koninklijke Bibliotheek – National library of the Netherlands, Deutsche Nationalbibliothek – German National Library and Nasjonalbiblioteket – National library of Norway, www.dnb.de/SharedDocs/Downloads/ DE/DNB/netzpub/kbLongtermPreservation.pdf?__blob=publicationFile.

Borbinha, J. (2010) Preservation Ready Systems: digital preservation and enterprise architecture. In Chanod, J.-P., Dobreva, M., Rauber, A. and Ross, S. (eds), *Proceedings of Dagstuhl Seminar 10291: Automation in Digital Preservation*, www.dagstuhl.de/Materials/Files/10/10291/10291.SWM11.ExtAbstract.pdf.

Burnhill, P. and Guy, F. (2010) Piloting an E-journals Preservation Service (PEPRS), *The Serials Librarian*, **58** (1–4), 117–26.

CASPAR (2007) *The CASPAR Review of the State of the Art*, http://casparpreserves.eu/Members/cclrc/Deliverables/ review-of-state-of-the-art-1/at_download/file.pdf.

Challis, D. (2010) *Notes on SITS – the Scholarly Infrastructure Technical Summit*, http://blogs.ecs.soton.ac.uk/webteam/2010/11/15/ notes-on-sits-the-scholarly-infrastructure-technical-summit/.

Chanod, J. P., Dobreva, M., Rauber, A., Ross, S. and Casarosa, V. (2010) Issues in Digital
Preservation: towards a new research agenda. In *Automation in Digital Preservation, Dagstuhl
Seminar Proceedings 10291,*
http://drops.dagstuhl.de/opus/volltexte/2010/2899/pdf/10291.Report.2899.pdf.

Chowdhury, G. (2010) From Digital Libraries to Digital Preservation Research: the importance
of users and context, *Journal of Documentation,* **66** (2), 207–23.

Chue Hong, N. (2012) Digital Preservation and Curation: the danger of overlooking software.
In Delve, J., Anderson, A., Dobreva, M., Baker, D., Billenness, C., Konstantelos, L. (eds)
The Preservation of Complex Objects, vol. 1, Visualisations and Simulations, 24–35,
http://pocos.org/index.php/publications/publications.

DARIAH (2010) *Collection Ingest, Management and Preservation,*
www.dariah.eu/index.php?option=com_docman&task=cat_view&gid=92&Itemid=
200DCC Curation Lifecycle Model. www.dcc.ac.uk/resources/curation-lifecycle-model.

Delve, J., Anderson, A., Dobreva, M., Baker, D., Billenness, C. and Konstantelos, L. (2012) *The
Preservation of Complex Objects,* vol. 1, Visualisations and Simulations,
http://pocos.org/index.php/publications/publications.

DigitalPreservationEurope consortium (2006) *D7.2 – Research Roadmap,* public deliverable,
June.

DPimpact (2009) *Socio-economic Drivers and Impact of Longer Term Digital Preservation,*
http://cordis.europa.eu/fp7/ict/telearn-digicult/dpimpact-final-report.pdf.

Gartner Hype Cycle (2011) www.gartner.com/hc/images/215650_0001.gif.

Gladney, H. M. (2008) *Durable Digital Objects rather than Digital Preservation.* ERPANET,
http://eprints.erpanet.org/149/01/Durable.pdf.

Gradmann, S. (2008) *Interoperability: a key concept for large scale, persistent digital libraries,* DPE
briefing paper, www.digitalpreservationeurope.eu/publications/briefs/interoperability.pdf.

Hitchcock, S. (2009) *Final Report of the PReservation Eprint SERVices: towards distributed
preservation services for Repositories Preserve2 Project,* http://preserv.eprints.org/
JISC-formal/preserv2-progressreport.doc.

ISO (2003) ISO 14721:2003 *Space Data and Information Transfer Systems – Open Archival
Information System – Reference Model,* International Organization for Standardization,
http://public.ccsds.org/publications/archive/650x0b1.pdf.

ISO/IEC (1993) ISO/IEC 2382-1:1993 *Information Technology-Vocabulary-Part 1: Fundamental
Terms,* International Organization for Standardization/International Electrotechnical
Commission.

KEEP (2009) *Preliminary Document Analysing and Summarizing Metadata Standards and Issues across
Europe (KEEP project deliverable D3.1.),* www.keep-project.eu/ezpub2/index.php?/eng/
Products-Results/Public-deliverables.

Kumar, A., Kaplan, D. and Rubinger, B. (2008) TIAMAT: an ingest service for the Tufts
Digital Repository. In *Third International Conference on Open Repositories 2008, 1–4 April 2008,
Southampton, United Kingdom,* http://pubs.or08.ecs.soton.ac.uk/75/.

Lavoie, B. (2004) *The Open Archival Information System Reference Model: introductory guide,* DPC
Technology Watch Report, www.dpconline.org/docs/lavoie_OAIS.pdf.

Lavoie, B., and Dempsey, L. (2004) Thirteen Ways of Looking at . . . Digital Preservation, *D-Lib Magazine*, **10** (7/8), http://dlib.org/dlib/july04/lavoie/07lavoie.html

Martin, J. and Coleman, D. (2002) Change the Metaphor: the archive as an ecosystem, *JEP (The Journal of Electronic Publishing)*, **7** (3), http://quod.lib.umich.edu/cgi/t/text/text-idx?c=jep;view=text;rgn=main;idno=3336451.0007.301.

Meyer, E. T., Eccles, K. and Madsen, C. (2009) Digitisation as E-research Infrastructure: access to materials and research capabilities in the humanities, *Proceedings of the 5th International Conference on e-Social Science, Cologne, Germany, 24–26 June 2009*, www.ncess.ac.uk/resources/content/papers/Meyer%282%29.pdf.

PARSE.Insight (2010) *D2.2 Science Data Infrastructure Roadmap,* public deliverable.

Quest Software (2011) *10 Predictions for Technology Trends and Practices in 2012*, www.dataprix.com/files/TEC_Survey_Whitepaper-2011.pdf.

Rajasekar, A. et al. (2010) *iRODS Primer: Integrated Rule-Oriented Data System,* Morgan and Claypool, www.morganclaypool.com/doi/abs/10.2200/S00233ED1V01Y200912ICR012.

Ross, S. and Gow, A. (1999) *Digital Archaeology: rescuing neglected and damaged data resources*, Library Information and Technology Centre, www.ukoln.ac.uk/services/elib/papers/supporting/#blric.

Rusbridge, C., Burnhill, P., Ross, S., Bozeman, P., Giaretta, D., Lyon, L. and M. Atkinson, (2005) The Digital Curation Centre: a vision for digital curation, *Proceedings of IEEE's Mass Storage and Systems Technology Committee Conference on From Local to Global: Data Interoperability – Challenges and Technologies*, http://eprints.erpanet.org/82/01/DCC_Vision.pdf.

Ruusalepp, R. and Dobreva, M. (2012) *Digital Preservation Services: state of the art analysis*, DC NET, www.dc-net.org/.

Simpson, D. (2005) *Directory of Digital Preservation Repositories and Services in the UK*, 2nd edn, Digital Preservation Coalition.

Strodl, S., Petrov, P. and Rauber, A. (2011) *Research on Digital Preservation within Projects Co-funded by the European Union in the ICT Programme*, http://cordis.europa.eu/fp7/ict/telearn-digicult/report-research-digital-preservation_en.pdf.

The New Renaissance (2011) *The New Renaissance: report of the Comité des Sages, Reflection Group on Bringing Europe's Cultural Heritage Online*, http://ec.europa.eu/information_society/activities/digital_libraries/doc/reflection_group/final-report-cdS3.pdf.

Thomas, S., Baker, F., Gittens, R., Thompson, D. (2007) Cairo Tools Survey: a survey of tools applicable to the preparation of digital archives for ingest into a preservation repository, http://cairo.paradigm.ac.uk/projectdocs/cairo_tools_listing_pv1.pdf.

UC Curation Center/California Digital Library (2010) *Merritt: an emergent micro-services approach to digital curation infrastructure*, Rev. 0.6–2010-03-25, https://confluence.ucop.edu/download/attachments/13860983/Merritt-latest.pdf?version=1&modificationDate=1269561985000.

Willemse, E. (2007) *DARIAH Challenges for Arts and Humanities Data Curation*, presentation, http://ipres.las.ac.cn/pdf/Ellen.ppt.pdf.

URLs for tools mentioned in the chapter

AQuA project: www.jisc.ac.uk/whatwedo/programmes/infl1/digpres/aqua.aspx

Archivematica: http://archivematica.org/wiki/index.php?title=Development_roadmap

CENDARI: www.geschkult.fu-
berlin.de/e/fmi/arbeitsbereiche/ab_janz/projekte/Cendari/index.html

CLARIN: Common Language Resources and Technology Infrastructure,
www.clarin.eu/external/. Short guide on preservation is available on
www.clarin.eu/files/preservation-CLARIN-ShortGuide.pdf

DARIAH: Digital Research Infrastructure for the Arts and Humanities, www.dariah.eu/.

DC-NET: www.dc-net.org/

DigiBIC: www.digibic.eu

Digital Records Forensics Project: www.digitalrecordsforensics.org/

Gartner Glossary: www.gartner.com/it-glossary/it-services/

Goportis: www.goportis.de/en/our-services/digital-preservation.html

IBM DIAS: www-935.ibm.com/services/nl/dias/

INDICATE: www.indicate-project.eu/

NEDIMAH: www.esf.org/activities/research-networking-programmes/humanities-
sch/current-esf-research-networking-programmes-in-humanities/nedimah.html

OPF: www.openplanetsfoundation.org/

SourceForge: http://sourceforge.net/

Tessella: www.digital-preservation.com/

TextGrid: www.textgrid.de/

CHAPTER 15

Digital libraries and information access: research trends

Gobinda Chowdhury and Schubert Foo

Introduction

Research and development in digital libraries (DLs) have progressed significantly over the past 20 or so years. A search on the Scopus database reveals a dramatic rise in the number of publications (articles, papers, reviews), from 436 publications between 1990 and 1999 to 7469 publications between 2000 and 2010 (Nguyen and Chowdhury, 2011). A number of reviews have been written to trace the developments and major areas of DL research. For example, Chowdhury and Chowdhury (1999) reviewed and classified DL research in the 1990s in the following major areas: collection development; development methodology and design issues; user interfaces; information organization; classification and indexing; resource discovery; metadata; access and file management; user studies; information retrieval; legal issues; social issues; evaluation of digital information; evaluation of DLs; standards; preservation; and implications for library managers.

More recently, Pomerantz et al. (2006) studied a sample of 1064 DL publications covering the period 1995–2006 and suggested that DL research and work can be broadly grouped into 19 modules (core topics) around 69 related topics. Another review of DL research, conducted by Liew (2008), was based on 557 publications covering the period 1997–2007. These publications collectively centred around five themes (core topics) and 62 related subtopics. These two studies provided fundamental frameworks of DL core and subtopics, with Pomerantz et al. (2006) covering core computer science and library and information science topics and Liew (2008) covering the organizational and people issues of DL research.

The most recent DL knowledge map proposed by Nguyen and Chowdhury (2011) includes 21 core topics and 1015 subtopics. In addition to the classic research topics in information and library science such as collection management, information organization, information retrieval, user studies, human–computer interactions and digital preservation, they noted several new research topics such as ontology and semantic retrieval, virtual technologies, mobile technology, the semantic web and social networking.

As discussed in the literature (see for example, Nguyen and Chowdhury, 2011;

Pomerantz et al., 2006; Liew, 2008) and in different chapters in this book, research and development activities in DLs are significantly influenced by several factors such as ICT developments, changes in the socio-political scenario, and new business models appearing within the information industry vis-à-vis new regulations (including copyright and access management regulations). Some recent research and trends in different fields and their impact on DLs are discussed in this chapter.

Design and architecture issues

Digital library research in the early days was initiated through projects funded under the first round of NSF (National Science Foundation) funding in the USA and Joint Information Systems Committee (JISC) funding in the UK (Chowdhury and Chowdhury, 1999). These research projects mainly concentrated on building architecture, tools and standards for managing large volumes and varieties of digital content such as text, audio and video coming from heterogeneous systems and services. Consequently, a large number of distributed DLs were built. However, some DL researchers focused on managing large quantities of data, for example, spatial data in the Alexandria Digital Library Project. Over the years, it has been increasingly realized that DLs should, wherever necessary, be able to handle and manage research outputs and research data in addition to those that previously existed.

As discussed in Chapter 2, DL researchers experimented on developing different alternative architecture for DLs, and in that process different metadata standards and harvesting protocols were developed. However, as discussed in different parts of this book, especially in Chapters 2 and 8, the design and architecture of DLs should be such that they meet the overall goal of making information accessible to everyone, irrespective of their geographical, technological and language barriers. Hence, in parallel to research on building large distributed DLs like the National Science Digital Library (NSDL), Europeana, the Networked Digital Library of Theses and Dissertations (NDLTD) and other DLs, researchers are also looking for alternative DL designs for people who have limited or unreliable access to ICTs and/or language or other barriers such as poor information skills.

For instance, the Greenstone DL software developed at the University of Waikato in New Zealand is supported by UNESCO in order to facilitate the design and development of DLs in developing countries (Greenstone.org, 2007). In Chapter 2, Suleman discusses SimplyCT, an alternative architecture for DL systems with a specific emphasis on low-resource environments, such as institutions in developing countries.

Given the increasing popularity and use of mobile technologies in our everyday life, and the penetration of mobile phones even among the poorer people in developing countries, researchers have now realized the significance of mobile technologies in

DLs. The potential use and benefits of mobile technologies in providing library and information services have been discussed in Chapter 9. Based on a case study of four selected institutions and university libraries in the USA, Mitchell and Suchy (2012) note that offering mobile access to digital collections is still a relatively new endeavour for libraries and museums, and the shift from desktop to mobile computing presents a challenge in providing service to our users.

Over the years, several large DLs and repositories have been built. Of late, researchers are working on building technologies and tools for integrating these DLs into useful and usable entities. The iSTEM project discussed in Chapter 11 shows research efforts in integrating various subject repositories in science, technology, engineering and mathematics (STEM) that both make use of the subject knowledge of professional indexers who have prepared the subject directory of each repository and facilitate better retrieval of information for end-users. Similar research activities directed towards the integration of institutional repositories and DLs are discussed later in this chapter.

Various initiatives are now being taken at national and international levels to facilitate access to and promote the use and reuse of research data. DataCite (www.datacite.org/), launched in December 2009, is a service that allows people to share and reuse research data. An international initiative with 20 members from 12 countries (as of February 2012), DataCite 'plays a global leadership role promoting the use of persistent identifiers for datasets' (Brase and Farquhar, 2011). Borgman, in her keynote address at the 2011 International Conference on Asian Digital Libraries in Beijing (Borgman, 2011a) and her article in the *Journal of the American Society for Information Science and Technology* (Borgman, 2011b), discussed the challenges associated with the management of digital research data. In order to integrate and manage the scholarly information and data of yesterday, today and tomorrow successfully, the DL community must make the necessary adjustments in its various activities throughout the information lifecycle, ranging from policies to information infrastructure as well as information retrieval and interactions.

As discussed in Chapters 2, 5 and 7 of this book, user-centred design of DLs, with a focus on language, social and cultural issues, has become a major area of research and development. Europeana is a prime example of a multilingual and multicultural DL. However, as discussed in Chapter 8, some DLs contain information and data that are culturally sensitive and therefore their design should follow some specific guidelines. Some such guidelines have been proposed for digital collections of specific materials (see, for example, ATSIRILIN, 2008; Nakata et al., 2008, for indigenous collections in Australia; and Sullivan, 2002, for indigenous collections in New Zealand)

Information organization and access

Since the beginning of DLs, information organization and information access have remained two major areas of research (Nguyen and Chowdhury, 2011). Two major types of access provided in DLs are based on metadata and full-text search. Consequently, as discussed in Chapters 2 to 4 of this book, interoperability and metadata crosswalks have remained a major area of research in DLs. Similarly, full-text and multilingual access features are also available in many DLs. As discussed in Chapters 6 and 7, social information retrieval based on social tagging, crowdsourcing, collaborative filtering and use etc. have also become important areas of research in DLs.

In parallel to DL development, a number of unique and very helpful information-access services have been developed by search engines. As discussed in Chapter 9, and also elsewhere in this book, typical examples of such services include Google Books, Google Scholar and Microsoft Academic Search. These services not only provide access to digital information, they add a lot of value to the retrieved information. For example, Google Scholar provides citation data related to the retrieved content, while Microsoft Academic Search adds more value showing the growth of publications as well as other citation information.

Many institutional repositories also provide valuable information based on usage logs. For example, the institutional repository Strathprints not only provides a simple and an advanced search interface with a variety of search features, but also allows users to generate a variety of graphs and tables summarizing the usage data for e-prints in the repository (University of Strathclyde, n.d.). Such data not only shows the usage of institutional repositories, but can also provide useful information relating to the performance of a given department, even an individual, in usage statistics.

Sustainability issues

Sustainable development has remained a major agenda of the United Nations for a long time. A special unit called the UN Division for Sustainable Development (DSD) was established in 1992 in order to promote activities for sustainable development at the national, regional and international levels. Economic sustainability is one of the major challenges of sustainable development. Maintaining the quality and standard of DL services and research activities in the face of global economic crisis and severe austerity measures has posed many challenges and, consequently, new ways of generating revenues for supporting DLs. In the UK, JISC has been playing a key role in promoting research for finding ways for developing sustainable DLs, especially institutional repositories (see for details, Jacobs, Amber and McGregor, 2008; JISC, 2011a). Similar efforts are being made in other countries to build and promote institutional repositories. However, many recent studies (see for example, Davis and Connolly, 2007; Connell, 2011; Cryer and Collins, 2011; Cullen and Chawner, 2011; Kim, 2011; MacDonald, 2011; St Jean et al., 2011) point out that the progress of institutional repositories has not been as much as was originally envisaged. There are many reasons for this, the primary one being the economic difficulties, i.e. lack of a continuous funding stream to support the development, management and preservation of content and data at the institutional level. Other difficulties facing open access DLs based on institutional repositories include: lack of understanding and commitment on the part of faculty members, various difficulties associated with the understanding and management of copyright issues, lack of proper evidence of better citation and academic rewards arising from institutional repositories, and the perceived additional workload on the faculty that is associated with the process of self-archiving of information.

Environmental sustainability is the second dimension of sustainable development. One of the most well discussed documents on environmental sustainability is known as Agenda 21, the Rio Declaration on Environment and Development. It was adopted at the United Nations Conference on Environment and Development held in Rio de Janerio, Brazil, 3–14 June 1992. This subsequently gave rise to several major international summits and conferences and resulted in a major policy document known as the Kyoto Protocol, which was adopted in Kyoto, Japan, on 11 December 1997 and entered into force on 16 February 2005. The Kyoto Protocol set binding targets for 37 industrialized countries and the European Community to reduce greenhouse gas (GHG) emissions. Unfortunately, despite several further initiatives, and government and international measures, it appears that the signatories are far from reaching their target of reducing the GHG emissions. Nevertheless, efforts are under way to build a new binding agreement for every country. At the UN summit on climate change held in Durban in December 2011, a decision was made 'to adopt a universal legal agreement on climate change as soon as possible, and no later than 2015'.[1] As shown in Chapter 10, DL projects require substantial use of ICTs, which collectively have led to significant demands on energy consumption, hence contributing adversely to environmental sustainability.

The third dimension of sustainable development is social sustainability, which is dependent on society and individuals, their customs and practices, interactions, rights and equality, freedom, peace, security, social justice, well-being and others. As part of the paradoxical equation, one should recognize that economic and environmental sustainability are the means and drivers that are required in order to achieve social sustainability and the overall development of individuals and society. The reader can refer to the DSD website, which provides a long list of topics related to sustainable development.[2]

The importance of information for sustainable development has been directly and indirectly mentioned in various contexts in the canonical text on sustainable development, titled *Our Common Future* (World Commission on Environment and Development, 1987). Information for decision making is the subject of Chapter 40 of Agenda 21, which emphasizes that,

> in sustainable development, everyone is a user and provider of information considered in the broad sense. That includes data, information, experience and knowledge. The need for information arises at all levels, from that of senior decision-maker at the national and

international levels to the grass-roots and individual levels.[3]

The importance of information for socio-economic development has also been recognized by organizations like the European Union and the Organisation for Economic Co-operation and Development (OECD) (see for example, European Commission, 2010; OECD, 2010, 2011). However, the importance of information has been ignored or downplayed in key policy documents on sustainable development, and within mainstream information science the issue of sustainable information has not been discussed or researched well (Nolin, 2010; Chowdhury, 2011a).

Cloud computing

While we recognize that extensive use of ICTs by DLs has a significant environmental impact, it should be noted that the appropriate use of ICTs can help in curbing CO_2 emissions. The report *SMART2020* by The Climate Group comments: 'while ICT's own sector footprint – currently two per cent of global emissions – will almost double by 2020, ICT's unique ability to monitor and maximize energy efficiency both within and outside of its own sector could cut CO_2 emissions by up to five times this amount. This represents a saving of 7.8 Giga-tonnes of carbon dioxide equivalent (GtCO2e) by 2020 – greater than the current annual emissions of either the US or China' (The Climate Group, 2008). The report further shows that improved and appropriate use of ICTs can reduce 'annual man-made global emissions by 15 per cent by 2020 and deliver energy efficiency savings to global businesses of over EUR 500 billion' (The Climate Group, 2008).

Hence, as discussed in Chapters 4 and 10, the use of green IT and, especially, cloud computing technologies is an encouraging sign of development in a direction that can significantly reduce the environmental impact of DLs. Cloud computing can be regarded as an IT utility service providing ICT facilities for the consumer. The notion of cloud computing as a utility service has been emphasized in the Berkeley definition of cloud computing:

> Cloud Computing refers to both the applications delivered as services over the Internet and the hardware and systems software in the datacenters that provide those services. The services themselves have long been referred to as Software as a Service (SaaS). The datacenter hardware and software is what we will call a Cloud. When a Cloud is made available in a pay-as-you-go manner to the general public, we call it a Public Cloud; the service being sold is Utility Computing.
>
> (Armbrust et al., 2009)

To date, very little systematic research has taken place in relation to the environmental sustainability of information services in general, and DLs in particular. Very recently, Chowdhury has conducted research into justifying how DL services can help to save universities reduce their environmental impact (Chowdhury, 2012); how green information services can be built using green IT and cloud computing services (Chowdhury, 2011a); and how to measure the environmental impact of information access and build green information retrieval systems (Chowdhury, 2012). By adopting the cloud computing model for DLs, in future the following benefits can be realized (JISC, 2011b; Chowdhury, 2011a, 2011b):

- reduced environmental and financial costs of managing DL services
- reduced cost of running large-scale research and experiments, especially for those that are needed for only short periods, like running large ICT experiments or increased volumes of activity at certain times
- load sharing where a DL research group wants to collaborate with other research groups and where neither has the required ICT infrastructure or investment
- cloud computing on the pay-as-you-go model, which will allow researchers to plan and run several DL research projects and experiments with reduced overheads and long-term investments
- being able to access data, content and services anytime from any location
- having the opportunity to conduct experiments with a variety of data and content-based services using virtual computing resources that can expand and shrink, based on demand.

Building sustainable DLs and digital preservation systems poses a number of technological, economic, environmental, legal and social challenges. New metadata standards and technologies are required in order to provide integrated content and data services through DLs. Some of these challenges are discussed in the literature, see for example:

- Wrenn, Mueller and Shellhase (2009), in the context of the economic sustainability of institutional repositories
- Li et al. (2011), in the context of institutional repositories
- Giglia (2011), in the context of open access data and content
- Li and Banah (2011), in the context of preservation of institutional repositories.

Socio-economic and legal issues

Internet and DL research and development activities have given rise to new social and legal challenges. As discussed in Chapter 9 and elsewhere in the literature (for example, Houghton et al., 2009; Chowdhury, 2011b), several new players and business models have emerged in the field of digital information products and services. Despite these new players and different business models, users of DL services still find it difficult to access and use information in the most convenient way. Over the years, Chowdhury and his associates have discussed these challenges and justified the need for a new digital content service network (for example, Chowdhury, 2009; Chowdhury and Fraser, 2009, 2011).

The need for new intellectual property (IP) rights, addressed in Chapter 13, to suit the needs of the digital age has been raised in different sectors. In the UK, the Hargreaves Review was commissioned by the British Prime Minister on the premise that the current IP laws did not adequately support the growth of the digital economy. In its statement of the context of the review, the report notes the following points (Hargreaves, 2011):

- 'our competitive edge depends on our capacity to innovate, especially in the high margin, knowledge intensive businesses which now exist across all sectors of the UK economy. . . . The UK's long term growth depends on these firms. These are also the companies most affected by our Intellectual Property (IP) system. That is the context for this review, which the Prime Minister launched in November, with a mandate to examine how to ensure that our IP framework does the best possible job in encouraging innovation and growth.' (10)
- 'Digital technology is probably the most important and transformative technology of our time. Because digital is fundamentally an information and communication technology (ICT), intellectual property rights lie at its heart. Not only has ICT adoption and use been among the strongest drivers of growth, but it has pushed content and communication technology into new uses, meaning the IP system has become part of people's daily lives.' (13)
- 'Because copyright governs the right to own and use data and information, as well as the output of authors, musicians, photographers and film makers, copyright law is now of primary interest to players across the whole of the knowledge economy, not just those involved in the creative industries. Digital technologies are based on copying, so copyright becomes their regulator: a role it was never designed to perform.' (14)

Thus the report acknowledges that the two key enablers of growth in these times are ICT and IP, which control access to and use of information. It also points out how the current IP laws are inadequate to promote the digital economy in Britain and, consequently, what measures need to be taken in relation to the IP laws to facilitate easy access and use of digital information. The Hargreaves Review makes ten specific recommendations, some with many sub-sections. One of its major recommendations is to set up a digital copyright exchange. The report recommends that:

> In order to boost UK firms' access to transparent, contestable and global digital markets, the UK should establish a cross sectoral Digital Copyright Exchange.

(8)

Although the Hargreaves Review recommends the establishment of a digital copyright exchange, the idea is not entirely new, and in fact the idea of a digital content network with a copyright switching system has been recommended before, specifically in 2009 by Chowdhury and Fraser in a series of publications and presentations (Chowdhury, 2009; Chowdhury and Fraser, 2009; Chowdhury and Fraser, 2011; Fraser, 2009,). The Hargreaves Review proposes that:

> A digital copyright exchange will facilitate copyright licensing and realise the growth potential of creative industries.
>
> (3)

A similar idea, in the form of a digital content service network, was previously put forward more explicitly by Chowdhury:

> a content service network (CSN) that will be complementary to traditional channels for content will enable users to choose information from a myriad of information channels and sources, with sufficient levels of granularity required for their use, and produce a new information package for access and distribution through a variety of media – institutional or personal computers, handheld devices, on-demand print, and so on, within the framework of a new and easy to implement business model.
>
> (Chowdhury, 2009, 216)

Summary

Digital library research and development have grown in scope as they have matured over the last two decades in evolution and use. Newer definitions of DLs, encompassing wider audiences and new application areas, and spawning new research areas, are all evident from the growing amount of literature on DLs. This book has selected to focus on the important and key areas of information access and interactions in DLs. The different chapters provide a current overview and projected trends in areas ranging from design and architecture to information organization and metadata, social aspects, user collaboration, interaction and open access, IP, usability and preservation. This final chapter has provided a summary of recent research and trends in a number of key areas of development.

Moving forward, it will be interesting to see how the new and emerging technologies and standards, cloud-computing technologies, reforms of the IP laws and associated developments such as new and emerging business models in the digital information world will influence the development and management of DLs. Alongside these, emerging user behaviour influenced by rapid developments in the web and in social-networking technologies vis-à-vis social tagging and collaborative search and retrieval techniques will also have a significant impact on the development, access and use of DLs of the future.

Note

1   http://unfccc.int/2860.php.

2   www.un.org/esa/dsd/susdevtopics/sdt_index.shtml.

3   www.un.org/esa/dsd/susdevtopics/sdt_infodecimaki.shtml.

References

Armbrust, M., Fox, A., Griffith, R., Joseph, A. D., Katz, R. H., Konwinski, A., Lee, G., Patterson, D. A., Rabkin, A., Stoica, I. and Zaharia, M. (2009) *Above the Clouds: a Berkeley view of cloud computing*, Electrical Engineering and Computer Sciences, University of California Berkeley, Technical report No. UCB/EECS-2009-28, www.eecs.berkeley.edu/Pubs/TechRpts/2009/EECS-2009-28.html.

ATSILIRN (2008) *Aboriginal and Torres Strait Islander Library and Information Resources Network Protocols*, www.wipo.int/export/sites/www/tk/en/folklore/creative_heritage/docs/atsilirn_protocols.pdf.

Borgman, C. L. (2011a) Drowning in the Data Deluge: digital library challenges for Asia, keynote address, *International Conference on Asian Digital Libraries, Beijing, ICADL*, http://works.bepress.com/borgman/252/.

Borgman, C. L. (2011b) The Conundrum of Sharing Research Data, *Journal of the American Society for Information Science and Technology*, 1–40, http://ssrn.com/abstract=1869155 or http://dx.doi.org/10.2139/ssrn.1869155.

Brase, J. and Farquhar, A. (2011) Access to Research Data, *D-Lib Magazine*, **17** (1/2), www.dlib.org/dlib/january11/brase/01brase.html.

Chowdhury, G. (2009) Towards the Conceptual Model of a Content Service Network, *Globalizing academic libraries vision 2020: Proceedings of the International Conference on Academic Libraries, Delhi, October 5–8, 2009*, Delhi Mittal Publications, 215–20.

Chowdhury, G. G. (2011a) Building Sustainable Information Services: a green IS research agenda, *Journal of the American Society for Information Science and Technology* (forthcoming).

Chowdhury, G. G. (2011b) Why E-books are not Common in Academic and Research Libraries even after Rigorous Research for Nearly Twenty Years, *International Conference on Digital Library Management, 13–15 January, 2011, Kolkata*.

Chowdhury, G. G. (2012) How Digital Information Services can Reduce Greenhouse Gas Emissions, *Online Information Review*, **36** (4) (forthcoming).

Chowdhury, G. G. and Chowdhury, S. (1999) Digital Library Research: issues and trends. *Journal of Documentation*, **55** (4), 409–448.

Chowdhury, G. and Fraser, M. (2009) Towards a New Service Model for the Content Supply Chain, keynote address, *The Seventh Book Conference, University of Edinburgh, 16–18 October*, http://booksandpublishing.com/author/admin/.

Chowdhury, G. and Fraser, M. (2011) Carbon Footprint of the Knowledge Industry and Ways to Reduce it, *World Digital Libraries*, **4** (1), 9–18.

The Climate Group (2008) *SMART2020: enabling the low carbon economy in the information age*, www.theclimategroup.org/publications/2008/6/19/smart2020-enabling-the-low-carbon-economy-in-the-information-age/.

Connell, T. H. (2011) The Use of Institutional Repositories: the Ohio State University experience, *College & Research Libraries*, **72** (3), 253–74.

Cryer, E. and Collins, M. (2011) Incorporating Open Access into Libraries, *Serials Review*, **37** (2), 103–7.

Cullen, R. and Chawner, B. (2011) Institutional Repositories, Open Access and Scholarly Communication: a study of conflicting paradigms, *Journal of Academic Librarianship*, **37** (6), 460–70.

Davis, P. M. and Connolly, M. J. L. (2007) Institutional Repositories: evaluating the reasons for non-use of Cornell University's installation of DSpace, *D-Lib Magazine*, **13** (3/4), www.dlib.org/dlib/march07/davis/03davis.html.

European Commission (2010) *A Digital Agenda for Europe*, Communication from the Commission to the European Parliament, the Council, the European Economic and Social Committee and the Committee of the Regions. Brussels, 19 May, COM (2010) 245, http://ec.europa.eu/information_society/digital-agenda/documents/digital-agenda-communication-en.pdf.

Fraser, M. (2009). Towards the Conceptual Framework of a New Knowledge Infrastructure, *Globalizing Academic Libraries Vision 2020: Proceedings of the International Conference on Academic Libraries, Delhi, Oct. 5-8, 2009*, Delhi Mittal Publications, 209–14.

Giglia, E. (2011) Open Access, Open Data: paradigm shifts in the changing scholarly communication scenario, conference report, *D-Lib Magazine*, **17** (3/4), www.dlib.org/dlib/march11/giglia/03giglia.html.

Greenstone.org (2007) *Greenstone Digital Library Software: About Greenstone*, www.greenstone.org/.

Hargreaves, I. (2011) *Digital Opportunity: a review of intellectual property and growth. An independent report*, www.ipo.gov.uk/ipreview-finalreport.pdf.

Houghton, J., Rasmussen, B., Sheehan, P., Oppenheim, C., Morris, A., Creaser, C., Greenwood, H., Summers, M. and Gourlay, A. (2009) *Economic Implications of Alternative Scholarly Publishing Models: exploring the costs and benefits*, JISC.

Jacobs, N., Amber, T. and McGregor, A. (2008) Institutional Repositories in the UK: the JISC approach, *Library Trends*, **57** (2), 124–41.

JISC (2011a) *UK's Open Access Full-text Search Engine to Aid Research*, 3 October, www.jisc.ac.uk/news/stories/2011/09/openaccess.aspx.

JISC (2011b) *Cloud Computing Increasingly Attractive to Universities, says JISC*, 16 May, www.jisc.ac.uk/news/stories/2011/05/cloud.aspx.

Kim, J. (2011) Motivations of Faculty Self-archiving in Institutional Repositories, *Journal of Academic Librarianship*, **37** (3), 246–54.

Li, C., Han, M., Hong, C., Wang, Y., Xu, Y. and Cheng, C. (2011) Building a Sustainable Institutional Repository, *D-Lib Magazine*, **17** (7/8), www.dlib.org/dlib/july11/chenying/07chenying.html.

Li, Y. and Banah, M. (2011) Institutional Repositories and Digital Preservation: assessing current practices at research libraries, *D-Lib Magazine*, **17** (5/6), www.dlib.org/dlib/may11/yuanli/05yuanli.html.

Liew, C. L. (2008) Digital Library Research 1997–2007, *Journal of Documentation*, **65** (2), 245–66.

MacDonald, R. (2011) Starting, Strengthening, and Managing Institutional Repositories, *Electronic Library*, **29** (4), 553–4.

Mitchell, C. and Suchy, D. (2012) Developing Mobile Access to Digital Collections, *D-Lib Magazine*, **18** (1/2), www.dlib.org/dlib/january12/mitchell/01mitchell.html.

Nakata, N. M., Nakata, V., Bryne, A., McKeough, J., Gardiner, G. and Gibson, J. (2008) *Australian Indigenous Digital Collections: first generation issues*, http://epress.lib.uts.edu.au/scholarly-works/bitstream/handle/2100/809/Aug%2023%20Final%20Report.pdf;jsessionid=E45981774E92A1FC816AB36326F1337E?sequence=1.

Nguyen, H. S. and Chowdhury, G. (2011) Digital Library Research (1999–2010); a knowledge map of core topics and subtopics. In Xing, C., Crestani, F. and Rauber, A. (eds), *Digital Libraries: for cultural heritage, knowledge dissemination and future creation, 13th International Conference on Asia-Pacific Digital Libraries, ICADL2011, Beijing, October 24–27*, 367–71.

Nolin, J. (2010) Sustainable Information and Information Science, *Information Research*, **15** (2), http://informationr.net/ir/15-2/paper431.html.

OECD (2010) *Committee on Information, Communications and Computer Policy (ICCP)*, www.oecd.org/dataoecd/18/39/37328586.pdf.

OECD (2011) *OECD Resources on Policy Issues Related to Internet Governance. OECD and the World Summit on the Information Society (WSIS)*, www.oecd.org/document/21/0,2340,en_21571361_34590630_35282901_1_1_1_1,00.html.

Pomerantz, J., Wildemuth, B. M., Yang, S. and Fox, E. A. (2006) Curriculum Development for Digital Libraries, *Proceedings of the 6th ACM/IEEE-CS Joint Conference on Digital Libraries (Chapel Hill, NC, USA, June 11–15, 2006). JCDL '06*. ACM Press, 175–184, doi=http://doi.acm.org/10.1145/1141753.1141787.

St Jean, B., Rieh, S. Y., Yakel, E. and Markey, K. (2011) Unheard Voices: institutional repository end-users, *College & Research Libraries*, **72** (1), 21–42.

Sullivan, R. (2002) Indigenous Cultural and Intellectual Property Rights: a digital library context, *D-Lib Magazine*, **8** (5), www.dlib.org/dlib/may02/sullivan/05sullivan.html.

University of Strathclyde (n.d.) *IRStats*, http://strathprints.strath.ac.uk/cgi/irstats.cgi.

World Commission on Environment and Development (1987) *Our Common Future*, Oxford University Press.

Wrenn, G., Mueller, C. J. and Shellhase, J. (2009) Institutional Repository on a Shoestring, *D-Lib Magazine*, **15** (1/2), www.dlib.org/dlib/january09/wrenn/01wrenn.html.

Index